Naming Theatre

Performance Interventions

Series Editors: **Elaine Aston**, University of Lancaster, and **Bryan Reynolds**, University of California, Irvine

Performance Interventions is a series of monographs and essay collections on theatre, performance, and visual culture that share an underlying commitment to the radical and political potential of the arts in our contemporary moment, or give consideration to performance and to visual culture from the past deemed crucial to a social and political present. *Performance Interventions* moves transversally across artistic and ideological boundaries to publish work that promotes dialogue between practitioners and academics, and interactions between performance communities, educational institutions, and academic disciplines.

Titles include:

Alan Ackerman and Martin Puchner (*editors*)
AGAINST THEATRE
Creative Destructions on the Modernist Stage

Elaine Aston and Geraldine Harris (*editors*)
FEMINIST FUTURES?
Theatre, Performance, Theory

Maaike Bleeker
VISUALITY IN THE THEATRE
The Locus of Looking

James Frieze
NAMING THEATRE
Demonstrative Diagnosis in Performance

Lynette Goddard
STAGING BLACK FEMINISMS
Identity, Politics, Performance

Alison Forsyth and Chris Megson (*editors*)
GET REAL: DOCUMENTARY THEATRE PAST AND PRESENT

Leslie Hill and Helen Paris (*editors*)
PERFORMANCE AND PLACE

D.J. Hopkins, Shelley Orr and Kim Solga (*editors*)
PERMANCE AND THE CITY

Amelia Howe Kritzer
POLITICAL THEATRE IN POST-THATCHER BRITAIN
New Writing: 1995–2005

Melissa Sihra (*editor*)
WOMEN IN IRISH DRAMA
A Century of Authorship and Representation

Performance Interventions
Series Standing Order ISBN 978–1–4039–4443–6 Hardback
978–1–4039–4444–3 Paperback
(*outside North America only*)

You can receive future titles in this series as they are published by placing a standing order. Please contact your bookseller or, in case of difficulty, write to us at the address below with your name and address, the title of the series and the ISBN quoted above.

Customer Services Department, Macmillan Distribution Ltd, Houndmills, Basingstoke, Hampshire RG21 6XS, England

---

Naming Theatre
Demonstrative Diagnosis in Performance

James Frieze

palgrave
macmillan

© James Frieze 2009

All rights reserved. No reproduction, copy or transmission of this publication may be made without written permission.

No portion of this publication may be reproduced, copied or transmitted save with written permission or in accordance with the provisions of the Copyright, Designs and Patents Act 1988, or under the terms of any licence permitting limited copying issued by the Copyright Licensing Agency, Saffron House, 6–10 Kirby Street, London EC1N 8TS.

Any person who does any unauthorized act in relation to this publication may be liable to criminal prosecution and civil claims for damages.

The author has asserted his right to be identified as the author of this work in accordance with the Copyright, Designs and Patents Act 1988.

First published 2009 by
PALGRAVE MACMILLAN

Palgrave Macmillan in the UK is an imprint of Macmillan Publishers Limited, registered in England, company number 785998, of Houndmills, Basingstoke, Hampshire RG21 6XS.

Palgrave Macmillan in the US is a division of St Martin's Press LLC, 175 Fifth Avenue, New York, NY 10010.

Palgrave Macmillan is the global academic imprint of the above companies and has companies and representatives throughout the world.

Palgrave® and Macmillan® are registered trademarks in the United States, the United Kingdom, Europe and other countries.

ISBN-13: 978–0–230–51770–7   hardback
ISBN-10: 0–230–51770–6   hardback

This book is printed on paper suitable for recycling and made from fully managed and sustained forest sources. Logging, pulping and manufacturing processes are expected to conform to the environmental regulations of the country of origin.

A catalogue record for this book is available from the British Library.

A catalog record for this book is available from the Library of Congress.

10 9 8 7 6 5 4 3 2 1
18 17 16 15 14 13 12 11 10 09

Printed and bound in Great Britain by
CPI Antony Rowe, Chippenham and Eastbourne

Contents

Illustrations

Acknowledgements

This book was generously supported by the Arts and Humanities Research Council. For critical guidance, I thank Elaine Aston and Bryan Reynolds. Thanks also to everyone at Palgrave, including Paula Kennedy, Steven Hall, Christabel Scaife, and Penny Simmons, for making the production of the book such an enjoyable process. Those who provided insights and materials include Theodora Skipitares, Jeanne Harrison, Will Adamsdale, Paula Vogel, Andy Lavender, Dan Rebellato, Ping Chong, Bruce Allardice, Jon Hough, David Woods, Cathriona Burke, and Liz Diamond.

Chapter 3 draws on two previous essays: 'The Mess Behind the Veil: Assimilating Ping Chong' (*Theatre Research International* vol. 31 no. 1, Spring 2006); and '*Imperceptible Mutabilities in the Third Kingdom*: Suzan-Lori Parks and the Shared Struggle to Perceive' (*Modern Drama* vol. xli no. 4, Winter 1998). For input on the material concerning postmodernism in Chapter 10, I am grateful to Baz Kershaw and Graham Ley. To members of the *Performance and the Body* working group of TaPRA, thank you for vital discussion.

For their wisdom and inspiring example, I cite Sally Banes, Mary Karen Dahl, Phillip Zarrilli, and Gerry Harris. Colleagues, former colleagues, and students of Liverpool John Moores University who supported this book practically and conceptually include Timothy Ashplant, Dymphna Callery, Ross Dawson, Charlie Dickinson, Oliver Double, Colin Fallows, Martin Griffiths, Colin Harrison, Elli Johnson, Siân Lincoln, Aileen La Tourette, David Llewellyn, Mike McCormack, Ros Merkin, Joe Moran, Jenny Newman, Joanna Price, Berthold Schoene-Harwood, Andrew Sherlock, Mark Smith, Tamsin Spargo, Yannis Tzioumakis, Roger Webster, and Andy Young.

People after whom I am named, or who are named like me, must share the blame: my late father Geoffrey, who could sew; my mother Patricia (who, despite performing her final stage role in Strindberg's *Dance of Death* when she was pregnant with me, continues to tread the boards of my life); my niece Jessica (whose writing accomplishments have cast a shadow over my efforts since she was five years of age); and the extraordinary Josephine, for whom no-one can stand in.

1

Introduction: Improper Naming

I began writing this book with a desire to understand what I perceived to be an obsession with naming in recent theatrical performances and texts. The naming in these plays and performances – of characters, settings, events, and phenomena – seemed to interrogate naming itself. How, I found myself asking, did this conspicuous name-play reflect on, and how did it intervene in, social experience of, and critical thinking about, identity, reality, and the mediation of identity and reality? The chapters that follow address this multi-part question through close reading of particular theatre-makers and works. In outlining the book's argument, this Introduction will contextualize those readings sociopolitically vis-à-vis critical discourse, theatre history, and performance theory.

Rich veins of analysis of naming run through philosophy, psychoanalysis, and linguistics. Emphasis within these disciplines has been on the mechanics of how a signifying symbol-set correlates to a signified object: on the relationship between an experience or phenomenon, conceived as singular and discrete, and particular labels that are attached to it. In other words, the focus has been on teasing out how a thing relates to its name. Saul Kripke wants us to think of names as rigid designators, which 'stick' due to causal habits amongst a community of speakers. He rejects descriptivist theories of naming propounded by the likes of Gottlob Frege, Bertrand Russell, and Ludwig Wittgenstein, each of which argue that names emerge from the properties of an object – as a descriptive synonym for, or sum of, those properties. *Naming Theatre* leaves that debate to linguistics and philosophy, but it is worth noting that, while their functional properties have been hotly debated for centuries, there is general agreement that names hide some 'things' (objects, rules, laws) and reveal others. Behind every name there are numerous stories.

The word 'behind' is crucial here. Names can stand in the way of, and render invisible, repositories of memory. Names are mnemonic, aiding memory; but they also forget. Names are the *shells* of stories, that which remains after stories are assimilated; but they are also the glue of the assimilation process, linking the way we absorb stories to our own absorption into society.

While analyses of naming have much to contribute to the study of theatre, theatre has much to contribute to the analysis of naming. When critical theorists and philosophers analyse the relationship between naming and identity-formation – what Judith Butler (see Chapter 2) terms 'the intersubjective relation' of 'the linguistic scene' – they often deploy theatrical metaphors in ways that bracket, or erase, theatrical practice itself. Theatrical practice has direct relevance to everyday speech relations, not least in its history of enacting the dynamics of concealing and making visible integral to naming. My examination of naming traces ways in which acts and rituals of naming that were once part of theatre's traditionally 'invisible' armoury (character names, stage directions, statements by narrators) function as objects of attention along with other 'invisibles' such as space and time. In the process, theatre reminds us that naming *is* spatial/geographical and temporal/historical.

The dynamics of naming are gestaltic: they entail interplay of figure and ground. In naming something, the namer establishes it as a figure against a ground that may or may not be visible before the act of naming occurs, but which is thrown into relief *by* the act of naming. Naming makes visible a particular configuration of parts, an entity. Other possible entities are overwritten or unwritten. Because naming is always also un-naming, all naming creates, in Coco Fusco's phrase (see Chapter 4), a 'zero space', erasing what was previously in view. Naming shepherds properties into nodes that focus perception. In drawing attention, concentrating the gaze, naming trains seeing to a logic of figure and ground, a perceptual geography in which meaning is clustered, or nodal, and what lies outside the nodes or clusters of meaning formed by naming demands less attention.

As the theatre-makers I read remind us, naming, including theatrical naming, structures knowledge most efficiently if its methods remain unnamed. The strongest message propounded in these works is that, for theatre to genuinely engage with and intervene in the re-framing of conceptualization, it must take demonstrable responsibility for its own naming systems. To an extent, such reflexive naming is continuous with, indeed a hallmark of, (varyingly mappable) avant-garde or experimental theatre, previous volleys of which are explicitly invoked in these works. At the same time, I posit these works as a group because they defamiliarize theatre's systems of enunciability, applying metaphors in ways that unravel metaphor. Citing and re-siting naming rituals and conventions, they interrogate the politics of naming, highlighting the name's emotive force as well as the mechanics of its operation.

Character and property

The vast bulk of character names that populate theatre history tend to perform the positivist function of identifying individuals by personality and locating them by group. This includes allegorical constructs like 'Everyman', and similarly metaphorical names like 'Volpone, or the Foxe', as Jonson describes his eponymous protagonist. While it is solipsistically easy to see recent practice as richer than that of bygone centuries, it is also true that the twentieth century is marked by radically new kinds of character-naming. Toward and into the twenty-first century, character-naming has become increasingly about the play of difference within, about the alienation of characters from themselves, the detachment of their present(ation) from their history. Character-naming has become ironic and dichotomous, marking desire, failure, and loss while staking out possibility, autonomy, and liberation.

A distancing of name from character begins in earnest with the impact of (what is conventionally labelled) expressionism on the stage. Sophie Treadwell's *Machinal* (1928), for example, is imbued with expressionist ideas about the effects of spiritually alienating and deindividuating urban industrialization. Building on European plays by the likes of Oscar Kokoschka and George Wedekind, and on American works like Elmer Rice's *The Adding Machine*, Treadwell deploys generic nomenclature to show the gap between individual freedom and the position available to a 'Young Woman' in a mechanized world. Treadwell draws attention to naming, putting her feminist stamp on the expressionist convention of generic nomenclature. The name 'Young Woman' stands in ironic relationship to the character 'Helen', who is herself something of a dramatic stand-in for the real-life character Ruth Snyder, the Long Island housewife executed for murdering her husband. In the intensely machinic first scene of the play, at the Office, the name of the boss and his firm is the most repeated of elements, courtesy of the Telephone Girl's continual, telephone-voice greeting to callers: 'George H. Jones..., George H. Jones and Company..., George H. Jones...' (Treadwell, 1993, p. 9). The boss's name rings in Helen's ear via dramatized interior monologues in which the oppressive prospect of marriage means, as the phrase goes, 'taking his name', which really means becoming his acquisition. A man who has made his name for himself, George H. Jones refers to everyone else in the most generic of code: Miss A, Miss B, Mr A, and Mr B.

A different kind of play on schematic, coded naming can be found in Beckett. Like so many aspects of his writing, Beckett's use of names is characterized by richness within simplicity. *Come and Go* (1965) features three women – Ru, Vi, and Flo – who adopt precisely delineated positions in a sequence of mini-conversations so brief and so tightly orchestrated that the orchestration rises above the substance of the conversation. Monosyllabic, colloquially ordinary, distinctly old-fashioned English names, 'Ru', 'Vi', and 'Flo' are also subject to Beckett's modernist referentiality, happening to allude to the flowers that adorn Ophelia in *Hamlet* – though only a few bright sparks or the research-prone might notice the allusion.[1]

Insofar as Beckett's naming layers colloquial and classical and Treadwell's plays positivism against expressionism in a sardonically quotational manner, both are examples that point toward, but stop well short of the play with, and on, character-naming in the examples I discuss from the late 1980s onwards. In schematic, quotational naming more extreme and more generative than that found in Beckett or Treadwell, authors like Suzan-Lori Parks and Paula Vogel extend (in historical terms) the use of name-play to construct and deconstruct identity. Like the name 'Young Woman', the name 'Third Man' is unspoken in Vogel's *Baltimore Waltz* (see Chapter 2). The unspoken status of the Third Man contrasts pointedly with the continual reiteration by him of the names of the play's other two characters. In the context of a play about the politics of the unspoken in the management of AIDS and homosexuality, the ex-nomination of 'the Third Man' is significant. In a different kind of occlusion by naming, 'Buffy', 'Muffy', and 'Duffy' are reiterated so zealously by their young bearers in Parks's *Imperceptible Mutabilities in the Third Kingdom* (Chapter 3) that their drilling attains military proportions: like all military drills, the effect is the swallowing of personality through systematic induction.

While Treadwell and Beckett are less extreme in their name-play than Vogel or Parks, any historical claims about the distinctiveness of late twentieth-century naming are mitigated by the work of avant-garde authors like Adrienne Kennedy and (earlier still) Gertrude Stein. As in Parks's, there is something immediately suggestive about naming in Kennedy's plays. *The Owl Answers* was first produced in New York in 1965 – the year that Beckett wrote (the first version, in English, of) *Come and Go.* *The Owl Answers* proffers characters with names like Bastard's Black Mother Who is the Reverend's Wife Who is Anne Boleyn and She Who is Clara Passmore who is the Virgin Mary who is the Bastard who is the Owl. These names advertise the play's acerbic exploration of quasi-schizophrenic self-perception. It is an exploration, as her name so vividly suggests, that entails a woman's obsessive quest to access and express her own history; an exploration that projects, onto our reading of character, a history of metaphor. Kennedy's note at the start of the play advises that 'characters change slowly back and forth into and out of themselves, leaving some garment of their previous selves upon them' (Kennedy, 1988, p. 25). The characters' severely enunciative names are garments in themselves – garments quilted, in Kennedy's distinctively uncanny, ritualistic fashion, from the Bible, history books, popular culture, and the contemporary experience of African Americans. As in Parks (see Chapter 3), character names in Kennedy seem to have been regurgitated from subjects who have been fervently but only speciously acculturated. Theatrically enacting acculturation, Parks and Kennedy offer characters who struggle to appear beneath a schema, the systematicity of which seems to keep them in place yet not to accommodate them. The enigmatic nature of these characters and their names poses a seriously playful challenge to the spectator/reader, stealthily bonding us to characters in a shared struggle to perceive.

Twenty-first-century audiences are more accustomed to conspicuous, sustained name-play than Stein's or Kennedy's (first) audiences were. American playwrights whose work straddles the twentieth and early twenty-first centuries frequently provide names that confront, that draw attention to themselves, that link the naming of character to the interpretation of events and phenomena, and to agency performed and revealed by iteration. Eric Overmyer's *Native Speech* (1985), for example, features Belly-Up, Loud Speaker, The Mook, and Hungry Mother, and names its setting as a radio studio 'constructed in the detritus of Western Civ: appliances, neon tubing, 45s, car parts, Junk' (Messerli and Wellman, 1998, p. 625). If *Native Speech* anticipates, and perhaps influences, Parks's *America Play* (1993) in its startling mixdown of urbane, literary referentiality and apocalyptic, pre-millennial, end-of-history tension, the characters anticipate another Parks play, *Death of the Last Black Man in the Whole Entire World* (1992), which offers characters named 'Before Columbus', 'And Bigger And Bigger And Bigger', 'Yes, and Greens Black-Eyed Peas Cornbread'. Like those in *Native Speech*, character names in *Death of the Last Black Man* sound like text has been untimely plucked from context. They are stridently improper proper names, an insult to the proper, but also hint at insult to the characters themselves, characters not afforded a 'real' proper name, merely a nickname, parenthetical phrase, or shard of discarded writing.

While Parks's and Overymyer's naming is, like Kennedy's, semantically rich even at first glance, it is important to note that for every *Owl Answers*, in which names are immediately complex, later twentieth- and early twenty-first-century theatre often strips names almost entirely away, as Sarah Kane's work progressively does,[2] or profers speciously simple, apparently unremarkable names like 'Buzz' and 'Annie'. By 'speciously simple', I mean that it is the *deployment* of the names which is decidedly layered, and which contradicts an initial impression of simplicity. Rather than the name itself, it is the deployment of naming in much of Martin Crimp's work, for instance, that generates meaning. To say that Anne/Anya/Annie/Anny/*Anny*/Annuska is the central character of *Attempts on her Life* (1997) is only partly to describe how the metastatic 'Annie' signifies in these '17 Scenarios for the Theatre' (as Crimp calls it). In one of the disturbing set-pieces that constitute the play, Annie becomes 'the new Anny', a literal and metaphorical vehicle: 'No one is ever dragged from the *Anny* by an enraged mob. No child's pelvis is ever shattered by a chance collision with the new *Anny*' (Crimp, 1997, p. 34).

Like 'Annie', 'Buzz' is the name of the central character in Ping Chong's *Kind Ness* (1986), but a name whose referential properties (as I discuss in Chapter 3) extend far beyond character. The other children see Buzz as radically removed from them, but Chong maintains ambiguity about what they see and/or pretend to see. At times, it seems that Buzz is a gorilla, at times that the gorilla suit is simply a distancing tool. Buzz and Annie are forcefields as much as characters: they cannot be squarely identified and deciphered; they are that which gets in the way of deciphering. As one character states in the 'Mum and Dad' scene of *Attempts on her Life*: 'She says she's not a real character, not a real character like you get in a book or on TV, but a *lack* of character, an *absence*, she calls it, doesn't she, of character.' Interpretation of the materiality of the self is thematically central to both plays, and, in both, it is the deployment of the name on which the drama of interpretation and the realization of character hinges. Through carefully orchestrated reiterations, the simple name can create a field of signification in which significance lies in the collision/tension between the mutually exclusive nature of different signifieds.

Proper names, as Derrida theorizes them, are marks of ownership, of a self-possession that anchors all systems of property. Along with ownership, the exigencies of propriety are competence (the ability to perform according to rules of language) and cleanliness (*propreté* means: to keep free of contamination). There are several characters who flout propriety in precisely these ways. The Naturalist in *IMTK* comes to restore propriety to Molly/Mona, who struggles to master English by reciting 'Mary had a little lamb' and lives in a house deemed to be filthy and cockroach-infested. Vogel's Anna's recurrent failure to master languages (including 'proper' AIDS discourse) compounds with the dubiety of her name, and with promiscuous sexual behaviour, to make her a stand-in who stands *out* as decidedly improper. 'Anna' is less a name than a palindromically compact 'I-position' within which bustle derivations and associations, the significance of which unfolds incrementally. A shamanic sequence of stand-ins as protean as her antagonist, the Third Man, Anna is an aggregate of the personal, historical, and fictitious. Taking her name from the author's real life childhood best friend,[3] but also modelled on Anna in the 1949 Graham Greene-scripted, Carol Reed-directed film, *The Third Man*, she is the alter-ego of the author within the play who then stands in for her/the author's brother in the play-within-the-play. Like Crimp's Annie, and Ping Chong's Buzz, she disobeys, in Derrida's terms, the law of the proper.

The names 'Anna', 'Molly/Mona', 'Annie (Anne/Anya/Anny/*Anny*/Annuska/Ann)', and 'Buzz' cannot hold as names, in the sense of 'accommodating' what they designate; but they are theatrically deployed to perform other kinds of holding function, opening fissures within congealed narratives, intervening in historical, geographical, and other disciplinary fields. As I describe in Chapter 3, Parks makes words like 'accommodate' function as pivots around which opposing forces wheel: these opposing forces are not resolved, tragically or comically, but are allowed to contend, co-mingling in ways that contaminate the proper.

Parks's strikingly inventive textual archaeology – riffing, in *The America Play*, on 'hole/whole', and on 'Founding Father/Foundling Father/forefather/foefather/fauxfather', co-mingles absence and presence, present and past, epic and vernacular, in ways that both re-member and incubate new history. Rather than fixing identification, names are used to highlight ephemerality, mutability, and difference. Across the chapters that follow, we will see the propriety of ostensibly proper names rooted out by naming that is provocatively partial/temporary/conditional/provisional, naming that interrogates the law of the proper name as something that, in designating, fixes in perpetuity.

Getting at language

The pitching of the improper into the proper is a formal and thematic tussle in which three major binaries consistently figure: the tonal plays against the designational, the subjective against the objective, and the deconstructive against the constructive. In stressing the tonal, subjective, and deconstructive, the improper naming I find in these works belongs, in Kristeva's terms, to the semiotic. The subject, in Kristeva's formulation (after Lacan) of her development, moves under pressure from the pre-Mirror stage of the semiotic, in which language use consists of instinctual play with prosodic elements, into the Symbolic, akin to Derrida's proper, the phallogocentric order of sense and meaning. The Symbolic has little truck with the semiotic, but the semiotic nonetheless irrupts into the order of the Symbolic.

Taking a line he presents as post-McLuhan, and which I would say is also neo-Artaudian, Hans-Thies Lehmann argues in *Postdramatic Theatre* (2006) that, in travelling through the 'media age', we have gone from a theatre in which the word was a privileged conveyor of sense to a paratactic theatre of textscapes in which the 'sonic' carries the meaning and language is free to exert itself in all its sensory force. Lehmann's useful phrase 'physis of the verbal' indicates the ways in which words can be re-embodied in performance, as does Kristeva's definition of the semiotic trace as 'that memory of being to which the music of the body brings testimony'. While I admire Lehmann's technical analysis of what (he claims) has happened to words and pictures, the tenor of his conclusions is seriously challenged by the works I read – and, I would argue, by some of the ones he reads. Parataxis allows for the interplay of different attitudes to the word within the theatre space: to claim that the word is rejected or escaped by paratactic textscapes is to draw the wrong conclusion. What Lehmann finds to be exceptional in Müller's *Hamletmachine*, a kind of 'out-of-timeness' of the theatre itself, a concentration on text that is behind the times, is actually far more common than the paradigm of postdramatic theatre (as he configures it) can allow. Like Robert Wilson, cited by Lehmann as the ur-figure of the postdramatic textscape, Parks's early works create a theatrical textuality in which, as it tries to assert meaning, focus, and intent, the written word is suspended in a kind of Derridean *espacement*, a *mise- en-scène* and soundscape of 'phonetic materiality [...] dispersion in space [...] loss of teleology' (Lehmann, 2006, p. 148). Like Wilson, Parks more or less makes text 'an exhibited object' in broad keeping with the example set by Gertrude Stein. In doing so, however, both Parks and Wilson systematically and self-consciously insert other (including logocentric, teleological, ratiocinatory) texts that collide in ways that demand attention, making the formation of text a focal concern. In *IMTK* (see Chapter 3), these texts include a history of trans-Atlantic slave-trading, a television nature programme, an anthropological treatise, and a dramatic script. The intense intertextuality of Parks's early works, and that of Wilson's problematically termed 'Theatre of Images',[4] are (each for their own artistic and political reasons) as concerned as Stein was *with* the verbal. Their dispersal and re-contextual collaging of words is not designed to escape the verbal, but with getting at it. As I argue in my discussion of Parks in Chapter 3, this 'getting at' the verbal entails reflexive use of the vertical, elaborative axis of language in conjunction with, and opposition to, the horizontal, narrative-forming axis. It is a reflexivity in which the 'physis of the verbal' plays a key part.

Theories and paradigms of performativity and performance have frequently attended to language and its relationship to matter. Despite, or perhaps because of, the prevalence of such theories within and across academic disciplines and other domains, the relationship of matter to language is more troublesome than ever. The phrase 'the linguistic turn' is a nice, academic understatement that helps to situate contemporary awareness of the constitutive role of language as the latest steps along a path bearing the footprints of Wittgenstein and Saussure. Drawing threads not only from analytic philosophy and Saussurean linguistics but also from Darwin on evolution, Marx on social structures, Nietzsche on morality, and Freud on the interior of the self, structuralism and poststructuralism accelerate the linguistic turn. Within that acceleration of the linguistic turn, Lacan shows how the unconscious is structured like language, and Foucault how power works through and inside discourse. 'Language' no longer refers to purely linguistic information and exchange, but to behavioural codes that structure the mind (psyche), the body (DNA), and society (culture). Coterminous with the colonization of all spheres by language is the probing of the ways in which language is an unstable system, including Derrida's explorations of how language systems are predicated on instabilities masked as stabilities. A sense that language is ubiquitous and stealthily constructive grows in tandem with a sense that language is manipulable. As Steven Shaviro puts it in a collection called *Posthuman Bodies*: 'it's not that language doesn't refer to anything real, but – to the contrary – that language itself has become increasingly real' (1995, p. 42).

Ambivalence about the constitutive power of language, and how to harness it, is integral to the theatre I discuss. On the one hand, the manipulability of what had been seen as innate, the feeling that control over language is up in the air and up-for-grabs is an opportunity: if language is appropriable, it serves the kind of rediscovery, repossession, and reclaiming that gets Smith, Wolfe, and others so excited. While naming usually facilitates identification, in these works it is used to explore the legacy of failure to identify, writing (in Parks, Chong, Lightwork, Ridiculusmus and Skipitares) a history of absent realizations that haunt and give the lie to apparent presence. On the other hand, as demonstrated by all the works I explore, language is treacherous in its capacity to disembody or to paper over, serving the interests of those who want to disguise the collateral damage of ethnic assimilation, medical progress, or military operations.

Language is a tool used to build a world of 'sound-bites' and 'spin' – words that marked discussion of politics and news production from the late 1980s, and continue to do so. As I discuss in Chapter 7, 'verbatim' and 'documentary' are posed as antidotes to a culture of spin and sound-bites in the production and interpretation of a significant amount of theatre in the 1990s. Anna Deavere Smith argues in her Introduction to *Fires in the Mirror* that her work should be seen as an intervention into 'sound-bite culture', which divides communities along the lines of what newspapers and tabloid television can perpetuate as lowest common denomination (1993a, p. xxxi). Cornel West's Foreword to *Fires* further politicizes Smith's performance of language, arguing that it recuperates 'the degradation of the public sphere by conservative elites in the past two decades'. In my final chapter, I discuss an essay by Anne Bogart that similarly calls for language that reclaims the public sphere. Chong, Parks, and Ridiculusmus each use words, interventionally, *against themselves* to target the neglect of language. The idea of language as a virus, complicit with implosion or dispersal of value – an idea propounded by Baudrillard, and in Jameson's account of late-capitalism's printing-up of increasingly valueless signifiers – is also theatricalized in *The Receipt*, where corporate-speak produces RotoPlas and infects all who work within its walls; and in Vogel's depiction of public 'education' agencies, whose alarmist propriety exacerbates rather than manages the onset of AIDS.

Whether emanating from corporations or politicians or denounced by academics as a hallmark of the postmodernism they may seek to control or refuse (see Chapter 10), spin is not an imaginary phenomenon, but it is one that preys on crises of perception. Exploiting and magnifying uncertainty, instability, and displacement, spin is both a symptom and a cause of identity crisis. As sociologist Kobena Mercer observes, 'identity only becomes an issue when it is in crisis, when something assumed to be fixed, coherent, stable is displaced by the experience of doubt and uncertainty' (1990, p. 43).

However reality is recalibrated vis-à-vis crisis, though, global and local factors undoubtedly conjoin in the late 1980s and early 1990s to precipitate intense forms of crisis. These factors are crucial to the critical obsession with naming, re-naming, and un-naming in the works I examine.

They include: globalization enabled by the loosening of national, political, and trading boundaries, by changing demographics as migrations proliferate (*Kind Ness, Imperceptible Mutabilities in the Third Kingdom*), by the rise of Neo-Conservativism in the US and its commitment to 'market democracy' (*Pugilist Specialist*), and by the opportunism of corporations (*The Receipt*); the breakdown of Communist regimes; the conspicuous softening of binary positions between left and right, communist and capitalist, democratic and republican, socialist and conservative, (*Fires in the Mirror, Say Nothing*); the impact of the AIDS epidemic (*The Baltimore Waltz; Under the Knife*); revolutionary developments in cybernetics, genetic science, and DNA technology (*Here's what I did with my body one day*); and the spread of poststructuralist modes in and beyond academia (*The Colored Museum, The World in Pictures*). Collectively, these events, trends, and phenomena engender destabilization of the grounds not only of identity, but of conceptualization itself.

The transition from identitarian to post-identitarian discourse is marked by the abating of emphasis on difference *between* selves/communities and a corresponding pursuit of difference *within*. In post-identitarian discourse, tropes of mobility hold sway. Post-identitarian perspectives recognize the social operation of – but unchain self and community from – the limits of positioning based on race, ethnicity, gender, and sexuality. While invoking the historical and contemporary effects of these aspects of identity, post-identitarian discourse aims to move before or beyond them, figuring identity as a fluid equation, self and other crossing and re-crossing a permeable boundary. The fluidity of such formulae is depicted as being starkly in contrast with the difference-collapsing effects of the identifications on which both the ego and the theatre are conventionally seen to be founded. Appearing as a character in Smith's *Fires in the Mirror*, Angela C. Davis – a Black Panther activist who became Professor of the History of Consciousness at Santa Cruz – explains that '[n]owadays', when she talks of 'race', she puts it 'in quotations'. This reflects her sense of abandoning 'the old notion of coalition in which we anchor ourselves very solidly in our specific racialized communities'. As Davis sees it, 'we still anchor ourselves in our communities', but these communities are more 'various' and 'the rope attached to that anchor should be long enough to allow us to move into other communities [...] to make more intimate these connections and associations' (Smith, 1993a, pp. 30–1).

By the mid-1980s, race, class, and gender are generally perceived to be unsustainable bases for both social activism and self-definition. The strategic value of an essentialist logic of difference between women and men, or Black and White, continues to be affirmed well into the 1980s, but is gradually eroded by insistence that binary logic cannot account for the experiential and mutable nature of difference. In theory and theatre alike, a form of naming is sought that, rather than suturing identification, holds identifications and investments in view, open to question, and subject to reversal. It is a search on which those whose work I read embark in their own distinctive ways, but with commonalities. Wolfe, Smith, and Parks, for example, all African American, offer formally very different kinds of theatrical experience, but each positions their own work in terms applicable to the other two. Wolfe eschews 'slogan theatre', and wants to use the past as a space in which to 'self-examine'. Smith bemoans the degradation of forums for the consideration of social tensions, the journalistic and televisual tendency toward arranging debate as a pattern of opposing sound-bites around which linking commentary is draped. In an essay sardonically titled 'An Equation for Black People Onstage', Parks insists 'the Klan do not have to be outside the door for Black people to have lives worthy of dramatic literature' because 'within the subject is its other' (1995, p. 19).

If identity politics is complex manoeuvring of sameness and difference within arenas such as the home, workplace, or judicial system, post-identitarian logic is equally but differently complex, involving play with binaries, caesuras, third or in-between terms. The shift from identitarian to post-identitarian discourse (on which I will say more in a moment) presents itself as epistemological, as more than a matter of finding new words, as a shift from making points that stake out positions to preparing fields in which positions can traverse and adapt, can be traversed and made to adapt. Davis's motif of being anchored in a community with a rope that roams typifies concepts of difference circulating in the late 1980s and early 1990s such as Benedict Anderson's 'imagined community' and Maria Lugones' 'world travelling'. In such conceptions, entrenchment, nostalgia, and retreat to first principles are the anchor; the roaming entails theoretical play on tropes of mobility and on the mobility of tropes. Play with and on mobility is desirous but also fugue-like, reflecting the extent to which movement, as an imperative of contemporary life, has changed the meaning of journey.

While Davis's rope encapsulates post-identitarian thinking, the 'new' binary it constructs is strangely familiar when considered in theatrical terms. While theatre has always entailed going somewhere while going nowhere, *attention* to that paradox of movement and inertia is prompted (in much theatre of recent decades) by destabilization of grounding concepts in the world at large.

Throughout the 1990s, as blocs and movements dissipate, the concern with mapping and taxonomy in theatre continues, often begging the question: has the conceptualization of difference become a more pressing concern than the particular content of difference? My argument is that theatre, over these two decades, does important things *to* conceptualization. The search for stabilizing concepts, or concepts with which to map instability, yields an obsession with renaming and redefinition, with the reshaping of old kinds of map and the development of new ones. In theatre, as in other domains, as binaries between male/female, Black/White, and left/right soften, great effort is made to theorize the relationship between individuals, and between individuals and their environment, in terms of literal and metaphorical mobility.

The agonism of mobility and stasis, which takes many theatrical forms, cuts across distinctions between genre. In Vogel's *The Baltimore Waltz*, Skipitares's *Under the Knife* (1993–95), and Lightwork's *Here's what I did with my body one day* (2006), a motif of opposing images of death and of dancing evoke ways in which individual and social bodies are read, written, documented, intextuated. In all three cases, a death/dancing opposition theatricalizes Benjamin's dictum that 'history decomposes into images, not narratives' (Benjamin quoted in Diamond, 1997, p. 146). My analysis challenges the view that a shift from opposition based on adherence to social, artistic, and intellectual movements to opposition based on concepts *of* movement is a retreat from action. The efforts of these theatre-makers *to situate desire* to act, or to *escape inability* to act are fertile, and (im)prove theatre's capacity to *stage the conditions of action*. In pointing desire to act, and staging conditions of action, these works echo, but also (as I argue in Chapter 10) extend critical theory of the time.

A central feature of experimental theatre from the mid-1980s is that, in extending identity politics, it pits mapping, taxonomy, and classification against mobility, transience, and evasion. It is an agonism via which, as playwright Mac Wellman argues, characters and theatre-makers alike pursue 'grounding in a paradoxical lack of groundedness'.[5] Wellman's phrase speaks to the works I discuss, not least Chong's *Kind Ness* and Parks's *Imperceptible Mutabilities* (1989), in both of which we see slides of 'made history' projected (to quote Parks) above characters 'mutating like hell' (Solomon, 1990, p.75), and Wolfe's overhauling of *The Colored Museum* (1986) by adaptable subject-positions that Wolfe refers to as 'silhouettes'. Those who bear hope in these three works are, conspicuously, not fully fledged and not properly named, the implication being that proper naming would foreclose the developing subject. Improper naming besuits a process of formation in which the developing subject tests the conditions of their own enunciability.

Systems of enunciability

Naming takes place through statements, or acts of designation, but does not simply spring from subjects who utter and perform. It is born of systems of demarcation and enunciability that make statements legible. Naming ordinarily demarcates a subject position, it provides the illusion of the whole, self-same subject, in control of objects on whose status *as* objects one's status as a subject, able to control and possess, is predicated. Through strategies such as the detachment of sign from effect, name from thing, shell from substance, attention is drawn in the works I read to the ways in which names construct subjects and objects. The materiality of the subjects and objects we will encounter is frequently mutable; manipulation of names, and strategic decoupling of name from thing, makes identities, spaces, and the reality of events coalesce and disperse before our eyes.

To name, as Foucault repeatedly detailed, is to participate in a classificatory schema, a practice of identification. To name is to endorse the rules that make names readable, but also to normalize and thereby conceal those rules. 'Greeks', the fourth and final section of Suzan-Lori Parks's *Imperceptible Mutabilities in the Third Kingdom (IMTK)* features the Smith family. Daddy, an Army Sergeant, sends countless letters home to a wife and two daughters whose prime activity, like that of their would-be hero, is waiting for the Commander to award him a 'Distinction'. To interpret correspondence with a precision appropriate to military matters, the three female Smiths construct a ledger, with multiple columns, which they fill in as follows: '"Subject": uh letter. Check thuh "non-bill" column ... "Contents?" ... Write – uh – general news ... Slash – "report of duties".' Then the final columns: '"Mention of Work": check: "yes".' When it comes to the category titled 'Mention of Family', an argument ensues, as Buffy was mentioned but Muffy not. Sandwiched in the middle of these formalities is the column 'Signs of Distinction'. Mrs Smith asks what they put last time. 'Last letter's Signs of Distinction were "On the Horizon"', informs Buffy. 'Before that?' asks the mother. 'Soon', says Buffy. 'Before that', she adds, with exemplary efficiency, 'he reported his Distinction to be arriving quote "any day now", unquote' (Parks, 1995, pp. 62–3). Buffy is the most adept of the female Smiths at co-ordinating the ledger, the one most deeply immersed in the lore of military intelligence. To comfort her sister Muffy, who is upset at not being mentioned, Buffy tells her of a family called the Censors. 'Mr. Censor', says Buffy, 'is a man who won't let Sergeant Smith say certain things because certain things said may put the Effort in danger.' She explains that Mr Smith 'deals in a language of codes – secret signs and signals' (ibid., p. 64).

So zealously does the ledger map the place-into-which-events-can-fall that, akin to the army's 'language of codes', the 'signs and signals' of the ledger take on a life of their own. The interpretative codes have become more substantial than the events to which they refer. In *The Archaeology of Knowledge*, Foucault states that:

> [t]he archive is not that which, despite its immediate escape, safeguards the event of the statement, and preserves, for future memories, its status as an escapee; it is that which, at the very root of the statement-event, and in that which embodies it, defines at the outset the system of its enunciability.
>
> (1972, p. 129)

What Foucault suggests is that the contours of the 'statement' are not fixed at the moment of its inception but develop over time, in ways that foreclose other ways. This mutability betrays, for Parks as for Foucault, the duplicitous nature of archival history and theology. The exposed face of the archive is that which smothers the fugitive quality of the utterance by recording it. The concealed face is that which attaches itself, unseen, at the moment the statement is born. By so doing, the archive provides an invisible framework within which the statement can be read. This framework – what Foucault calls a 'system of enunciability' – inscribes a logic which confines future analysis to a narrow realm of possible interpretations. Mr Smith proclaims to himself: 'Thuh events of my destiny ssgonna fall untuh place. What events? That I don't know. But they gonna fall into place all right' (Parks, 1995, p. 58). The Smiths reflect Parks's belief that indoctrination is not an instilling of knowledge, but of ways of knowing. She wants her spectators to see that refreshing perception of identity depends less on redefining particular events than on interrogating the machinery of enunciability that hold identities and events in their proper 'place'.

As I argue in Chapter 4, these works might be seen as equivocating with Brecht's (modelling of epic theatre on) demonstrative techniques that use commentary to name the action represented. Diverse theatrical experiences though they are, there is a similarly conspicuous naming of scenes in works such as *Baltimore Waltz, Under the Knife, The Travels, Two Undiscovered Amerindians,* and *Venus* (Suzan-Lori Parks, [1996] 1998), a naming that plays on a tension normally played down in theatre: between commentary and representation; between what we see, hear, and smell, and what we are told we are witnessing. An embedded irony compromises the ability of commentary to *manage* representation, as in *Venus* when the continual, ritualistic countdown of scene numbers articulates theatrical anatomy with the textualization of Saartje Baartman's body, or in *Under the Knife* when the announcement of the scene name both diagnoses and confers existence, as if the matter represented has no existence prior to diagnosis. Rather than a seamless weaving of representation and commentary that would secure characters and events to their proper place, there is, in all these works, an opposition of statement to proof, set-up to ensuing action. It is an opposition that 'outs' the ordinarily invisible, promissory nature of what (in Chapter 5) I call 'en-scening': the naming of where and when action is set, and who is performing it, a naming that invisibly shapes what it frames and enters us as spectators into a particular contract.

The compromising of that contract ties us to the characters depicted. Without commentary that neatly frames the representation of character, we are left with characters who struggle to signify as we struggle to decode them. They struggle to articulate and disarticulate, to forget and to re-member, to do so in and at the proper, 'standard' time. Their efforts are linguistically inventive: they turn words over in their mouths and try embodying them in different ways, unchaining them, piecing them together, breaking them down into parts and reassembling them into new wholes. We find characters in moments of crisis, moments in which they try to remember who they are, to reground themselves. These moments of crisis make registering their private thoughts in the public domain imperative and palpably difficult. Their effortful play with words might be seen as lingering in a semiotic space of possibility. Certainly, characters like Miss Faith, Principal Conklin, the Third Man, to name but three such authority-figure-cum-narrators, have little truck with the struggle of the characters they keep in place, characters whose efforts nonetheless irrupt into their pristine Symbolic Order. Readings of feminist writing by Kristeva, and other second-wave French feminists such as Cixous and Irigaray, show how the pressure on the developing subject to move from semiotic to Symbolic is inscribed in the text. In that respect, such readings are a useful reference point for the interpretation of many of the theatrical characters we encounter in *Naming Theatre*. Name-sets like 'Muffy, Duffy, Buffy' and 'Mona, Chona, Verona' seem to ensign the passage from semiotic to Symbolic realms, just as the characters themselves are torn between the improper and the proper. However, they, like all the characters we meet, demand to be seen as their *own* reference points – a point I make in various chapters and reiterate in the final one.

In several chapters (including 4 and 6), I explore the idea that theatre-makers jam, or attempt to jam, the machinery of enunciability. Sometimes, as in *The America Play* and *IMTK*, it is verbal naming of characters, places, and events that jams the machinery. Parks's riffing on proper names exploits in post-Derridean fashion the expectation that the proper name must confer singularity – a singularity (as Derrida theorizes) that is paradoxically translatable and based on correspondences. In tandem with verbal naming structures (character names, stage directions, and so on), other sonic sign-systems, along with visual elements such as costume, props, and lighting, play a crucial role in the naming of scene that is theatre's machinery of enunciability. Wolfe articulates theatre with museums, Chong with zoos, and performance artist Mimi Goese (whose work I discuss only fleetingly here; see Frieze (1998) for a fuller description) with circuses: all three imply that theatre is no more a mirror up to nature than any of these other arenas that taxonomize and fetishize the subjects they purport to accommodate.

If Barthes knelled the death of the author, these pieces are autopsies, inquests, and resurrections. Confusing 'reader' and 'author' (an opposition that Barthes paradoxically perpetuates), these works reconstruct authorship as the modelling, or enactment, of interpretation.[6] At their heart is a desire to use theatre to model the kind of productive reception needed to live in a world in which identity seems increasingly fused with textuality, a world in which, as Stuart Hall argues (see Chapter 2) there is increasing pressure to root identity in 'the symbolic', a pressure which always involves 'displacement'. It is in the struggle to interpret coded systems, these works suggest, that identity forms. Parks's unwitting archivists, the pilgrims to nowhere in Forced Entertainment's *The Travels* (2002), the daydreamers exposed to the public by Vogel and Chong, and the interviewees copied by Anna Deavere Smith (see Chapter 7): they are all, conspicuously (in a Barthesian sense, 'shockingly'), authored by interpretation. Belying the paradigm shift described by Barthes from 'writerly' to 'readerly' text, these works enact the futility and danger of separating authorship from reception.

As I discuss in Chapter 7, Anna Deavere Smith is an influential propo-
nent of a particular brand of theatrical authorship that models reading.
Emphasis placed by Smith and some critics on the fact that the only
words she uses are those spoken by her interviewees only emphasizes,
in the view of many, the intensely authorial work of editing. Smith's
method draws heavily, in ways that have not been investigated by critics of her work, on television editing. She describes herself as having
grown up at the same time as television grew up, and she consciously
taps into ways of seeing developed through the format of the television
programmes of her youth (the 1970s and 1980s), in which a host, or
anchor, mediates video clips for the audience. Like the host, or anchor,
in the studio, Smith is the home plane; the extracts she performs are
'foreign'. That Smith does not explicitly position herself *as* a host (in
the manner, according to Barthes, that omniscient authors of novels do)
makes her strategies all the more worthy of scrutiny. More explicit positioning occurs in *Kind Ness*, which begins with the words 'Good evening',
spoken by an unreliable, official-sounding Narrator. He proceeds to take
us, over a loudspeaker, through a series of pairs of images, training us
to read difference. Brandishing their ear-trumpets (Lucy in *The America
Play*) and their ledgers (the Smiths in *Imperceptible Mutabilities*), characters in Parks's plays are keen receivers, whose obsessed readiness to
read is characterized as a pathetic sign of the extent to which they are
'authored', their work with texts intextuating them. A form of *theatrical*
authorship emerges in these pieces in which the author is no longer an
'originator of meaning' (to quote the *OED* definition of 'author'), but
rather an editor of systems.

In some of the texts, there is a deliberate fusion and/or confusion of
authors with performers and/or characters, a renunciation of originary
meaning. Goese's personae seem to be the sum of their interpretation
of taped music/spoken words/noise played over a loudspeaker: their
actions appear to be driven by the sound tape and by items of clothing that they find themselves wearing. Every now and again, she seems
to step out of character, as if to remind us that the whole thing is a
product of her imagination – before reminding us again, in ways that
remind me of Forced Entertainment (Chapter 6), that her supposed rev-
elations are just performances of authenticity, promises of intimacy that
will not be kept. As has increasingly become the case in Forced Entertainment's (FE) work,[7] the detritus of what she has performed a minute
or two ago becomes a stationing agent for the present Goese, one that
she performs herself trying to escape even as it fascinates her, as if it
were alien material. As for Goese's work, FE's play with pseudo-found

material is periodically interrupted by moments of self-consciousness, explicit reminders of being part of a performance tradition. In reading *The Travels* in relation to Happenings in the 1950s and 1960s (Chapter 6), I discuss how FE's self-consciousness plays out within a paradoxically programmed performance of intuitive responses.

Naming failure/failure to name

In several of the works I discuss, the key events and phenomena are those pointedly *not* named. Tension between this ex-nomination and the hyper-nomination of pseudo-events and pseudo-phenomena generates drama in *Kind Ness, IMTK, Fires in the Mirror, Say Nothing,* and *The Baltimore Waltz*. No-one mentions that Buzz is a foreigner/gorilla in *Kind Ness* but they treat him accordingly. No-one mentions AIDS in *The Baltimore Waltz*, Acquired Toilet Disease standing in for Acquired Immune Deficiency Syndrome and Sexually Transmitted Diseases in a ludicrous ex-nomination that echoes Ronald Reagan's (see Chapter 2). The scandal of dirty toilets is also discussed *ad nauseam* in *Say Nothing*, as is the niceness of traditional Irish breakfasts, but no-one dares mention 'the Troubles'.

There are many examples in the pages that follow of failure to name and failure to perform, examples that collectively point to the breakdown of systems of enunciability. While it is tempting to shepherd these examples into a totalizing paradigm or ethic of failure, I veer toward stressing their diversity. Freud taunts Stein in *Pugilist Specialist* by accusing her of having 'FTA' – Failure to Adapt. Ironically, given the coruscating account of medicine's visual economy in *Under the Knife*, an economy in which tools of visualization such as the microscope and the x-ray have paramount value, it is the failure of a device rigged to *prevent* her from seeing that allows Fanny Burney to view the performance of the mastectomy operation on her: she peers through a cambric handkerchief, a totally inadequate barrier to her observation. In Goese's pieces, it is usually costume which breaks down. At first busily designating the character she is to perform, the seemingly endless layers of her ceaseless transformation overwhelm our ability to keep up the decoding. Each outfit tells us 'this is who I am now', but each layer revealed tells us we were wrong to assume. In *Kind Ness*, the Stage Hand puts down rocks to mark out the diorama that must be in place before we are allowed to see the gorilla only to be told by the Narrator 'no, not yet', making us wonder what, in the play's narrative of assimilation, is not yet in place. That Chong has the Stage Hand repeatedly move to lay down the rocks at the wrong time is his reflexive practise of a philosophy broadly similar to that which underscores the theatres of Meyerhold and Brecht: that glitches in systems make processes more visible, and that when signifying apparati work without glitches, those apparati remain invisible. Chong's dialogue is geared less to the use of speech as communication, and more to the creation of an unsettling negative space of miscommunication. Like Ridiculusmus in *Say Nothing* and Adamsdale and Branch in *The Receipt*, he pushes the phatic function of language to excesses that unravel communication.

There is an argument to be made that failure is an ethic. While Anna Deavere Smith herself regards it as a mark of her successful unlocking of 'American character', Smith's framing of her *Search for American Character* valorizes that negative space of performance, what she calls 'the gap', that results from the performer's failure: '[c]haracter lives in the obvious gap between the real person and my attempt to seem like them' (Smith, 1993a, pp. xxxvii–viii). If failure has hit the United States, where both mainstream and counterculture have tended to be goal-oriented, it is not surprising that it has hit the United Kingdom with a more resounding bang (whimper?). Goat Island (whose Matthew Goulish, along with Tim Etchells, co-founded the Institute of Failure in 2001) reflect on failure, but Etchells's Forced Entertainment have luxuriated in it, and in an increasingly explicit, focused manner. From 2001's *First Night* to 2008's *Spectacular*, both of which crucially quote more successful theatrical performances than the one they are able to achieve, Forced Entertainment have not only dwelled on how theatre cannot communicate, but put out press packs and issued spectators with DVDs that strive to pinpoint their focus on effort and failure.[8]

It is all too easy, though, to talk in blanket terms of an 'ethic of failure'. Failure may not exactly be the new success, but it in some respects it is the new power. In one of the most frequently cited passages from Foucault, he writes: 'One needs to be nominalistic, no doubt: power is not an institution, and not a structure; neither is it a certain strength we are endowed with; it is the name that one attributes to a complex strategical situation in a particular society' (1992, p. 93). Judith Butler paraphrases Foucault's discussion of the word 'power': 'It is the name that one attributes to a complexity which is not easily named' (1997, p. 95). While the word 'failure' serves, or fails, to describe an array of strategies and dispositions, these are even more disparate than the branches identified by Foucault's formulation of 'power'.

Rather than theorizing an ethic of failure, I have begun, and will continue, to describe how naming is used, in various respects, *against itself*, that negativity providing a platform for the articulation of ex-nominated connections. My reading is informed by Jon McKenzie's notion of 'catachristening'.[9] 'Catachristening (catastrophic naming) engages the interminable death and birth of performative referentiality' (McKenzie, 2001, p. 212). Via catachristening, the name, as deployed by Chong, Parks, Vogel, Ridiculusmus, Riot Group, and Forced Entertainment, 'becomes an event' as its 'catastrophic effects register the inherent ability of performatives to fail and misfire, and, in misfiring, to link up with other referents, other contents, other performances' (ibid.). In Chapters 4 and 6, I consider the idea that failure in (particular works of) performance jams the performance machinery of hegemonic culture. In Chapter 8, I extend Noël Carroll's philosophy of monsters within horror genres to global corporations, arguing that confusion and bluntness are valuable tools of dissimulation that allow corporations to function and to grow. When it comes to creating a company like RotoPlas, evacuation of substance passes as provision. The non-communicative language and non-service services alienated in *The Receipt* are potent ways for corporations to constrain social channels. Recognizing failure as an engineered *part* of the corporate machinery of globalization means that any performance of failure in terms of the *in*corporation of accidents and glitches can as equally be seen to play into the hands of corporate power as to transgress its laws.

Even if, making less-activist claims for it, we see failure as a reflection rather than an agent of breakdown, it is still fraught with contradictions as a descriptor. As Jean-Luc Nancy opines in *The Inoperative Community* (1991), what are traditionally named 'communities' in what is conventionally called 'the West' have, over centuries, increasingly found themselves united only in a common failure to unite. At its most potent, perhaps, theatre's engagement with failure, and I would claim this for many of the works I consider here, can articulate something along the lines Nancy draws, and can model a way to deal in and with that common failure to unite, something like Wellman's 'grounding in a paradoxical lack of groundedness'.

Making history, making geography

This book is about acts of naming that take place in theatrical texts and performances; but the theatrical acts of naming I explore crucially engage with naming practices in domains such as television and print journalism, the justice system, tourism, advertising and brand development, semiotics, cultural theory, anthropology, corporate statutes, urban planning, peace and reconciliation fora, military training, cybernetics, genetics, histories of medicine, and histories of nationhood. As well as spilling into one another, some of these domains, such as advertising and cybernetics, push beyond the term 'domain': they are naming practices that construct platforms or arenas *for* naming.

Here's what I did... and *The Receipt* (see Chapter 8) suggest that naming after (both personal and vocational) has been superseded by what might be called 'naming across', in which value, and often a kind of colonial, cross-domain authority, is obtained by the borrowing of names, the extension of naming conventions from one domain to another. 'Why', asks Wiley in *The Receipt*, 'is technology increasingly named after fruit?' The conference that David attends in *Here's what I did ...* is sponsored by multi-national corporation GenTechnica, whose businesses range 'from genetic engineering to music sales'. GenTechnica represent , in Baudrillard's terms, the viral, or 'trans-apparent' nature of branding.[10] In familial 'naming after' the logic is one of continuity, and in vocational naming one of attribution: in both cases, naming works to fix the named individual to a particular achievement or family line. In corporate 'naming across', naming corporealizes a named entity by *un*fixing it from achievement, family line, domain.

Continuing the work of the twentieth-century's last, the first decade of the twenty-first century was an era in which it was not just products that were subject to intense branding and re-branding, but concepts and *forms* of conceptualization. As the grounds of individual and communal identity are called into continuing question, authors of and characters in these works create new names to incubate new phenomena and viewpoints. But they also 're-remember' the referentiality of signs overwritten or rendered dormant by re-branding, histories of signification on which formative identifications and investments were built.

Instead of the Aristotelian *peripeteia* and *anagnorisis* (reversal and recognition), based on an identification with the protagonist cemented by the unities, these works exert a different kind of identification, based on a shared struggle to perceive. If identification for Aristotle depends on being immersed in the protagonist's journey, in these pieces it depends on the alternation between being immersed and being distanced. Immersing the spectator in and removing them from the narrative via de- and re-familiarization techniques allows the likes of Ridiculusmus, Lightwork, Vogel, Chong, Parks, and Bobby Baker (see Chapter 4) to effect contextual jolts. The technique highlights the relationship between the way individuals assimilate stories and the way they are themselves assimilated into society through reading.

In lieu of Aristotelian dramatic irony, in which we know before s/he does what is coming to the protagonist because it is there all along, naming in these works fosters mnemonic irony, in which we alternately forget and re-remember what is there all along. The latex gloves of the Baltimore doctor are worn by The Third Man throughout Anna's dream, but tend to become invisible until adjusted. Vogel states that the gloves are not about allowing us to see as if for the first time, but are about noticing our own serial 're-remembering' – forgetting to see; remembering; forgetting again; remembering again – which is the flipside of denial: 'As cultural animals, we do not forget because something is hidden, we forget because something is in our face and we don't want to see it anymore. That's what forgetting is. Forgetting is a way of not looking' (Savran, 1999, p. 271). Anna's alternate denial and recognition of her circumstances parallels our own immersion in and detachment from the narrative. The gloves are formalist devices that Burke and Shklovsky would recognize, but are also pieces in a game of re-remembering and denial that is topical in its focus on the politics of cultural memory. For Vogel, as for Chong and Parks, performative restoration brings to life both the remembered events and the instruments of remembrance. It is not just props and costume but, by virtue of their cathectic investment in these objects, characters themselves that are formalist devices. The gorilla suit worn throughout by Buzz, not so much a costume as a signifying game, occasions all kinds of play with dis- and reinvestment in gorilla as signifying metaphor. In a phrase that speaks for Vogel, Parks, and others of the theatre-makers I read, Chong describes his allegorical works of the 1980s as 'waking public dreams', in which unmoored figures play at de- and re-attaching themselves to available reality, seeing themselves from a distance as strange figures on familiar ground, or familiar figures on strange ground. The distancing that name-play can engender allows characters to establish a viewing position, they remove themselves in order to see themselves, to recognize or re-remember that they are assimilable beings in a cultural field.

Many of the names we encounter – like 'Founding Father' (see Chapter 3), 'Roentgen' (Chapter 5), or 'Roland Barthes' (Chapter 9) – are names that, in Bordieu's phrase, *'font date'*: they 'make history' as time marked by names. Bordieu elucidates how proper names 'make history' by figuring history as a canon, establishing canons as timelines marked by names that *'fait date'*.[11] In *Here's what I did …* (see Chapter 9), Lightwork use Barthes's writing on name/sign relationships to look at what that traditional figuration of history means for those, like Barthes himself, who make a name for themselves, but whose names outlive them as historical signs. In thinking through, and resisting, the construction of history as the marking of time by names, Lightwork, like Skipitares and like Parks, interrogate the role of naming practices that brand people and their labour to institute character and to 'characterize' institutions. Interrogation of 'naming after' in *Here's what I did…*, *Under the Knife, IMTK,* and *The America Play* – a son after his father, a disease or a technology after its discover or developer, an impersonator after their subject – links exploration of personal identity to consideration of how museums, archives, and institutions of learning discipline labour.

Against the time-honoured tradition of 'making history' by 'making a name for oneself', the practice that upholds the proper, the works I discuss set the making public of that which does not, within the regime of the proper, make a name for itself. This kind of *making public* is what documentary theatre often nominates, naming its own naming, as I argue in Chapter 7. Making public in these instances is an intervention into making history, the naming of that which history has excluded from view. Because exclusion from the public realm is maintained by the law of the proper, making public means challenging those laws. Founded as it is on a self-possession that anchors all systems of property, on competence (the ability to perform according to rules of language), and on cleanliness (keeping free of contamination), the proper, as marked by proper names, ex-nominates its own history-making. In contrast, documentary theatre works like *My Name is Rachel Corrie*, *Talking to Terrorists*, *The Laramie Project*, and *The Vagina Monologues* nominate their portrayal of subjects who trouble propriety. As well as playing up, and playing on, the challengingly contradictory nature of the characters they study, these works, I argue, name their own theatrical questioning of what is regarded as polite, or proper, discussion (often this means, amongst middle, or theatre-frequenting, classes), their transgressing of social and linguistic norms and taboos.

Several other chapters indicate, and reflect on, theatre's tendency to make public, make history, and make geography. While Lightwork allow the intimate (the private thoughts of famous, French, public intellectuals) to undermine the epic (familiar, historical perspectives on these public figures) as they intercede in the making of history, Forced Entertainment set the intimate communication of interior monologue against the public places listed in the A–Z of Britain as they 'make geography', in decidedly improper fashion, in *The Travels*. As in the work of a number of American playwrights, such as Charles Mee and Sarah Ruhl, *The Travels* pits the classical against the modern in ways that reveal constructions of classicism and modernity.[12] *Eurydice* (2003), an inventive rendition by Ruhl of the story of Eurydice and Orpheus, applies contemporary rhythms, idioms, and preoccupations in a wittily incongruous, playfully unclassical manner. Like Forced Entertainment, Ruhl loves to effect a kind of joyous melancholy via vertiginous oscillation between romantic storytelling and cool, anti-romantic urbanity. Both *Eurydice* and *The Travels* recuperate a contemporary sense of disconnection from the past by importing the romantic otherness of the classical. In both cases, names *allow* play by acting as the stimulus for language games that improperly classicize the modern and modernize the classical. Contriving some doable activities appropriate to the names 'Oracle' and 'Delphi' in her A–Z, Cathy Naden decides to look for a fortune-teller. Remembering where she is, she worries that 'getting all this to happen in Salford is going to be hard' (Forced Entertainment, 2002, p. 15).

A lecture by geographer Doreen Massey, whose books (including *For Space*, 2005) have made an impact on dance and site-specific performance practitioners and theorists, informs several of my readings.[13] Massey's lecture describes how, in globalization, romantic notions of space bolster its commodity value by/while erasing historical differences from present perception. Her ideas about the ways in which globalization over-writes space by trading on romantic ideas of space as possibility, making tourists of us all, resonates with *The Travels*. The participant-performer-tourists of *The Travels* enjoy the romantic feeling of exploration while reflecting with a dry, plaintive wit on the obscene discrepancies between exotic, august, expansive place names and the cramped lives to which the actualities of place testify. The title of Massey's talk, 'Is the World Really Shrinking?', reminds me also of watching *Say Nothing* (see Chapter 8), in which a ridiculously tiny rectangle of turf is the putative, inadequate 'stage' on which the characters trade names of places they both might know in a performance of establishing common ground.

Forced Entertainment and Ridiculusmus are not alone in exploring the ways in which traditions of naming manage connections between mental and physical space. Several of the theatre-makers I discuss examine how mental and physical compartmentalization work in tandem in material and political ways, and how theatrical metaphors intervene in that compartmentalization. Many of the theatre-makers want to clear space, to create 'gaps' – a word iterated many times in the pages that follow. Anna Deavere Smith positions her interview-and-impersonation technique as opening a space in a 'sound-bite culture' that forecloses doubt, shepherding difference into seamless divisions. 'Character', she suggests, 'lives in the obvious gap between the real person and my attempt to seem like them' (Smith, 1993a, pp. xxxvii–viii). I suggest (in Chapter 7) that what is most valuably dialogic about Smith's work, however, is not the 'gap' she identifies, but the one between her framing of the work and the work itself. While Smith nominates a lack of space as somehow a *cause* of a degraded public sphere, Parks takes a step back, implicating metaphors that *lead to the experience* of a lack of space. In the mini-essays that preface *The America Play and Other Works* (1995), she touches on some of the ways in which, as the plays in the volume enact, temporal and spatial metaphors intersect to station identity. As I discuss in Chapter 3, several of her plays and comments on them implicate metaphors of linearity and horizontality in serving to train readers/spectators to receive a play as a system according to which events are perceived *as* eventful only by falling into place. Her characters are readers and spectators of their own time-lines. Mr Smith's family use the letters he sends home from the army to plot his destiny 'falling into place'. For Mr Smith, time, which the army has led him to believe is a vista of possibility, runs out. The character of time itself appears, from Mr Smith's perspective, to have deteriorated:

> MR SERGEANT SMITH: Time for somethin noble was yesterday. There usta be uh overlap of four hours. Hours in four when I'd say 'today' and today it'd be. Them four hours usta happen together, now, they scatter theirselves all throughout thuh day. Usta be uh flap tuh slip through. Flaps gone shut.
>
> (Parks, 1995, p. 65)

It is not until this point, late in the day of his destiny, that Mr Smith thinks beyond the spatial metaphors in which he has been drilled, beginning to get a grip on his situation by applying his own metaphors.

In all the works I discuss, space is a spectral commodity: it often seems to be running out, or to have been degraded or devalued; characters struggle to access real, or pure space, and complain of a cheapened or illusory form. Attempts to regain a sense of space involve refusal or, as in Ping Chong's allegories, a Martianist/ phenomenological bracketing of accepted ways of naming space, and of naming history via spatial metaphors. Often, there is a desire to start again, to un-write space, to erase its codes, to start again. It is an impulse that informs the rush of documentary theatre at the turn of the millennium, a wave of work that wants to excavate a space before spin. In her 'Other History of Intercultural Performance', Coco Fusco describes *Two Undiscovered Amerindians* as a performance located at the '"zero degree" of intercultural relations, in an attempt to find a point of origin for the debates that link "discovery" and "otherness"' (1994, p.148). A character in Parks's *Death of the Last Black Man in the Whole Entire World* expresses a desire to un-map his world, to return it to a state 'before uh demarcation made it mapped' (Parks, 1995, p. 114).

The problem with 'zero degree' discursive space (as I discuss in Chapter 4), is that it entails an erasure (albeit heuristic) of history. One person's strategy to seek a point of origin is another's complicity in forgetting. The idea of the performance space as a blank slate, an erased tablet or physicalized mind-space from which knowledge has been wiped clean, has a history beyond the scope of this discussion. More tendentiously than Peter Brook's *Empty Space* (1977), the empty spaces on view here are conspicuously constructed in their emptiness, in contra-distinction from, and resistance to, constructions of spatial metaphor that take place within. Though their works are quite diverse in form (including durational pieces, scripted narratives, and interactive web-based environmental works), Forced Entertainment's brand of performance features a use of space marked by a *lack* of representational decor invoking a fictional world, and by the presence of sardonically effortful tools for presentational communication (cardboard signs, disco lights, and microphones on stands or on a desk). While the physical and mental geography discussed in *The Travels* is rich – full of imagined spaces triggered by names in the A–Z, and detailed reporting of actual space – the presentation space itself is a presentation of non-space, a kind of despatialized zone.

The utopias (literally, 'non-places') presented by Smith, Parks, Forced Entertainment, Ridiculusmus, Wolfe, and Fusco are far more varied than the phrase 'empty space' implies. Rather than seeing them as a particular *kind* of space, I suggest that more coherence lies in what these presentation spaces evince: a desire to free space from, or empty it of, commodification and dead metaphor. Graeme Miller's site-specific performances and installations (to which, in Chapter 6, I compare *The Travels*) have often sought to reclaim spaces that have become 'unnamed'. Of one of his works, *The Desire Paths* (1993), Miller writes:

> [The] starting point was that a place does not exist until it is imagined and named and that all of the copses, knolls and paths that have been walked and named are the mark points of human experience and the markstones of lives lived. These real spaces have become 'unnamed' with the passing of time, becoming less plausible than the centralised reality of the media and the transitory, frantic nature of living today. *The Desire Paths* was a theatre work that re-named the city.[14]

Pseudo-naming in *The Receipt* and *Say Nothing* (Chapter 7) trades on a veneer of efficiency that is the opposite of, and over-writes, those 'real' spaces that have become unnamed. It is a kind of pseudo-naming that indicates a shift in late-capitalist societies from a metaphysics of substance to a metastasis of value.

Wolfe's method in *The Colored Museum* is a post-Brechtian detachment of sign from effect. Rather than offering another form, or shell, *The Colored Museum* spews calcified forms from the history of African-American self-representation. Having regurgitated these forms, Wolfe ends (in 'The Party') by salvaging their shells, which should be seen, he states, not as fossils, but as 'silhouettes', reformable.[15] The 'silhouettes' are the characters themselves, the inhabitants of the museum: they wear the shells of dead iconography like the casing of a Trojan horse, hiding the agency within. The spaces in which the characters hang out are emblems of this subterfugal force. Miss Roj's Bottomless Pit, like Parks's Great Hole of History, is a hidden, interior space of un-naming that accommodates an elsewhere beyond the hegemonic gaze – an elsewhere not outside discourse, but in which discourse is materially unpacked and re-figured.

.

2
Authorship: A Trick of the I

In her Introduction to *Excitable Speech*, Judith Butler writes that the subject is:

> brought into social location and time through being named. And one is dependent upon another for one's name, for the designation that is supposed to confer singularity. Whether the name is shared by others, the name, as a convention, has a generality and a historicity that is in no sense radically singular, even though it is understood to exercise the power of conferring singularity.
>
> (1997, p. 29)

Naming, and the subjectivity it bolsters, requires 'an intersubjective context', states Butler, because 'the very possibility of naming another requires that one first be named'. To name is not simply to offer oneself up as an individual subject, but to participate in a 'dyadic relation' with another who also offers themself up. That is not to say, however, that those who participate in this intersubjective relation are generally aware of how it constitutes them: 'the time of discourse is not the time of the subject' (ibid., p. 31). The system of the subject's enunciability, as Butler portrays it, is a 'linguistic scene', a stage whose spatio-temporal frame is ordinarily invisible.

In so much theatre of recent decades, it is the condition of 'being subject to' that has become the subject. In this chapter, I cast Butler's metaphorically theatrical scenario of how naming constitutes subjectivity alongside Paula Vogel's theatrical scenario. The playwright's brother, Carl, died of AIDS-related illnesses on 9 January 1988. *The Baltimore Waltz* (*BW*) is a self-conscious memorializing of Carl's life and public mourning of his death. Though the siblings it depicts, Anna and Carl, are the playwright's alter ego and a version of the playwright's brother, *BW* is less an autobiography than a play that explores the limits of autobiography in the theatre *circa* 1990. Traumatized by the loss of her brother, the playwright attempts to bring him to life. In the course of trying to make Carl present, she gets caught up in the instabilities of (what Vogel refers to as) the 'postmodern': 'the awareness that all texts are battlefields of contradictions and that each work, when examined, implodes' (Dixon and Smith, 1995, p. 94). These instabilities become the subject of the play.

Not just because it is the most clearly autobiographical, *BW* is Vogel's most reflexive play. In its meditation on the uses of textual, and specifically theatrical, artifice, the play accords with Herbert Blau's observations of a theatre in which immersion in fantasy is a way not to escape truth, but to prove that truth exists. Referring to his own theatre practice, Blau reflects:

> the appearances from which theatre is made and upon which it reflects are conceptually elaborated and in turn reflected upon until there is a denial, or refusal, by means of theater of the distressing and maybe crippling notion that in life there is nothing but theatre.
>
> (Benamou and Caramello, 1977, p. 62)

Vogel's Anna exerts the 'denial, or refusal', that Blau describes. Wishing to assure herself that she has a past, a centre, Anna throws herself into the 'conceptual elaboration of appearances', a whirlwind in which she tosses herself between fantasy and reality. Along the lines of the paradox that Blau elucidates, Paula/Anna strives to situate herself in her reality by constructing a veil of artifice and then dramatizing herself piercing that veil. She feels her past, her remembered experience, to be hers only because it is so artificial that she can lose herself in its luxuriant 'elaborations'.

Vogel's enmeshing of her projected self in artifice, proceeding from the construction of an alter ego who immerses herself in imaginatively quilted textual worlds, resonates with Foucault's conceptions of the space of writing. Foucault uses the word 'écriture' to designate writing seen not from the standpoint of intended meaning, or of the act of writing, but according to 'the space across which writing is dispersed and the time in which it unfurls'. In the wake of the death of the author and the death of the subject, 'the point' of writing, states Foucault, 'is not to pin a subject within language; it is rather a question of creating a space into which the writing subject constantly disappears' (Foucault, 1991, pp. 101–20). He describes a scenario acutely applicable to *BW*, in which writing 'unfolds like a game *(jeu)* that invariably goes beyond its own rules and transgresses its limits' (ibid., p. 102).

A series of items precede the printed text of *BW*: a dedication; an epigram; an autobiographical note from the playwright explaining the circumstances that led her to write the play; and a letter from Carl that she encourages 'all future productions to reprint' in their 'accompanying program'. Though they memorialize the play, these precursors mark the insufficiency of the play as a memorial. The dedication reads:

> *To the memory of Carl – because I cannot sew.*
>
> (Vogel, 1996, p. 3)

The sewing reference is an allusion to the established practice of making quilts to memorialize AIDS victims. The epigram is a quote from actor Ron Vawter, who also died of AIDS-related illness:

> I always saw myself as a surrogate who, in the absence of anyone else, would stand in for him.
>
> (Vogel, 1996, p. 3)

The playwright's note explains that, a year or so before he died, Carl invited her on an 'excursion to Europe. Due to pressures of time and money, [she] declined, never dreaming that he was HIV positive'. The phrase 'never dreaming' is apt. Most of the play stands in for the dream that the playwright did have, waiting in the hospital as her brother lay dying: it is a daydream in which the author's alter ego imagines an exhilarating trip through 'a Europe that exists only in the imagination' (ibid., p. 4). The final item preceding the play, a letter containing Carl's directions for his funeral, conveys his personality vividly. His taste in music, the hypothetically dead author states, runs 'to the highbrow: Faure's 'Pie Jesu' from his *Requiem*, 'Dance of the Blessed Spirits' from *Orfeo*, 'La vergine degli Angeli' from Verdi's *Forza*'. As for 'the piece of me I leave behind', he offers a comprehensive set of options including '[o]pen casket, bum up (you'll know where to place the calla lilies, won't you?)'. In permitting all productions to reprint Carl's letter in her capacity as 'executor of his estate', Paula explains that she 'would appreciate letting him speak to us in his own words' (ibid., p. 5).

From the moment that the first words of *BW* are spoken, however, the contingencies of such speech are apparent. The play opens with Anna speaking to the audience/practising a foreign language:

> 'Help me please.' (*Anna recites from memory*.) Dutch:
> 'Kunt U mij helpen, alstublieft?' 'There's nothing I can do'.
>
> (Vogel, 1996, p. 7)

The 'I' of the language lesson is emblematically foreign, a quotational 'I'. Derrida argues that the self 'becomes a speaking subject only by making its speech conform to the system of the rules of language as a system of differences'.[1] In everyday life, the manoeuvres required for appearance as a speaking subject are not visible: the death of Carl, and the desire to resurrect him, prompts a crisis of subjectivity in which those manoeuvres become the subject. (The language lessons that Mona/Molly fails to grasp in *Imperceptible Mutabilities in the Third Kingdom* (*IMTK*) – discussed in the next chapter – work a similarly Derridean insight into the effortful cultural training of a conspicuously unstable identity.)

Read in conjunction with the dedication, 'because I cannot sew', Anna's statement, 'there's nothing I can do', might be seen as a symbolic switching over from the playwright 'I' to the character 'I'. The switch seems to be motivated by Paula's acknowledgement that she can only help Carl vicariously. Moments later, when Carl receives his diagnosis, a second switch occurs:

> DOCTOR: ...And there is usually rapid destruction and metastases.
> CARL: Anna –
> ANNA: I'm right here, darling. Right here.
> CARL: Could you explain it very slowly?
> DOCTOR: .....Often seen with effusions, either exudate or transudate.
> ANNA: Carl –
> CARL: I'm here, darling. Right here.
>
> (Vogel, 1996, pp. 9–10)

As the Doctor describes the progress of disease through Carl's body, Vogel/Anna arrests his diagnosis through a quasi-shamanic substitution, Anna becoming the patient. The 'standing-in' alluded to in the epigram thus takes on a redemptive quality as Anna takes on Carl's disease. Carl is diagnosed with Acquired Toilet Disease (ATD), a ludicrous stand-in for Sexually Transmitted Disease (STD) and Acquired Immune Deficiency

Syndrome (AIDS). Anna switches places with Carl and redeems him textually by taking on the substitute illness. The symbolic switching over from the playwright to the alter ego, from the Paula 'I' to the Anna 'I', seems to be motivated by Paula's acknowledgement that she can only 'help' Carl vicariously. Already a stand-in for Paula, Anna proceeds to stand in for Carl, performing the role of the patient throughout the play-within-the-play, the palimpsestic 'treatment' that constitutes most of *BW*.

All but the first few and last few minutes of the play is an exteriorization of what takes place in Anna's mind while she waits in the stark wings of Johns Hopkins Hospital in Baltimore, where Carl lays dying. In the original published text of the play, Vogel states that it takes place 'in a hospital (perhaps in a lounge, corridor or waiting room) in Baltimore, Maryland'.[2] The 'lounge, corridor or waiting room' is a limbo that reflects the state of Anna's mind. The mental journey she undergoes is an imaginative, quasi-transcendent reflection on Carl's passing. It is an exhilarating one for siblings and spectators alike: Anna throws herself with abandon into culinary and sexual indulgence, while Carl delights in the paintings and buildings that Western Europe has to offer. Motifs of vicarious presence, and of standing-in, multiply throughout a quilt-like inner narrative fashioned from memories of novels, travel guides, plays, and films.[3] The dominant palimpsestic source is the 1949 Graham Greene-scripted, Carol Reed-directed, post-war noir espionage thriller, *The Third Man*. In trying to cope with death on a personal level, and with the mediation of AIDS on a political level, the author propels her alter ego into a web of textual and performative substitutions in which finding the truth seems to depend on surrender to fantasy.

Writing in the year that *BW* received its New York premiere, Stuart Hall reflects on the 'expansion of the notion of text and textuality, both as a source of meaning and as that which escapes meaning'; and 'of textuality and cultural power, of representation itself, as a site of power and regulation; of the symbolic as a source of identity' (Morley and Chen, 1996, p. 271). Hall identifies a paradox crucial to the drifting of attention within cultural studies away from analysis of social stratification and toward the effects of image-making systems. That paradox can be expressed thus: there is ever more urgency to root and find one's own and others' identity in coded systems, in what Hall calls 'the symbolic'; but to turn to the realm of the symbolic is to turn to discursivity and textuality, which always involves 'displacement' (ibid.). In *BW*, Vogel enacts herself trying to overcome the 'instabilities' and the 'displacement' that textualizing experience entails. The impulses that led to the play are redemptive and compensatory: Paula wants to bring Carl to life. This desire, however, is chased by the need to express, comprehend, and come to terms with the fact that Carl has gone, and cannot be brought to life. The play enacts Paula finding cunning ways to make Carl present by inserting bits of text – from sources such as films and travel guides – into the gaps in her shared experience with, and memories of, her brother. With every wave of invention, though, there is a counter-wave of negativity, a recurrent and inevitable marking of Carl's absence. The ebb and flow of absence and presence itself marks the ways that subjects can and cannot be animated and constructed in language and in theatre. As she adopts the authority of the playwright to conduct a kind of personal autopsy in public, she finds that, to come to communicative terms with her brother's death, she must first accommodate the Death of the Author.

After Vogel becomes Anna, and Anna stands in for Carl, autobiography increasingly merges with a theatricality infiltrated by film iconography. A third performer plays a myriad of roles, most of them as slippery and duplicitous as the Orson Welles character in *The Third Man*. Vogel's Third Man wears the latex gloves of – and, in dream logic, 'is' – the Johns Hopkins Doctor, but calls himself Harry Lime (as the Welles character does), as he takes on all the personae the siblings encounter: an Airport Security Guard, a string of fly-by-night lovers, the odd waiter and concierge, and various doctors. In Platonic philosophy, The Third Man is a notional figure, hypothetically placeable between the Ideal Man and the Particular Man. Because The Third Man is a synthesis of the Ideal and the Particular, he is not a concept in the pure sense that the Ideal Man is, nor a concrete entity like the Particular Man. The problem, Plato muses, is that between Third Man and the Particular Man, another man can always be inserted. Plato's Third Man is as slippery as Vogel's: he is not real but is not unreal; not apparent, but based on appearances.

While it is The Third Man who is most conspicuously duplicitous, Anna herself is an exceedingly slippery central figure. She is interpellated not as a true 'I', but as a projection of the playwright that allows her to function. Vogel's stepping into her own and then her brother's shoes, propelling her on an imagined version of a journey she wishes she had actually taken with him, is a far cry from the smoothness of conventional autobiography 'wherein', as Elin Diamond puts it, 'past experience is made to testify to the subject's self-consciousness' (1997, pp. 148–9). Anna inhabits, in Diamond's thinking (which draws on Walter Benjamin), 'an I-position' that 'decomposes into dialectical images' that are 'trans-historical' and that 'help us to read history against the grain – and read the body against the grain' (ibid., p. 154). The I-position allows Paula/Anna to suspend time and consciousness, to transcend the space and the reality of the Hospital, to stand outside herself. Creating an alter-ego allows Paula to 'produce' an 'I' that is 'dialectic' in several senses: Paula is gay, Anna is straight; Anna speaks words that Carl said to his sister in real life; the character Anna is based on Paula's real-life best friend. The personality that Paula attributes to her friend describes the character of Anna in the play:

> I decided to model Anna on my best friend – who had been an elementary school teacher, and who, although certainly not naïve, was very alive and appreciative of life – the opposite to blasé.[4]

The I-position of Anna, then, is, as Vogel puts it, an 'amalgamation' – a word used, also, by Butler to describe the process of naming – that is deeply strange but deeply familiar, intensely comforting but intensely unstable.

When Anna swaps places with Carl to become the patient, the author function passes to Carl. Carl and The Third Man switch and collude to fix Anna in third-person object position, prizing her from the 'I-position' of the image-maker that she occupies at the start of the play. The Third Man's use of the first-person pronoun emphasizes the fact that 'I-ness' is paradoxically mutable in *BW*: it is the position from which the story is told, but is not fixed to stable subjectivity. On the contrary, Vogel exploits every opportunity to use the I-position as a site of contest, a place in which reading is always 'against the grain'. It is striking that the first-person pronoun is used in the play precisely at the point where subjectivity is occluded, where the self is silenced, as in the language lessons. As in *Under the Knife* (see Chapter 5), the 'I' is more often than not quotational, often conspicuously so, except in those moments where the subject *speaks of being silenced*.[5] The speaking of being silenced that is so key to the I-positions constructed by Vogel and Skipitares highlights the translations on which theatre's mechanisms of identification are predicated.

As the European journey begins, Anna often regains the author function, but another change of subject-object positioning is always just around the corner. Vogel alternately suspends and reveals evidence of her character's voice and of her own authorial self-consciousness. Anna, in parallel with her author, tries to free herself from painful consciousness, but finds, in what she thought was escape, a deeper consciousness. Vogel dwells on the development of the ego, the interface of psychic and social, the cusp in which thought becomes behaviour and is thereby laid open to interpretation. Scene VIII (early in the daydream that is the play-within-the-play) begins:

> THE THIRD MAN: At the hotel. (*Simultaneously with Carl's next lines:*) Lesson Six: Direct Pronouns. I am tired. And my sister looks at herself in the mirror.
> CARL: Sixieme Leçon: Pronouns – Complements Directs. Je suis fatigué. Et ma soeur elle se regarde dans la glace.
> CARL climbs onto a double bed. [...] ANNA stares into a mirror. [...]
> THE THIRD MAN: The first separation – your first sense of loss.
> (Vogel, 1996, p. 17)

The author translates her first-person experience into the hypothetical possessive ('your first sense of loss'), which makes no distinction between first- and third-person pronomination. Address is in limbo, poised between the shared warmth of identification and a clinically distancing transposition. Naming here is a sea of translation, a compressed, oneiric version of Butler's quasi-theatrical scenario in which 'the name is offered, imposed by someone or by some set of someones, and it is attributed to someone else' so that the 'subject of speech who is named becomes, potentially, one who might well name another in time' (Butler, 1997, p. 29). In her unpacking of how naming works, Butler makes a statement that could be a critique of Vogel's code-switching: 'This suggests that such a subject in language is positioned as both addressed and addressing, and that the very possibility of naming another requires that one first to be named' (ibid.).

In the next scene, the switching continues as Carl takes on naming duties and The Third Man becomes the demonstrator:

> CARL: Medical Straight Talk: Part Two.
> *(THE THIRD MAN becomes a Public Health Official)*
> THE THIRD MAN: Here at the Department of Public Health, we are announcing Operation Squat.
> (Vogel, 1996, p. 18)

The re-entry of the sardonically named 'Medical Straight Talk' to speed things up, and to distract Anna just at the point where she begins to come to terms with loss, runs parallel to Butler's account of the importance of time in naming. In Butler's scenario, the subject never quite attains determinate awareness of being constituted by language, which means that 'the time of discourse is not the time of the subject'.

In this sea of translation, in which the baton of the subject's self-naming is passed from one stand-in narrator to another, Anna, much like Holly Martins tracking Harry Lime in *The Third Man*, navigates the serial displacement and conflation of identities as we try to keep up. When Anna forgets to reflect, and immerses herself in the 'daydreamt' action, Carl takes over the role of the decoder:

> CARL: Although he began his career by studying in the classical tradition, his later paintings reveal the influence of the Italian style.
> ANNA (*muffled*): Ah! Yes!
> GARÇON (*also muffled*): Ah! Oui!
> CARL: He traveled extensively around the world, and in the salon of 1827 his privately lauded techniques were displayed in public.
> ANNA: Yes, oh, yes, yes!
> GARÇON: Mais oui! [...]
> ANNA: Yes – I – I – I – I – !
> GARÇON: Je – je! Je!! Je!
> (*Pause.*)
> CARL: In art, as in life, some things need no translation.
>
> (Vogel, 1996, pp. 22–3)

Anna's bodily exploits and Carl's cerebral ones may seem poles apart, but both point to escape, to solace, to forgetting in this typically Vogelian conjunction of farce, genuine passion, and reflexive irony.

The motif of 'the translated I' frames Anna's sexual escapades as a metaphor for the play as a whole. Earlier in the play, after diagnosis and before entering the journey of the imagination, Anna announces that she intends 'to fuck her brains out' (Vogel, 1996, p. 12). While this is a character's statement about how she plans to spend her time abroad, it is also a metaphorical statement by the author about the function of the play. The daydream-as-theatre, through which Paula/Anna sublimates her mental turmoil, chimes with Gavin Bolton's theory that artistic expression is driven by ludic desire that cannot be satisfied in the everyday scheme of life:

> In a game the pain of life can safely be recaptured, encountered and switched off as required, for [...] a game and all other forms of playing including the arts are deliberately created second-order experiences, removed from the rawness of living.
>
> (Bolton, 1984, p. 105)

While they seem to be opposites, Anna's mindless sex tour and Carl's erudite critique of Corot both function as sublimations within a bigger 'game' in which Vogel generates 'second-order experiences' to 'remove' herself 'from the rawness of living'. Vogel explores the idea that theatre is a medium rooted in contingency: it 'operates in the present tense' (Bigsby, 1999, p. 310), but 'there is no you or he or she' (Savran, 1999, p. 271) fully present.[6] Vogel's public daydream is a fundamentally interrogatory form of theatre, marking rather than closing the gap between personal consciousness and public discourse.

As well as enacting the constraints upon subjectivity that the experience of her brother's diagnosis and treatment brings into critical consciousness, playwriting affords Vogel an opportunity for *heteroglossia*, Bakhtin's name for the productive refraction of authorial experiences through another's language. Vogel turns to playwriting as a refuge within a sound-bite culture in which hyperactive currents of imagery dressed as information seem to answer questions before we have had a chance to form them. Sound-bites in the form of titular clips – 'As children they fought' and 'Dolls are for girls' – are smothered by moments of insight and reflection that establish Anna as the spectator's partner in perception. She does not really connect with any of the characters played by The Third Man. She does not talk meaningfully to Carl once the daydream has begun. Moments of reflection, in which Anna refers to herself in the second-person pronoun 'you', as opposed to the first-person 'I', have a testimonial quality that temporarily cuts through the frenzy of the narrative:

> ANNA: You hear the doctor through a long-distance corridor. Your ears are functioning, but the mind is numb. You try to listen as you swim towards his sentences in the fluorescent light of his office.
>
> (Vogel, 1996, p. 12)

Occurring in Scene 3, almost immediately after Anna has assumed the role of the patient, this is the first of Anna's reflective addresses to the audience. Immediately, the focus is on perception, on being connected and disconnected to language and to presence. Though the 'you' pronoun and the use of the present tense invite the audience to insert themselves into Anna's position, they also underline the barriers to intimacy and complicity because they underline the fact that Anna is not fully present, even to herself: the 'ears are functioning, but the mind is numb'.

It is to attain a quality of perception that is embodied, rather than merely mechanical ('ears functioning [...] mind numb'), that the play leaves the hospital and enters the imagined world. Like works of the period discussed in other chapters – *The Colored Museum, Kind Ness, IMTK, Fires in the Mirror, The Travels, Under the Knife, Pugilist Specialist, The Receipt, Here's what I di...* – *BW* heuristically pits intuitive, embodied perception against seeing and hearing that are merely mechanical. The play asks: what kind of diagnosis do we, and should we, trust? Vogel's portrayal of diagnosis and perception assaults the material operation of, but determinedly unchains the self from, the limits of positioning based on race, ethnicity, gender, and sexuality. Carl and Anna's daydreamt European journey figures the 'I' in post-identitarian fashion, as a fluid equation, 'self' and 'other' crossing and recrossing a permeable boundary.

Anna's daydream casts the spectacle as a dialectic of fixity and movement, between going somewhere and nowhere. The lack of scenery and of scene changes imposes a sense of immobility; this mood is counterpointed by action which travels ceaselessly, taking in a multitude of milieux. The play's title is an emblem for this counterpoint: 'Baltimore' stands for hospital, being an object under observation; 'Waltz' signifies the free, highly subjective play of the dream. Interplay between the cold sobriety of truth and the warm airiness of fantasy is the underlying dynamic of a narrative that is brisk and frenzied, but suddenly 'implodes' into moments of reflection. Benjamin states that, despite the endless stories that people construct about events, 'history decomposes into images, not narratives' (Benjamin quoted in Diamond, 1997, p. 146). In *BW*, the propulsion of theatrical narrative is set against the stasis of theatrical imagery.[7] In a kind of perceptual tug-of-war, the pull of the Baltimore waiting-room and hospital-bed contends with the pull of the imagined journey. Vogel continually points to tension between the stasis, specificity, and grounding of the image and the narrative diversion of travel. It is useful to note that Vogel had never been to Europe when she wrote *BW*. As the tension inherent in the title suggests, the daydream explores the liberties with actuality that translating images into narratives entails. In the structural interplay of image and narrative, stasis and movement, meaning is palpably constructed.

Connections and tensions between juxtaposed images and statements form and dissipate within a structure that edges toward, but never settles into, narrative cohesion. Narrative is an active force, antagonistic to Paula/Anna's desire to find a cure for Carl's absence. Never allowed to take the narrative at face value, the spectator is drawn to see character being obscured, rather than heightened, by narratological structuring.

The conspicuously mysterious Third Man is crucial to the play's mordantly agonistic schema. The Third Man 'plays' (Vogel's term in her stage directions on p. 6) a string of characters who physically and emotionally come between Anna and Carl in the story: he is the wedge that repeatedly inserts itself between the siblings, the personification of self-concealing authorities that keep them apart. Some of the characters 'played' by The Third Man, such as the Johns Hopkins Doctor, try to fix Anna in the object position of diagnosed patient; others, like Harry Lime, try to keep things on the move, the promise of revelation and resolution always just around the corner. The Third Man tries to force events into a narrative, but Vogel repeatedly leaves images hanging as narratives break down.

The play's 30 short scenes each begin with a rhetorical trope of identification or comparison that frames the ensuing action within an ironically authoritarian narrative voice. In the early stages of the play, the generic title phrases are derived from language textbooks:

> THE THIRD MAN: Basic dialogue. The phone call. Hello. I would like to speak to Mr. Lime, please?
> CARL: ...Wie geht es dir?! ...it's my sister. ATD.
> THE THIRD MAN: ATD? Jesus, that's tough, old man. You've got to watch where you sit these days. She's a sweet kid. Yeah. Yeah. Wait a second. (*Offstage.*) Inge? Inge, baby? Ein Bier, bitte, baby. Ja, ja. You too, baby. (*Pause.*) Okay. Dr. Todesrocheln? Yeah, you might say I know him. But don't tell anybody I said that...Do you still have the rabbit?
>
> (Vogel, 1996, p. 13)

Though the language lesson promises transparency, the use of multiple languages, the background action involving 'Inge, baby', and the mysterious allusions to a 'Dr. Todesrocheln' and 'the rabbit', all raise more questions than they answer. The private and side-references form images that hang. These hanging images counteract The Third Man's reductive narrative constructions, including the use of titular phrases such as 'The phone call', that strive to render Carl and Anna exemplary, normal, typical.

While the demonstrative clips that start the scenes promise monologue, Vogel's strategies conspicuously struggle to foster dialogue:

> THE THIRD MAN: As children they fought.
> CARL: We never fought, really.
>
> (1996, p. 43)

As The Third Man claims to fix causes and symptoms in childhood that account for adult behaviour, Vogel disarticulates his formulations. Arresting the momentum of The Third Man's demonstrative efforts, Carl often takes over the role of narrator, forcing moments of reflection in which linguistic ambiguities undermine the certainty of what is stated:

> You were not permitted to play with dolls; dolls are for girls. You played with your sister's dolls until your parents found out. They gave you a stuffed animal – a thin line was drawn. Rabbits were an acceptable surrogate for little boys.
>
> (Vogel, 1996, p. 34)

For Carl's parents, rabbits stand in, or are 'a surrogate', for 'dolls', because normal little boys do not play with dolls. In the context that Vogel builds around it, however, the line '[r]abbits were an acceptable surrogate for little boys' is subversively double-edged. It is a pointedly sententious sentence that exemplifies Vogel's testing of the rules of, to destabilize the neatness of, binary logic.

BW counters the reinforcement of entrenched binary thinking that characterized mediation of the AIDS epidemic in the United States. At a time when binary narratives were being challenged by the breakdown of the Cold War, and by the achievements of (30 or so years of) race- and gender-focused activism, AIDS was an excuse to revive such narratives. Making Anna a first-grade schoolteacher allows the playwright to substitute children, whom society tends to see as innocent, for practices, such as gay sex, and drug use, which are often seen as threatening to society's moral fabric. In hushed tones, the Doctor explains early on to Anna that '[f]ive year-olds can be deadly' (ibid., p. 11), the play with stereotypes forcing us to read medical authority against the grain. By swapping a gay man living in San Francisco with a straight elementary-school teacher living in Baltimore, the playwright replaces homo- with heterosexuality, and defamiliarizes the paranoia generated by AIDS. Disarticulating promiscuity from particularity of sexual orientation, location, and occupation, her play with opposites conflates the attributes of innocence and corruption that the parents, who draw the line between rabbits and dolls, endeavour to keep separate.

Railing against the fervent articulation of AIDS and homosexuality in America's cultural image bank, Vogel creates her own signifier: the stuffed rabbit. Stuffed only with mystery, the rabbit is speciously important: icon, catalyst, deceptively empty vessel, and red herring masquerading as The Answer that will lead to The Cure. Like so many images in the play, it refuses to fit into the narrative while promising to complete it. The connection of the rabbit with the chase for a cure is cemented by the parallels with the chase for Harry Lime in *The Third Man*, who exploits an underground trade in penicillin. It is Vogel's Harry Lime – an old friend of Carl's who remains unseen – who first mentions the rabbit in the telephone call, cited above. The rabbit is then smuggled around Europe by Carl, who keeps fervently arranging to meet Harry. Anna, despite her brother's best efforts, knows about the rabbit, but has no idea why it is significant. She attaches herself to the sign of the rabbit like a greyhound chasing an effigy of a rabbit around a labyrinthine track. As she chases it, the rabbit multiplies, Carl and The Third Man furtively exchanging rabbits and Anna finding it impossible to determine which is the original one. Confused by the furtive offstage activities of Carl and The Third Man, Anna asks: 'What is it they do with those rabbits?' (Vogel, 1996, p. 21). Vogel parodies the prurient paranoia that equates gay men with voracious 'offstage activities' such as the clandestine solicitation of sex in public toilets. Her refusal to name satirizes Reagan's fatal refusal to talk about AIDS in public – long after its magnitude demanded address – not only fostered paranoia and misinformation about AIDS, but revived paranoia and misinformation about gay male sex.

The passing through Customs, which completes the substitution of Anna into the role of the patient, is a symbolic switching over into the fantasy world of the daydream. A blast from childhood past, a passport to a potential cure or resolution, the appearance of the rabbit foreshadows the rampant but illusory momentum of Anna's fantasy – the daydream that takes her everywhere and nowhere. The rabbit is a kind of baton, carriage of which takes Anna out of the mundane time and place of the waiting-room and into the spatial and temporal elasticity of the day-dream. Christopher Bigsby observes that fantasy, for Vogel, is 'not an evasion of the real but an extension of it' (Bigsby, 1999, p.293). That is particularly true in relation to *BW*. While Paula/Anna's daydream is motivated in part by a desire to 'evade' the reality of the actual situation, it 'extends' that reality in several respects. On a personal level, it takes her beyond the walls of the waiting-room on a vertiginous, interior version of an itinerary that Paula wishes she and Carl had travelled, carrying her backwards to childhood to confront the spectre of a future in which she will have to come to terms with Carl's death. The daydream's estrangement devices contextualize Paula/Carl's particular situation and the specific Johns Hopkins waiting-room within a broader socio-cultural context: analysis of the effects of medical language; attitudes to AIDS; attitudes toward sexual behaviour.

Early scientific, political, and journalistic mediation of AIDS was characterized by officious discourse that disembodied disease by covering AIDS in rhetoric to avoid dealing with experiential, bodily reality. *BW* depicts the effects of that discourse, alienating individuals from one another and from themselves. In the face of disembodying and alienating treatment that preys parasitically upon, rather than ameliorating, the symptoms of, disease, the play's theatrical substitutions reassert connectedness and embodied presence. Look again at the passage quoted earlier:

DOCTOR: ...And there is usually rapid destruction and metastases.
CARL: Anna –
ANNA: I'm right here, darling. Right here.
CARL: Could you explain it very slowly?
DOCTOR: .... Often seen with effusions, either exudate or transudate.
ANNA: Carl –
CARL: I'm here, darling. Right here.

(Vogel, 1996, pp. 9–10)

Anna's escapist strategies – the dream itself, and the sexual and gastronomic binges within it – are a quest for a cure from the effects of the treatment, effects which attach themselves to the disease, exacerbating alienation of patient from carer. Food and sex provide some comfort, but, as finding a cure becomes increasingly unlikely, Anna is forced to find solace in reflection, interpretation, decoding. This pattern resonates with Roland Barthes's lament that the quest to translate the world into signs, and the experience of individuality as the mastery of those signs, is specific to the late-capitalist era, and compensates for a lack of embodied connectedness between people.[8]

Wrecked by the disembodying effects of rhetoric and obfuscation, Anna finds paradoxical solace in the only kind of cure available – a semiological journey. The tour of Europe, in which Anna 'fucks her brains out', is a quest for a lost sense of wholeness: in that quest, escapist sex is continually juxtaposed with escapist decoding. The process of decoding is not the means to an end for Anna that it purports to be: it is cathartic in and of itself, and as much of a release as the sex. *BW* depicts a society in which touch is neurotically codified, 'a thin line drawn' between acceptable and unacceptable contact. Despite the libertarian rhetoric of his pronouncement that 'fucking is a revolutionary act', the Radical Student Activist is a mechanical lover and an equally mechanical thinker. The strict code within which he conducts his sexual activity is violated when Anna reveals that she is 'a schoolteacher from low-income housing' – a far cry from his fantasy of storming the bourgeoisie. Anna replies, sarcastically, that 'the missionary position does not a revolution make' (Vogel, 1996, p. 46). Another neurotic masquerading as a libertine, the Garçon, picks up Anna after waiting on her in a bistro. He is happy to explore and be explored by her, until she trespasses the no-go area:

ANNA: And this?
GARÇON (*Scandalized*): Non. There is no word en français. *Pas du tout.*
ANNA: For this? There must be –
GARÇON: Non. Only the Germans have a word for that.

(Vogel, 1996, p. 25)

For the Garçon, the anus is both out of bounds and unnameable. Anna's hands-on French lesson, a pastiche of the Henry and Katharine scene of intimate royal encounter in Shakespeare's *Henry V*, invokes the deep-rooted link within cultural consciousness between disease and foreigners. Noting that dirt is matter out of place, sociologist Mary Douglas asserts that associations between foreignness and contamination are psychically and socially fundamental (Douglas, 1984, p. 36).The link between fear of foreigners and fear of contamination in *BW* is a reminder of how similar was the mediation of the threat of AIDS to the mediation of potential invasion by foreign ideologies that characterized the preceding Cold War era. AIDS rhetoric and Cold War rhetoric fix vague but abiding fears about innocence and transgression. For nearly half a century, Americans were led to believe by politicians and dominant sections of the media that Soviet Communism was a murky threat to the liberty, democracy, and prosperity fundamental to the identity of the United States. Even into the 1980s, the Iron Curtain of Communism in Eastern Europe acted as a backdrop, against which the United States distinguished itself. In the late 1980s, that Curtain was drawn – and in some sections torn down – at precisely the time that the management of 'multiculturalism' within the United States climbed to the top of the political agenda. Multiculturalism, like Communism, like the anti-Vietnam counter-culture of the 1960s, and like AIDS, provokes the biggest fear of all for US hegemony: the fear of losing a generation, the fear that America's children will be contaminated by foreign bodies.

The parodic content of the dream – in which a first-grade schoolteacher beds every waiter she meets, while two men engage in furtive activities with childhood toys that have nothing to do with sex – conspicuously estranges such fears. Viewing a slide of Heidelberg, Carl comments: 'Every cobblestoned street, every alleyway, was so pristine and clean. Wasn't it, Anna?' *'(Deadpan)'*, Anna replies: 'Yes, sterile' (Vogel, 1996, p. 38). The country which figures prominently in the play, often as a symbol of paranoia and sterility, Germany is also the one that looms largest in the playwright's own heritage. Germany's presence is therefore apt in a play about 're-remembering'. 'Vogel' is German and Dutch for 'small bird', yet, when Dutch and German are spoken in the play, Anna cannot comprehend them. Articulating sterility with disembodiment, and playing on her own 'forgotten' roots, Vogel analogizes the struggle to learn a lost language with diminution of subjectivity that is the price of security. It is only through the alter ego that she can regain composure in the face of a crisis of subjectivity; but, as Foucault warns, creating space and time involves surrendering, or 'disappear[ing]' inside, a textual 'game' that annihilates the subjects who play it.

As if possessed by an animating spirit, a single piece of furniture transforms in protean fashion throughout the play, to conjure whatever needs to be conjured. This solitary item – a hospital gurney as Vogel imagines it, but a sofa in Anne Bogart's production – constantly changes but never changes. Like the latex gloves, worn at all times by The Third Man, it is equivocal between stasis and flux, absence and presence.[9] Together, the gloves and the gurney maintain the shadow presence of the waiting-room throughout the journey. As Ann Linden observes, they are a quintessentially Vogelian spin on prop-as-formalist device, allowing us to see as if the first time, but are about noticing our own serial 're-remembering' (Linden, 2002, p. 242). They take us on a phantom journey, an anti-escape, in which Anna's denial of her actual circumstances informs our own immersion in and detachment from the narrative. Vogel's deployment of stage properties to target denial is rooted in notions of resistance that underlie her attitude to theatre. Several related aspects of the playwright's thinking about resistance emerge in the course of an interview with David Savran in *The Playwright's Voice*. Acknowledging the influence of Theodore Lipps and Vernon Lee – early twentieth-century philosophers of aesthetics – Vogel explains her preference for negative empathy 'in which we resist the empathy we feel towards the protagonist' (Savran, 1999, p. 273). Creating tension between identification and moral judgment, negative empathy is essential for the elasticity of perspective on which Vogel insists. Vogel contrasts her paradigm with 'sensationalism', based on 'positive empathy without any resistance', that leads to 'avoidance and denial' (ibid., pp. 273–7).

The resistance Carl works to his sister's textualization of him becomes critical in a scene that occurs precisely half-way through the play, and half-way through the journey within the play. The pivotal Dutch Boy episode – in which Anna encounters the Little Dutch Boy of the children's story, now aged 50 and the worse for wear – is the lacuna, or crest, of the dream, the point at which Anna begins to wake up. Vogel uses the folk tale to brilliantly articulate dreaming with resistance:

> Here in Noord Brabant there are three walls of defenses against the cruelty of the North Sea. The first dyke is called the Waker – the Watcher; the second dyke is de Slaper – the Sleeper; and the last dyke, which had never before been tested, is known as the Dromer – the Dreamer.
>
> (1996, p. 31)

The 'walls of defenses' correspond to layers of resistance within Anna's psyche. It is a correspondence made clearer at the end of the scene, when The Dutch Boy At 50 asks about Carl:

> DUTCH BOY: Wo ist dein bruder?
> ANNA: Oh, he stayed in Amsterdam...
> DUTCH BOY: And you did not go?
>
> (ibid., p. 32)

The exchange refers to the guilt that Vogel feels about the journey she never took with Carl, and to her subconscious realization that, while she daydreams, he is dying. The veil of the daydream is further pierced a couple of scenes later, during a slide presentation that Carl attempts to make to the audience. The images that Carl glosses – of the German countryside – have been mysteriously replaced by images of the hospital and its Baltimore environs, interspersed with images of Disneyland.

A couple of scenes after that, the veil is more violently ripped: the visit to Dr Todesrocheln breaches the narrative fantasy once and for all. If the dream is the theatricalization of Carl's death throes (as perceived by Paula/Anna), then the visit to Dr T is the final throe. In the search for a cure, it is the final throw of the dice. Literally translated, 'Todesrocheln' means 'Deathrattle' or 'Deathspluttering'. Todesrocheln specializes in 'uriposia', purification through the drinking of one's own urine. 'Let us', he explains, 'look at the body as an alchemist, taking in straw and mud und schweinefleisch and processing it into liquid gold which purifies the body' (Vogel, 1996, p. 53). The determinate wake-up call for Anna comes as Todesrocheln imbibes her urine with distracted and unbalanced relish:

ANNA: I don't believe that's your real hair.
DR. TODESROCHELN: I will need first of all twenty-four hours of your time for a uronocometry –
ANNA (*Increasingly scared*): You look familiar to me –

(ibid., p. 55)

A few moments later, his disguise punctured, Dr T 'takes off his wig and glasses and appears as the Baltimore Doctor from the first scene, peeling off the black gloves to reveal latex gloves underneath' (ibid., p. 55). In the unmasking of Todesrocheln, Anna is released from the journey back to the waiting-room of Johns Hopkins. Reflexive awareness seems finally to have breached the daydream. By describing Dr T's specialty as 'uriposia' – which, Anna points out, sounds like a form of poetry (ibid., p. 15) – Vogel suggests that the drinking of the urine is a metaphor for the daydream-as-theatre. Anna and the playwright both purify themselves by passing through their own image bank. In writing the play, Paula recycles herself as Anna; in the daydream, Anna recycles herself as Carl. As the daydream gives way to Johns Hopkins, and the Carl/Anna (patient/carer) substitution is reversed, the relationship between alter ego and playwright is reinscribed.

Tension between absence and presence, and between fantasy and reality, crystallizes in the play's final throes. Into the glaring banality of the Baltimore hospital, to which we have only just returned, the frenzy of the dream again irrupts. Anna gives escape one last go. She tries to stir Carl as a Strauss waltz begins to play, but Carl, in his pyjamas, is 'wooden'. As Anna repeatedly tries to animate him, he becomes manically mechanical, '*like the doll in E. T. A. Hoffman*' (Vogel, 1996, pp. 55–6). An alarm clock sounds. The Doctor enters, covers Carl with a sheet, and attempts to console Anna. As Anna begins to exit, the Strauss sounds again, this time without the dream-state lighting. Carl, calmly and 'perfectly well, waits for Anna. He is dressed in Austrian military regalia. They waltz off as the lights dim' (ibid., p. 57).

If the initial attempt to dance is a struggle that Anna cannot control, the final dance is celebratory and funereal. The first attempt seems to symbolize denial-bound and desperate fantasy: it is Anna still locked in her own romanticism. The final waltz is the beginning of learning to live with Carl's death. Only by learning to live with his death can she successfully animate him in her imagination. The literal Baltimore waltz crystallizes the tension between absence and presence, pointedly leaving that tension unresolved. The daydream helps Anna to come to terms with her situation, but is not a real escape. Her imagination, as the playwright's surrogate, has revealed connections which more mechanistic discourse obscures.

3
Assimilation: Sounding Through the Surface

Writing in 1993, Jill Dolan notes: 'Numerous play anthologies published recently mark a new geography of American theatre as it hyphenates itself in print – *On New Ground* (1987), a volume of Hispanic-American plays; *Between Worlds* (1990), Asian-American; *Out Front* (1988), gay and lesbian; even Lenora Champagne's edited collection of women's performance art pieces, *Out from Under* (1990), all use metaphors of location to title themselves in conjunction with identity positions crossed by gender, race and sexuality' (p. 420). She observes that 'the hyphenates of these anthologized identities also point to a possible recuperation into the fabric of something more recurrently, hegemonically 'American', that the 'hyphens serve as temporary connectors that are bound to either separate or assimilate the terms' (ibid.).

The processual indeterminacy that Dolan associates with 'hyphenated identities' is acute in Ping Chong's *Kind Ness* and Suzan-Lori Parks's *Imperceptible Mutabilities in the Third Kingdom* (*IMTK*). The name 'The Third Kingdom' indicates a desire to place, to map, to particularize; but, also, a recognition of the ineluctable mystery of the universe as a place that is in limbo and in flux. The play is set, insofar as it *is* 'set', between a new world inhabited after the Middle Passage, and an old world left behind. The four sets of characters that inhabit Parks's Third Kingdom never meet. Structurally, the most explicit link between the four groups lies in verbal echoes, things said in one section repeated by a character in another. Everything in Chong and Parks – including historical events, images of the future, cultural artefacts, and characters – is a 'shard' (Parks quoted in Drukman, p. 73) of found culture, detached from any familiar ideological, temporal, and spatial context. Characters bring with them local (geographical and historical) contexts which the authors attach to a sweeping purview in which the mythical and the vernacular are entwined, so that an epic moment can become startlingly intimate, and vice versa. The characters act as (to use Dolan's word) 'connectors' between the intimate and the epic; but their own perception of connections is fragile at best. Chong and Parks offer cryptic motifs of the failure to recognize oneself. Chong sends Daphne ('100% American, pure bred') out star-gazing with Buzz, thinking she recognizes Cassiopeia, a queen of Greek myth thrown into the sky to learn humility, but getting the wrong location. Parks gives us a family of diggers (in *The America Play*), who appear to have subsumed their own identity in the relics they unearth; and, in *IMTK*, a startlingly oneiric quintet of Seers – abstractions as much as characters, and paradoxical abstractions at that – visionaries who cannot see. Both authors allude to the attempts of some naturalistic theatre to construct a natural habitat for the viewing of behaviour. By making the living-room of the women in 'Snails' into a 'nature study', the Naturalist in *IMTK* purports to 'accommodate' his 'subjects' (Parks, 1995, pp. 27–9). A third, and then two-thirds of the way through *Kind Ness*, as Buzz seems to be assimilating, a Stage Hand crosses with foam rocks to set up the diorama for a gorilla. Whether the gorilla is Buzz, or a different gorilla, is deliberately ambiguous, open like the question of whether Buzz really has assimilated. At the end of the play, he is finally given permission by the Narrator to set the rocks down. Buzz, seemingly fully assimilated having married Daphne and with a baby, stares at the gorilla in its natural habitat, poised in the limbo of the hyphenated subject in the process of assimilation. It is a moment, like so many in *Kind Ness*, and like so many in Parks's plays, in which an embodied gaze of genuine recognition contends with the cultural gaze of the assimilated subject. (Re)cognition of distance travelled in assimilation sounds through the void of amnesia. It is a sounding through that allows Chong and Parks to play formations of 'natural' habitat against what such formations leave out.

Chong and Parks figure naming as a mask through which character sounds. 'Sounding through', a literal translation of the Greek word 'persona', refers to the way that character sounds, or resonates, through the mask. The masked performer uses both the mask itself and the overcoming of the mask to register personality. Drawing explicitly on this use of the mask in Greek theatre, Jung used the term 'persona' to denote the outermost part of consciousness, the skin of personality through which inner thoughts and feelings are filtered and presented to the world. The (1980s) allegorical works of Ping Chong and the early works of Suzan-Lori

Parks bring that Jungian 'sounding through' into dialogue with post-identitarian naming of identities.

* * *

From *Lazarus* in 1972 to *Elephant Memories* in 1990, Chong produced two dozen allegorical works for the stage. Since 1990, he has produced three series: the stylistically eclectic *East/West Quartet* (*Deshima, Chinoiserie, After Sorrow: Viet Nam, Pojagi*), exploring interactions of particular Asian countries with particular European countries and with the United States; a trio of large-scale, multi-media puppetry pieces (*Kwaidan, Obon,* and *Cathay*); and the ongoing *Undesirable Elements* documentary project, each incarnation of which assembles diverse groups whose personal histories catalyse autobiographical ensemble performances following a template that has evolved over two decades. The allegorical works of the first half of Chong's career (my focus here) betray a range of influences as diverse as postmodern dance (he has collaborated extensively with Meredith Monk) and Peking Opera (in which both his father and grandfather directed and performed), but bear Chong's signatory style. His storytelling has a dry, grotesque quality of 'laughter through tears' that calls to mind European theatre practitioners such as Meyerhold, Brecht, and Dürrenmatt.[1] Long-standing interest in the specific vocabularies of a range of visual media – painting, sculpture, and especially cinema – inform what Chong refers to as the visual and thematic 'plasticity' of his theatre, which appropriates for live performance the conventions of painting, sculpture, and film. He sounds through technologies of, and obstructions to, seeing. While *Nosferatu: A Symphony of Darkness* (1985) refers to Murnau, *Maraya~Acts of Nature in Geological Time* (1987) alludes to the films of Japanese directors Mizoguchi and Ozu. In both *Maraya* and *Nosferatu*, Chong deploys obstructions to the spectator's gaze to highlight acts and ways of looking. In *Maraya*, the audience sees the stage through a white wooden grid, a device which, as in Ozu's films, helps to define the space of the image like squares on a chessboard.

In spite, or perhaps because, of this eclectic array of influences, Ping Chong is very much an *auteur* with a highly distinctive stylistic and thematic signature. There is an elegant economy to his *mise-en-scène*. Light, in brilliant colours, is used to pick out small, powerful visual details – such as recurrent images of knives in *Nuit Blanche* (1981) – on a stage free from clutter or complication, more closely resembling a modern dance space than the set of a play. The subtitle of *Nuit Blanche*, *A Select View of Earthlings*, aptly conveys the martianist quality of Chong's staging. For the spectator, it can feel like seeing human life stripped bare, looking for the first time at the world and at the tools we use to represent it.[2]

Despite the spareness of his aesthetic, Chong is fond of, and has a particular way with, things: tools/props, iconographic details such as typefaces, bits of scenery or couture. In remediating 'things', he elicits the role of iconography in displaying, and thereby solidifying, culture. Objects of consumption are endowed with a ghostly agency that projects itself onto those who consume. Like Wolfe in *The Colored Museum*, Chong dramatizes from the outside in, presenting a naïve, pop-culture surface from beneath which there are rumblings and irruptions of the psychologically and socially repressed, evoking the extent to which (in the Parks phrase I cited in my Introduction) 'within the subject is its other'. Chong's method might be seen as counter-quotational: he isolates and provocatively de- and re- contextualizes spatial, temporal, and stylistic codes. Quietly, but tendentiously, he estranges culture by distancing its codes: the effect tends to be amusing and disturbing at the same time. His innocent, martianist eye is naïve, not in the Western sense of naïvety as emptiness, but in the Buddhist sense of naïvety as integral to wisdom. He describes the way that he presents himself to experience as a 'Confucianist ethic, not as aggressive as a Western ethic' (Chong, 1990a, p. 65). In his late 1980s work, Chong sounds grandiose significance through light-hearted vehicles. By looking naïvely at what is already naïve, Chong creates spectatorial distance and a lonely wisdom. He is drawn to popular texts and images that are resonantly shallow: apparently fatuous, but redolent with acculturation. *Elephant Memories* (1990) uses a television game show format to ironize the packaging of history as trivia; in *Kind Ness (KN)*, he uses the iconicity of the gorilla suit and the yellow ponchos of the schoolchildren to signify, but also to unravel signification, stripping layers of significance from over-familiar signifiers. Dress, music, and other elements that characterize 1950s and 1960s American suburbia are deployed not to create verisimilitude, but as bits of iconicity laid thickly onto the blank canvas of the stage: costumes are in lurid, primary colours against the white floor and empty space; silence is pierced by loud bursts of popular songs of the day. These bits of iconicity do inform the narrative's evocation of milieu but do not melt into that evocation: they hang in the air, demanding attention.

Like Parks, Chong treats the personal and mythic as embroiled, the distance of the mythic giving insight into the intimate chamber of the personal. The thematic layering of the everyday and epochal plays out visually as a tension between what Misha Berson calls the 'acrylic surface' of Chong's work and what is conspicuously not fully seen and heard beneath it: shadowy projections, shrouded and silhouetted forms; off-stage and loudspeaker sound.[3] Thematically and aesthetically, Chong conveys a sense that the self-identical surface of cultural order belies the constant shifting of sedimented texts and performances.

In *KN*, in front of and at each corner of the white (inner) stage floor, there are small, white, upright squares which catch the colours of light projected onto each of the scenes. These blank plaques frame the inner space, and give spatial definition to the stage; they also 'suggest that the audience is watching human specimens in a zoological environment'. As we observe the characters becoming saturated with culture, the white squares at the corners are saturated with colour. Chong's articulation of theatre with zoo can be seen to inform many of his works, but is most explicit in *KN*. The play sketches the coalescence and dissipation of six schoolmates, from second grade to early adulthood. While Chong has dealt elsewhere with growing up, and with this period of history, this is, both thematically and formally, the most strikingly American piece in his oeuvre: it is explicitly about American rites of passage, and is suffused with the lurid, specious innocence of the *Archie*[4] comic books that were an initial stimulus for the devising of the play.[5] It consists of 12 scenes that sketch a singular line of action:

Scene 1	A slide lecture
Scene 2	Daphne's garden
Scene 3	First Day of School
Scene 4	Slapstick #1
Scene 5	Chez Buzz
Scene 6	Introductions
Scene 7	Slapstick #2
Scene 8	Questions and Answers
Scene 9	Bus Stop
Scene 10	Prom Nite
Scene 11	Testimonials
Scene 12	At the Zoo

As some of these scene titles indicate ('First Day of School'; 'Prom Nite'), a familiar narrative, or at least the idea of a familiar narrative, is a key element of *KN*. The First Day of School and Prom Nite are landmarks whose contours are cross-cultural, but which are filled with culturally specific detail. As milestones, displaying the progress of the individual, they exhibit a society's norms as a narrative of growing-up. While

Chong promises a story, he also compromises it. The play's interruptions, backtracks, tangents, and ellipses coerce the spectator to ask what theatrical, personal, and cultural narratives leave out, and why. The ludicrous formality of the social rituals which constitute 'Introductions' and 'Prom Nite' is underscored by the fact that the characters' movements are severely choreographed. They walk in geometric patterns, often diagonally and/or backwards, in fast motion. Semiological prisms, the characters are mechanically immersed in, but have no psychological purchase on, the culture they are learning to perform. They are ensigns, displaying the codes of 1950s suburban childhood to excess. Speech and movement take on a life of their own – expressing but ultimately transcending the psychology of each character – to directly articulate the culture they are learning to perform. 'Acculturation', as Sally Banes comments, 'becomes palpably physical',[6] each movement, to apply Meyerhold's language, 'a hieroglyph with its own peculiar meaning' (Leach, 1989, p. 56).

At the end of 'Introductions', in another of the play's hanging moments, Dot is left behind when her over-excited friends run off. For comfort, she begins to name what she would like to eat:

> I'd love some pop! And some hot dogs, and some ice cream, and some candy, and some Juju Bees, and some Hum Hums, and some Tic Tacs, and some Snoo Snoos, and some Yo Yos and some Bim Bums...
>
> (Chong, 1988, p. 19)

Through Dot, Chong equates immersion in culture with a narcoticized, consumptive desire. Like the other children, her speech and movement display to a grotesque extent the consumption that constitutes her cultural training. Naming here, as so frequently in Chong's work, is conspicuously quotational, used in close relationship to physical objects as a mask of culture through which individuals sound. It is worn rather than mastered, put on like a piece of clothing, and with something of the same materiality. Whether it is the frantic recitation of numbers and cities in *Nosferatu*, or (as I will discuss) hate terms, lists of countries, or candy in *KN*, Chong pushes the phatic function of language to excesses that unravel communication. Names are like units of capitalist culture – they establish value, but are never really possessed by those who circulate them.

Chong has always been fascinated by the relationship between assimilation and the encoding of meaning into signs. He cites Lévi-Strauss, who states that, '[w]hereas concepts aim to be wholly transparent with respect to reality, signs allow and even require the interposing and incorporation of a certain amount of human culture into reality' (Lévi-Strauss, 1966, p. 18). Like many of Chong's pieces, *KN* begins with a prologue: here, it is a slide lecture which, in preparation for what is to follow, purports to teach the audience to 'tell the difference between what is alike and what is not alike, what is harmonious and what is dissonant' (ibid., p. 1). The Narrator, a male voice heard over a loudspeaker, interprets a series of slides, each of which displays a pair of images side-by-side. Slide One is simple enough: {Red Rectangle | Blue Rectangle}. The Narrator explains: 'What is alike is that both are vertical rectangles, they are both colours. What is dissimilar is that one is a hot Color, the other is a cool Color.' As the series progresses, the limited nature of the Narrator's explanations becomes increasingly evident; the images then become ever-more culturally loaded. The Narrator greets Slide Seventeen {Woman from Este Lauder ad | Woman from Algeria} with the information that the 'image on the right is of a woman who had to remove her veil in order for this photograph to be taken. The woman on the left did not have to remove her veil at all' (ibid., pp. 1–5). Seeing this Slide Lecture in a class-room, along with a number of other graduate students, was the first exposure I had to Ping Chong's work, and I have since shown it to a number of classes myself. I find myself, like the professor who taught me, helping students to 'tell the difference' between the prologue and the rest of the play, between this play and the rest of Chong's 'oeuvre', between what they are seeing here and what they would see in the theatre.

As *KN* progresses, it will become clear that Chong sees culture itself as a veil of myths and symbols that cannot itself be seen, but which, for those who are acculturated, normalizes what is seen through it. What Chong refers to as 'the artifice of human culture' is a veil, or mask, of normality that we must wear to attain a sense of identity, to feel like cultural insiders.[7] That mask is held in place by naming rit-uals. Chong weaves names – labels, insults, and names of consumer goods – into a veil of artifice that is lifted in fits and starts to reveal complexities beneath. The similarities and glaring differences between the children are foregrounded by Chong, and by the gang themselves, from the start. Dot is a blind, Jewish girl. Rudy and Lulu are both Irish Catholics – he a 'smart aleck', she 'a dumb blonde [...] with a Barbie-doll quality'. Daphne, a descendent of a Mayflower family (the original pilgrims), is a WASP (White Anglo-Saxon Protestant) who describes her-self as 'American ... 100% ... pure bred' (Chong, 1988, p. 25). She revels in her socio-economic superiority over would-be suitor Alvin, a

French-Canadian whose father struggles to find work as a coal miner. Immediately after the 'Slide Lecture', a stichomythic exchange of names ensues:

> DAPHNE: Let me explicate the situation for you ... My mother is a
> Johnson.
> ALVIN: My mother is a housewife!
> DAPHNE: My family is coal in this country, Alvin.
> ALVIN: My Uncle Emile, he died of black lung!
> ....
> DAPHNE: I'm afraid my taste runs more to Die Zauberflote and Cosi
> Fan Tutte!
> ALVIN: I go for spumoni myself!
> DAPHNE (*finally exasperated*): Tennessee Williams
> ALVIN: Tennessee Ernie Ford!
>
> (Chong, 1988, pp. 7–8)

The markers of difference weave a veil of easily recognizable opposition. As the characters journey through high school, however, they neglect to perform these identities according to the schema.

The catalyst for the disruption is the arrival of a new pupil, Buzz, who – though the children often seem, or pretend, not to notice – happens to be a silverback gorilla, from Rwanda. Hauntingly, Chong never lets us be sure what Buzz's peers and teachers see when they look at him. Enigmatically, he is at times addressed by other characters as a person, at times as a gorilla. We are never quite sure exactly what the characters see, and whether it is the same as what we see. Is the gorilla suit supposed to alienate ex-nominated racial difference, like the proverbial elephant in the living-room that no-one mentions? Bunny Conklin, the School Principal's wife, bludgeons diplomatically away as she shoves America (in snack form) down the throats of its youth: 'Your people don't eat cheese, do they?' (Chong, 1988, p. 16). Are we implicated as the subjects of the gaze, or should we regard ourselves as wiser than Buzz's peers and teachers? Maybe they see things we cannot? For the most part, whether or not Buzz is a gorilla seems irrelevant compared to other factors of difference, such as his fondness for European opera, which his peers find odd. Not to be outdone by Buzz's reputed opera singing, Dot exhibits her intention to become a rhythm and blues singer 'like my people: Blind Lemon Jefferson, Blind Willie McTell, Blind Boy Fuller...' As she bursts into a spirited rendition of 'John Henry', Rudy reminds her that these are black rhythm and blues singers and she is 'a white Jewish girl from Scarsdale' (ibid., p. 35). Sick of being ribbed by her so-called friends, the generally peaceable Dot explodes: 'what about Buzz?! He's a fucking monkey and you don't give him half the shit you give me!' (ibid., p. 37) The iteration of the name 'Buzz' embeds the enigma. Buzz is a not uncommon first name for generations of Americans, not least in the 1950s and 1960s, when *KN* is set. Like Buzz Lightyear in the CGI block-buster *Toy Story*, Chong's Buzz seems trapped in the 1950s and 1960s of astronaut Buzz Aldrin's heyday, but our Buzz's story roams into the future, mocking the effects of nostalgia in normalizing a culture's sense of itself. Phonetically, the name 'Buzz' connotes the desire to be appealing to one's peers, and the children whose class Buzz joins love saying his name: they do so often, exploiting its sonic force to the max. On another level, though – and the play is all about contrasting layers of awareness, about recognition that lies just out of view – 'Buzz' is not a proper name at all, and as such signifies the invisible disturbance that the other creates, the pulse of difference, that which needs to be deciphered but which gets in the way of deciphering.

The major journey, or through-line, of the play is the transformation of Buzz from object to subject of the gaze. On the First Day of School (Scene 3) and at Principal Conklin's Party (Scene 6), Buzz is the exotic object, continually introducing himself, an embarrassed figure in a sometimes actual, sometimes metaphorical spotlight. Scenes 4 and 7 are vaudeville-style 'Slapstick' scenes in which a white hunter is tricked by the ape that he is trying to poach. These scenes comment on, but are not joined to, the main narrative. They are scenes in which tension between different possible readings of Buzz intensifies: the gorilla is like Buzz, but not like Buzz; the hunter is played by the same actor who plays Alvin. The Slapstick scenes' partial similarity to and partial difference from the main narrative imbues these scenes with an oneiric feel. They step us out of the time-line of the play just at the points when we are likely to immerse ourselves in identification with Buzz, to suspend disbelief in the fact that he is an actor in a gorilla suit. They stand out from and re-contextualize the foregoing action but are not fully assimilated.

In Scene 9, the children, further into their second-grade year, wait after the end of the school day at the 'Bus Stop'. Movements are less robotic, but still quite mechanized. Clad uniformly in yellow ponchos – costumes that are both faithful to 1950s suburbia and almost archetypal badges of childhood – the group plays games centred on insulting each other along gender lines. The crudity of the insults, and the desperate attempts to

win the game, make it a light-hearted, only faintly disturbing scene to
watch:

RUDY: Oh, go blow it out your ass, Daphne.
LULU: Oh yeah? Well, your ass looks like my face.

(Chong, 1988, p. 28)

Each time a teacher walks by, the children form a neat line. Conscious
and crafty disobedience is now evident, a rumbling within the neat social
order; but it is a subversion that is permissible, part of that order. A deeper
rumbling begins when Daphne is called away by an (invisible) teacher.
Throughout the scene, she has been trying to hold on to a letter from
'overseas' from her brother, clutching it away from her nosey classmates.
From offstage (literally beyond the frame) – we hear Daphne screaming
as a teacher tells her of her brother's death. It is revealed that he has
been 'dropping bombs on the gooks'. Neither Korea nor Vietnam are
named, but Korea is the war that fits the scene's place in the play's time-
line. The five visible characters, and Daphne's scream, freeze as the stage
recedes into semi-darkness. The six actors then line up along the cyc.
Still wearing their yellow ponchos – but no longer playing children, or
playing any obviously matrixed character – they walk and speak, in uni-
son, delivering a litany of (mostly racial) epithets: 'Yellow belly commies,
gooks, pinko chinko, greaseball, Arab wog bastards, honkie, nigger, spear
chucker, Irish mackerel snapper, jungle bunny, faggot, jigaboo, red neck,
Jew bastard, Turk-' (ibid., p. 32). The speech and movement is cold and
rhythmically emphatic. An irruption of the epochal into the everyday,
the litany of hate terms parallels and reflects back on the child's play and
our enjoyment of their game.

   This kind of contextual jolt typifies Chong's technique of immersing
and removing the spectator, another kind of game that can metasta-
size from hilarity to horror. Between Scenes 9 and 10 ('Bus Stop' and
'Testimonials'), Buzz enters as the sound of rain and many images of
the word 'RAIN' are projected through transparent drops, along with the
names of nations for whom killing is 'currently a daily event, like the
weather'. These hanging moments, in which Buzz is imaged alone, reflect
the fact that Buzz himself is a presence that the narrative does not contain, highlighting what churns beneath its 'acrylic surface'. If the 'Slide
Lecture' at the start is a fake reading-lesson, Buzz is a genuine exercise
for the spectator: he accommodates so many investments that multiple
dis- and reinvestments in the course of the play illuminate the motions

of signification – how associations, or signified 'effects', coalesce and disperse. During the play, Daphne, the ultimate insider, barely interacts with Buzz, the most obvious outsider. At the end of the play, however, Daphne and Buzz appear to be a suburban married couple, familiar and niggly, with a baby in tow. The baby's name, Chippy, connotes similarity to Buzz ('a chip off the old block'), but also, and more pointedly, the deep-rooted bitterness of one forcibly assimilated. The final scene takes place at the zoo, where Buzz is momentarily intrigued by a gorilla. He stares at it with a dim cognizance, in the liminal state of the hyphenated subject in the throes of assimilation. Meanwhile, the Stage Hand – who has been trying to put down his (fake) rocks throughout the play and has been repeatedly told by the Narrator 'not now' – is finally allowed to install the flimsy 'natural habitat'. Once the rocks are down, a tyre is lowered for the gorilla to swing on. S/he swings, reluctantly, on the tyre. But the second time s/he does so, the tyre returns and the gorilla has gone. By this point, Daphne and Buzz have also moved on. The play ends with the tyre swinging back and forth from on- to offstage (Chong, 1988, p. 43).

Deploying a cinematic metaphor of framed space, Teresa de Lauretis describes 'the movement in and out of gender' as 'a movement between the (represented) discursive space of the positions made available by hegemonic discourses and the space-off, the elsewhere of those dis-courses' (de Lauretis, 1987, p. X). Chong schematizes acculturation in a similar manner, also deploying a cinematic frame of reference to figure immersal in, and removal from, the 'in and out of' culture, movement between the sanctioned, framed space and the obscured 'elsewhere' of 'hegemonic discourses'. Chong articulates the filtering mechanisms of theatrical production and consumption with the zoo. A scopophilic envi-ronment analogous to the theatre, the zoo reflects the place of seeing back on the spectator, leaving the audience with a sense of the interre-latedness of the(ir) gaze and processes of assimilation. Chong reminds us of first principles: that our desire to see things naturalistically is a way to fix the unassimilated subject from the perspective of the insider. Just when we feel competent to view the gorilla and his habitat, he will disap-pear beyond the frame; all we can see are the meanings and associations we project.

In the denouement to *KN*, it is not Buzz's assimilation, but rather the relationship between seeing-lessons and social integration, that takes centrestage. Immediately after the Dionysian excesses and purgings of the ritual that is 'Prom Nite', we are left in the pathetic restoration of Apollonian order. Just as momentum appears to be building toward a resolution of the narrative and the characters' journey, a chronological sequence of slides is projected, a radically jarring compression of time:

> *The cyclorama and plaque lights come up, gelled blood red. The STAGE-HAND, carrying the rock, crosses the stage in silhouette from upstage right to upstage left; he reenters from centerstage left, exits centerstage right. Meanwhile, slides are projected, each one showing a year:*
>
> *1959, 1960, 1961, 1962, 1963, 1964, 1965,1966, 1967, 1968.*
>
> *STAGEHAND reenters downstage right and is about to put the rock down.*
> NARRATOR: No, not yet.
>
> (Chong, 1988, p. 38)

As Chong sardonically evoked in the 'like/not like' Prologue, slide projections are a medium geared to efficient delineation. Partly through usage in lecture-type presentations, we are trained to see slides as authoritatively deictic. Far from smoothing the jump in time by summarizing what happens to the characters in the intervening years, Chong simply displays a list of dates. It is a deliberately unsatisfactory form of deixis that highlights, rather than accounts for, what is missing. In using a communication tool to delineate that which is lost from view, Chong renders the slides agential, their efficiency a cover for reification.

After this slide 'non-show', a bookend for the slide-show at the beginning of the play, the characters enter in a line, as for an identity parade, and stand downstage, each in their own box of stark white light, facing out as they are asked to account for the nine 'missing' years. The Narrator asks Rudy, Lulu, Dot, and Alvin, now in their late twenties: 'when was the last time you saw Buzz?' They take it in turns to answer the question with a story, or set of remarks, about Buzz – each testifier leaving after providing their testimony. The final testifier is Daphne, who we expect will have little to say on the subject. As Daphne thinks about the question, the other characters leave, the stark white squares drop out, and a mottled, evening state comes up to indicate a tranquil evening in the country:

> DAPHNE: Oh ... the last time I saw Buzz. Hmmm.
> *(BUZZ enters. DAPHNE walks over to him, sits on ground next to him, takes off sandals. Looking at night sky, BUZZ sees a shooting star.)* Oooh! *(Pause. She points.)* Buzz ... is that Cassiopeia right here overhead? *(BUZZ moves her arm over.)*
>
> (Chong, 1988, p. 40)

Chong identifies Daphne with what she sees (or thinks she sees): Cassiopeia, a queen of Greek myth thrown into the sky to learn humility. Unfortunately, Daphne gets the wrong location. Having spent the entire play asserting the self-identical purity of her own 'star' and subjecting the other characters to her punitive gaze, she is corrected by Buzz, whose view of the world has conspicuously not been portrayed, as he has always been the object of the gaze. In the following and final scene, 'At the Zoo', Buzz become the bearer of the gaze. But, as he stares at the gorilla with a distant recognition, we may wonder whether assimilation makes hyphenated subjects of us all.

Through the union of Buzz and Daphne, Chong makes spectatorship sound. Like all his work, *KN* connects the way we absorb stories to the way that we are ourselves absorbed into society. In attempting to absorb the play, we fill in the blanks, the missing links, by projecting our own assimilated stories. In that process, do we recognize the effects of our own projection? From the mythologist's perspective, identity is in the veil and in the mess behind the veil.

* * *

Like Chong, Parks plays different notions of innocence against one another, espousing a martianist aesthetic that is quasi-phenomenological but which exaggerates the strangeness of certain elements with which we are familiar. She describes her approach as a clearing of pre-conceptions about what the world looks like, and what the form of a play should look like: 'I'm saying that the inhabitants of Mars do not look like us. Nor should they. I'm also saying that Mars is with us – right on our doorstep and should be explored' (Parks, 1995, p. 8). *Imperceptible Mutabilities in the Third Kingdom* (written in stages between 1986 and 1989) and *The America Play* (written in stages between 1990 and 1993) trace continuities of survival and transformation in an elliptical world, unpicking the idiosyncratic shapes and patterns that events make in the minds of her characters. Born conceptually resourceful, their capacity for conception has been stifled by the institutions – religious, scientific, governmental – on which they depend to know how to interpret themselves and their environment. As the interpretative templates they have come to rely on crumble, they try out new strategies. Slowly, barely perceptibly, they shed their ingrained ways of knowing, analysis of their failures causing them to read back, to question their certainty, their ways of seeing. This retrospective questioning comes to a head in veiled epiphanies and fragmented visions.

Parks returns identity to its basic meaning: coalescence. The dynamics of dispersal and coalescence with which she engages create interpretative situations in which agency, and causal links, can suddenly become visible. She writes in a mode I will call 'epic vernacular', a mode in which the same metaphor or motif figures in, and bridges, macrocosmic (epochal) and microcosmic (everyday) events. The epic and everyday are entwined via physical images and phrases. Parks generates motifs, allowing them to resonate through the text, and uses characters and situations to attach them associatively to recognizable contexts. Like Chong, she peels and chips at layers of discourse that have sedimented into a symbolic order. 'Snails', the first section of *IMTK*, features three roommates named Mona, Chona, and Verona – or rather, they used to be. In the first scene of the play, Chona, now named Charlene, states that '[o]nce there was uh robber who would come over and rob us regular' (Parks, 1995, p. 26). A few lines later, Mona, now Molly, says: '[o]nce there was uh me named Mona who wanted to jump ship but didnt'. The third scene of the play begins:

> MOLLY: Once there was uh me named Mona who wondered what she'd be like if no-one was watchin. You got the Help Wanteds?
> CHARLENE: Wrapped thuh coffee grinds in em.

> (ibid., p. 27)

Like the 'coffee grinds', Mona is a series of residues packaged for urban convenience. Physically and ontologically, the used coffee conjures images of black identity being ground down and wrapped in discourse. From her first appearance – at the very start of the play – Mona herself is symbolically buried beneath language as she recites her enunciation lesson:

> MONA: 'S-K' is /sk/ as in 'ask.' The little-lamb-follows-closely-behind-at-Marys-heels-as-Mary-boards-the-train. Shit. Failed every test he shoves in my face. He makes me recite my mind goes blank.

> (ibid., p. 25)

After beginning, here, by showing the effects of narrative, Parks goes on to uncover those effects, to peel away accreted discursive layers in search of the sense of 'me-ness' that Mona has lost. The Mona/Chona/Verona scenes are interspersed with monologues by a character named The Naturalist, who discusses his strategies for 'researching' his subjects with the aid of a 'fly' – a device used by anthropologists to study subjects in their natural environment. The Naturalist gains entry to the Mona/Chona/Verona household in the guise of 'Lutzky the PhD exterminator', who promises the women he will take care of the enormous cockroaches that reside in their living-room. Lutzky's claims to cleanse the living-room read back on, and are as euphemistic as, the question that the Naturalist (Lutzky's double) poses in his first appearance in the play: 'How. Should. We. Best. Accommodate. Our subjects?' (Parks, 1995, p. 29) The ghettoization of each word makes this a sentence in the sense of a severe pronouncement. Bearing in mind that the human-sized roaches in the living-room are placed there by Lutzky, his equivocation with the word 'accommodate' is far from accidental.

Parks's riffing on words, like 'accommodate', pregnant with both epic and vernacular resonance, works in tandem with images such as Charlene wrapping coffee grinds in newspaper, which first appear trivial, but become increasingly charged as the play progresses and similar motifs recur. Kin-Seer's dream, in which he is 'uh black black speck in thuh middle of thuh sea' (Parks, 1995, p. 38), links the visions of the Seers – their dreams of sequential 'swallowin'' and 'becamin'' that evoke the epochal trauma of the Middle Passage, and the continuing struggle of African-Americans to 'become' – back to the wrapped coffee grinds, themselves 'black speck[s]', and to Charlene, a 'real-life' African-American trying to find a place for herself with the aid of the Help Wanteds. Parks provocatively ties the materialities of urban and suburban life to the archaic and the metaphysical. While the Mona/Chona/Verona scenes grow out of and recede back into domesticity, the Seers inhabit a poetic limbo between the archaic and the urbane.

Embodying the turbulent legacy of forced African migration to the United States, the Seers are a bridge – albeit rickety – between domesticity and archaism. Habitants of the 'Third Kingdom' of the play's title, they are interspersed between the three longer sections of the play. They image a form of seeing which is unwittingly poetic, a visionary capacity which is startlingly vivid but horrifyingly incomplete. In Chong's phrase to describe his own work, Parks gives us 'waking public dreams': when director Liz Diamond first read *IMTK* she 'felt like it had to be a really wild hallucinogenic, sort of nightmarish event' (Drukman, 1995, p. 70). In the 1989 production of the play directed by Diamond at BACA Downtown in Brooklyn, the Seers were presented as voices on tape. The stage was dark, except for black-and-white photographic slides projected onto a black screen. Historically aspecific, the first slides featured fragments of bodies, hands and feet in thick mud. Later, more intelligible images are projected.[8] As the Shark-Seer (voiceover) recalled his dream of being swallowed by a fish, and of 'uh me that then becamin that fish and [...] that fish becamin uh shark and ... that shark becamin uhshore', the slides depicted bejewelled and well-dressed women, lending a concreteness to the social commentary lurking in the text.

Over-Seer's name and authoritative bearing resonate with the slave masters of the Middle Passage, but he might also be a community leader. Us-Seer seems to embody the home body, standing in both for those left behind when slaves depart and those, within the diaspora, who are themselves left behind by practices that divide to conquer. In their disorienting 'glass-bottomed boat', Kin-Seer, Shark-Seer, and Soul-Seer ride ('navigate' would over-state their command) an ambiguous sea of symbolism which frequently mires them in confusion. All the Seers find it hard to recognize themselves and their environment, but it falls to Over-Seer to fill in the gaps in their knowledge. He informs the others that when half the world fell away, a wet place was inscribed between the two worlds called 'the Third Kingdom'. This topographical narrative is complicated by Over-Seer's qualification that 'the second part comes apart in 2 parts'. The compulsion of Kin-Seer and Soul-Seer to read the dynamics of identity mirrors the audience's pursuit of meaning, a caution against reading things in a mechanically habituated manner.

The Seers are out of focus, mangled archetypes, elliptical points of reference. This impression is reinforced by the structural fact that they appear in relatively short bursts in the play, interspersed between the three longer, discrete sections. Parks's theme-phenomena engage notions of integration, and its structural counterpoint, separation. Like the motifs of enclosure, images of integration and separation accumulate so that they become charged and, fleetingly, coalesce into specific social contexts.

Assimilation and its shadow, ghettoization, are highly charged with past and continuing struggles of African-Americans in the United States for, with, and against, social integration. The legacy of these struggles is most explicit during the central 'Open House' section, in which Aretha, a freed slave, hangs around an apartment that the children of her former owner are looking to purchase. It is the nature of Aretha's presence – as a kind of ghost, or, as Parks puts it, a 'figment' – that is crucial. As she tries to concretize the reality of what is happening to her by piecing together her fragmented memories and visions, we are able, through Aretha, to piece together the associations that Parks generates. The family to whom Aretha is enslaved are the Saxons: Charles Saxon and his children, Anglor and Blanca. The names are emblematic of contradiction: though they contain clear associations with (Anglo-Saxon) heritage, there is a tension between these associations and the name Aretha. For many, the name 'Aretha' connotes Aretha Franklin, who began singing as a girl attending black gospel services and who became a mainstream success despite often being seen as too Black to assimilate. Aretha Saxon is far from fully assimilated: she hovers in scenes, and we do not know quite how aware she is of her own situation. She is, like Buzz in *Kind Ness*, a narrativistically hanging figure, not quite contained by her own signified environment, or by the signifying environment of the play.

When Aretha learns that her time as a guardian has come to an end because 'her lease has expired', she insists on taking photographs of the family with toothy grins. This task of preservation proves tricky as her subjects are truculent. Aretha is undeterred: 'Dont matter none at all. You say it's a cry I say it uh smile. These photographics is for my scrapbook. Scraps uh graphy for my book' (Parks, 1995, p. 54). The pictures she describes horribly echo pictures of 'happy' slaves. Under Miss Faith's supervision – literally under it, as Miss Faith sits on a high platform overlooking her – Aretha measures space to assess how many slaves they will be able to accommodate. Alluding to the fact that Aretha's own term as a slave is about to 'expire', Miss Faith extracts Aretha's teeth with a pair of pliers. This diligent dentistry proceeds despite Aretha's screams. Taking words out of Aretha's mouth, Miss Faith informs her patient: 'if we didnt pluck them, we couldnt photograph them' (ibid., p. 46). While the extractions allude *specifically* to the use of dental records to identify slaves and corpses, they are also a poetic allusion to the fact that Miss Faith's archival gathering is a 'system of enunciability' that, as in Shark-Seer's dream, swallows everything Aretha says and does.

In a scene prefaced (in the printed text) with the word 'Dreamtime', Aretha goes to meet her maker, who turns out to be her earthly master, Charles Saxon. He asks for her papers, which state that her name is also 'Charles Saxon'. She informs Charles that her husband is dead, but is told that she too is also called Charles. Her proper name is confirmed by Miss Faith, it is after all signed in her book. Signatures are as important for Miss Faith as they are for Derrida, and are equally tied to scriptural truth. Miss Faith insists that Aretha can prove (and continue to remember) who she is by looking at her signature in 'the book'. Derrida describes how the confusion of proper names derives from the story of Babel. To cut this long story short, God wants the Shems to hear his name and obey his voice (which means translating it into terms they can understand), for he is God. But he also wants them *not* to understand his name, for he transcends their worldly codes (Derrida, 1985, pp. 100–2). The elusiveness of Aretha's surname foregrounds the paradoxical nature of the proper name on which Derrida dwells: its propriety is predicated on it being both singular/non-translatable and communicable/translatable. But Parks also foregrounds how the ordinarily paradoxical function of the proper name is put into particular crisis by both slavery and so-called 'emancipation' proclamations. Male slave-owners routinely used (un-)naming to mark ownership of their 'favourite' slaves while trying to cover up evidence of sexual congress with them, robbing slaves and their descendants of autonomous identity.

Parks's naming of systems of enunciability chisels at the culture in which Aretha is entombed. Aretha may have swallowed the rhetoric that valorized slavery, but in digesting she rearranges, so that Miss Faith's book becomes more 'scraps uh graphy for [her *own*] book'. Messy, reflecting the fragmentation of Aretha's life, Aretha's book contrasts with Miss Faith's, which is as pristine and unyielding as the proper must pretend to be, swallowing everything into its system of enunciability. Aretha's book is falling apart at the seams.

While Parks's plays contain forward-moving narratives, and often feature establishing scenes, middle passages, and denouements, the plays do not arc in an exposition → conflict → catastrophe manner. Rather, they mine the gaps between what has happened and not happened, what is lost in memory and what is over-familiar. Parks's method is a ritual calling to memory antithetical to Miss Faith's book, a theatrical means of 'creating history where it is and always was but has not yet been divined' (Parks, 1995, p. 5). Her plays are purgatories of (mis)reckoning and (mis)recognition.

As commentators including Genevieve Fabre have observed, words in Eurocentric drama are primarily vehicles for logic, units to be laid together horizontally to build meaning. In modern Afrocentric drama, where ties to oral traditions tend to remain stronger, the vertical axis of language – repetition and elaboration – is crucial: in any act of naming (any invocation of 'Nommo'), emotional investment 'counts' as much as rational delineation. Emphasis is on the force with which words are iterated, so that they can attain the incantatory power to conjure previous iterations. A consequence of the decline of orality is the loss of a connection between speech and breath, embodied language. Parks's plays mourn, and yearn to recuperate, that loss. In *IMTK*, the opposition between Aretha and Miss Faith is most evident in the language they use:

> ARETHA: Three two thuuup one n one. Huh. Twenty-one and one and one. And thuh little bit. Thuuup. Thup. Thirty-two and uh half.

MISS FAITH: Footnote #1: the human cargo capacity of the English slaver, the *Brookes*, was about 3,250 Square Feet. From James A. Rawley, *The Transatlantic Slave Trade*, G. J. Mcleod Limited, 1981, page 283.

(Parks, 1995, p. 43)

Parks sets the physicality of Aretha's speech against the disembodiment of Miss Faith's referential insistence on the written word. Parks's rendering of Aretha's words bears the marks of bodily expression, whereas Miss Faith's speech continually points to the act of writing.

In interviews, Parks has referred to the spectatorial pleasure of deciphering familial and thematic connections to make meaning as 'digging' (see Drukman, 1995; and Jiggets, 1996). As the *America Play* audience is immersed in the serious fun of semantic digging, a family of 'real' diggers ply their trade on stage. In the first of the play's two acts, the father of the family tells his story of being a black man who makes a meagre living as a fairground attraction in which he impersonates, ad nauseam, Abraham Lincoln being shot by John Wilkes Booth at Ford's Theatre. Once the money has been paid, the shots fired, the dying performed, and the guest assassin has uttered their version of Booth's mythical line ('The South will be avenged'), up gets the 'Lesser Known' Lincoln ready for the next customer. In Act 2, we see his wife and child, Lucy and Brazil. While Lucy listens for echoes of her husband's presence with the aid of an ear-trumpet, Brazil follows in his father's spade marks, digging up treasures including accoutrements that once belonged to Lincoln. Brazil has also pursued his father's other occupation – as a designated mourner – wailing, weeping, and gnashing with virtuosity.

The America Play is set in a sort of archaeological theme-park 'out West', described in the printed text as 'an exact replica of The Great Hole of History'. To fill the void that is the historical past and their own present, the family excavate *tsatskes* – bits of costume and other artefacts whose theatrical sheen is authoritative and alluring. Parks has explained that the linguistic friction between the words 'hole' and 'whole' was the seed for the (w)hole play (Pearce, p. 26). The Great Hole that Brazil mines is a re-creation of the Original Great Hole that his parents discovered on their honeymoon 'back East'. While his son (the copy of himself), works the Hole (the copy of the original Hole), the Foundling Father relates his original enchantment:

THE FOUNDLING FATHER: You could look intuh that Hole and see your entire life pass before you. Not your own life but

someones life from history ... *Like* you, but *not* you. You know:
Known.

(Parks, 1995, p. 197)

Mesmerized by spectral, absent celebrity, the Lesser Known becomes
a stranger to his own family. Instead of spending time with them, he
spends (and re-spends) his life being repeatedly shot by visitors – including honeymooners like he and Lucy once were. Lucy spends her time
perambulating the space of the stage, listening with her ear trumpet
for echoes of her husband. Brazil bases his life around following in the
spade marks of a father he never knew, but regards (much as the father
regarded Lincoln) as someone to emulate, to mythologize, a Figure possessive of the sheen of 'reality' precisely because he is absent, a historical
treasure.

The play is full of responses looking pathetically for a call: the Lesser
Known looking for a sign from The Greater Known to help him in his calling as an impersonator; Lucy with her ear trumpet listening for echoes.
Call and response is a key feature of African ritual and subsequent theatre, in which naming hinges on concepts of possession, of being moved
by a force powerful enough to invoke Nommo, the word or seed of god
(Fabre, 1983, p. 205). In their display of grief, Brazil and his father fake
as if they are possessed, but they seem to be hollow, almost dead; for all
their histrionics, no passion passes through them. African-American art
is propelled by ascendant visions of the future promising liberation from
the difficulties of the past and present. As they dig for evidence of the
past, the characters in *The America Play* seem not to consider the future,
so that the present continually slips through their grasp. Their digging,
the opposite of transcendence, seems to bury them.

Named Foundling Father, a bathetic allusion to the Founding Father
of the United States, our impersonator continually refers to himself in the
third person, and always explicitly in relation to Lincoln. Lincoln he calls
the 'Great Man', himself 'the Lesser Known', proudly and pathetically
implying that all he has is his relationship to Lincoln. Parks writes in
signifying echoes and near-echoes, the effect of which is that statements
seem not to die, but to resonate with a life of their own. The Foundling's
speech acts implode meaning and agency, burying his identity in an icon
of Lincoln and his experience in 'The Great Man's'. He refers to himself in
the third person (as 'he' or 'The Lesser Known'). In contrast, Parks's riffing
produces accidental associations that work like small explosions across
the surface of the characters' speech. She opposes his antiquating devices
with her animating ones. *The America Play* begins with the following

four bits of Lincolnesque rhetoric, that are as pompous as the footnotes spouted by Miss Faith in *IMTK*:

THE FOUNDLING FATHER AS ABRAHAM LINCOLN:
'To stop too fearful and too faint to go.'
(Rest.)
'He digged the whole and the hole held him.'
(Rest.)
'I cannot dig, to beg I am ashamed.'
(Rest.)
'He went to the theatre but home went she.'

(Parks, 1995, p. 198)

These pronouncements, invoked by the Foundling to strengthen his connection to the Founding Father, are the agents of depersonalization, the means by which he attaches his own flimsy identity to one that is more 'Real'. The Foundling Father uses Lincolnesque rhetoric to lay the ground for an authentic rendition – antiquated and varnished – of the Great Man. There is a completeness to each of the Lincolnesque declarations by which the Foundling grounds his performance. Each sentence contains two clauses, separated by a caesura, in perfect balance. 'Rest[s]', a musical notation, render every sentence self-contained, and give an air of finality. The overall formality of this series of speech acts is such that pronouns become almost irrelevant: the self becomes a figure of speech. I say 'almost' because agency does remain – in the image of the Lesser Known *wanting* us to confuse him with Lincoln. For Parks, however, language is soil to be turned. Her word play, polemical and whimsical, dis-members and re-members the speech acts and conventions that give the performance its authenticity. As well as 'The Foundling Father', the stand-in for Lincoln is referred to, for example, as the 'faux-father', a play on 'forefather' and on falsity; and as 'foefather', connoting animosity (Parks, 1995, p. 184). Parks's riffing (or in Gates's terms, discussed in the next chapter, 'signifying') on 'forefather' un-names the icon of Lincoln named by the Lesser Known.

In Act 1, it is the deconstructive, relativist nature of the naming that stands out, the fact that his identity is paradoxically defined by his relationship to Lincoln. For most of Act 2, however, the Foundling Father is absent, referred to by his wife Lucy and son Brazil as 'daddy', 'papa', 'the Father', and 'your fathuh'. These identifiers give him an identity, albeit one dependent on a role, and on confirmation by a family who provide him with a matrix. As the Act progresses, though, the absence of the father deprives him of stable identity – a sense of absentness that only increases when he appears on stage, both 'live' and on a television screen that Brazil has excitedly dug up, a screen that is replaying Act 1, 'The Lincoln Act', in which the Foundling Father continually replays that shard of history that is the shooting of Lincoln.

As his televised image enthrals Brazil, The Foundling Father reappears in live form. He is dead, but has come back to check that Brazil has organized his funeral properly, and 'to say a few words from the grave' as his televised self continues to play out. Lucy and Brazil watch the Foundling Father being repeatedly shot and rising up again. Brazil quickly realizes that he is 'dead but not really' (Parks, 1995, p. 194). But when the Foundling Father appears in person next to them, Brazil has no idea whether 'zit him' and, then, whether 'he's dead?' For Brazil, as for the women in *IMTK*, television is a safe world that can be read more easily than the world around him. It provides the illusion that the viewer is in control; whereas the truth about his father's status, and even about his own and his father's identity, confuses Brazil.

Parks has described how theatre helps her bring the dead to life each evening in an act of messy animation; whereas television, as it features in her work, tends to commodify and sanitize, disembodying individuals and neutralizing conflict. Parks's theatre 'makes the bones sing': her digging, and that of the audience, are preparatory phases, the re-membering of the bones. Television, in contrast, entraps what is alive, as betrayed in *IMTK* by Chona's lines: 'Once there was uh woman on thuh lookout. Still trapped. *Wild Kingdoms* on' (Parks, 1995, p. 31). Like Brazil, Chona fails to see the connection between what is on TV and what is happening right next to her. On TV, Marlin Perkins is in Africa observing savage beasts; in the living-room, Lutzky, 'thuh exterminator with a PhD', is secretly observing the women, whom he refers to as 'mundus primitivus'.

The challenge that Parks sets herself and her spectators is to use theatre in a way that allows history to reverberate. Her plays suggest, though, that before theatre is to liberate the past, she and her spectators must steer theatre clear of theme-park 'Reconstructed Histories'. In a synthetic analysis of theatre, theory, and architecture, Elinor Fuchs describes 'postmodern' buildings in which there is a schematizing of 'historical into stage, the contemporary into auditorium' (Fuchs, 1996, p.146). In other words, there is a collapsing of time into space, but a continuation of the association of primitivism with objects, static in time, and of subjects with development, in progression. It is a construction which Parks alludes to throughout *IMTK* and *The America Play*. The Naturalist first appears after a few short scenes of interaction between Mona,

Chona, and Verona. Addressing the audience very directly, his first line – 'Thus behave our subjects naturally' – puts him in the narrator position. Though he refers to them as 'subjects', he puts the women very much in the object position. When he poses his research imperative, the positioning continues:

> THE NATURALIST: Having accumulated a wealth of naturally occurring observations knowing now how our subjects occur in their own world (mundus primitivus), the question now arises as to how we of our world (mundus modernus) can best accommodate them.
>
> (Parks, 1995, p. 29)

The Naturalist aligns himself with the audience, which he equates with the contemporary, which is seen as advanced ('mundus modernus'). He positions the women as spectacle, which he equates with the past, which is seen as primitive ('mundus primitivus'). By making him a 'naturalist', a word rich in theatrical as well as scientific connotations, Parks draws attention to a relationship that preoccupied theatre scholars in the late 1980s and early 1990s: between the framing devices that induce theatrical spectatorship and (what James Moy, Coco Fusco, and others have referred to as) the anthropological gaze. Moy elucidates an 'anthropological gaze [that] emerged as the mechanism by which the common man came to participate in national dreams of empire' (Moy, 1993a, p. 7). The idea of the gaze as an image-*conjuring* mechanism, creating 'dreams of empire' in 'the common man', informs Parks's portrayal of Mr Smith waiting on a foreign island for his Distinction, of the Seers, and of the 'Reconstructed Histories' that never leave 'the minds eye' of the Foundling Father.

Parks uses *Our American Cousin* (*OAC*), the play-within-*The America Play*, to explore the construction of stage and auditorium in relation to the historicization of identity. These scenes, interspersed with the meanderings of Lucy and Brazil, are introduced by the Foundling Father as Host, much like the Masterpiece Theatre Host in *The Colored Museum*'s pivotal 'Last Mama-on-the-Couch Play' (which I will discuss in the next chapter).[9] As the first of the two *OAC* scenes ends, with overblown taped applause, the Foundling Father is left, looking our way, sounding through time: '"Hellloooooooo!" (*Rest. Waves*).' In the second, he takes a role in the action as the cantankerous Mrs Mount, whose daughter Augusta is being wooed by the play's hapless protagonist, Mr Trenchard. A role markedly different from his own persona in gender and demeanour, the performance creates an almost surreal clash of performative idioms – Black Man-as-Abraham Lincoln-as-Mrs Mount. In Diamond's definitive Yale Repertory production of 1993, the two *OAC* scenes, each titled 'Echo' in the printed text and in the production programme, were performed on a red, raised-platform inner stage. The stage became a surrogate auditorium for a moment, foregrounding the theatrical packaging of 'history'. Though the play-within-a-play scenes are short, the trope of stage-as-surrogate auditorium hangs over the listening of Lucy, and of Brazil, that occupies much of Act Two. Making Lucy and Brazil function as surrogate spectators is another way in which Parks frames spectatorship. While Lucy and Brazil try to discern signs of communication from beyond their metaphorical island, we too are led to listen for echoes.[10]

4
Demonstration: Illustrative Irony

In the previous chapter, I discussed performances by Ping Chong that link slide presentation, as an early information technology, to identity formation. Twenty years later, in 2006, Forced Entertainment's *The World in Pictures* contains its own set-piece slide-show. Jerry Killick, still wearing his caveman wig from an early phase of the show, clicks on a laptop that emits electronic quacks, keytones not unlike those emitted when performer-technicians in The Wooster Group's *House/Lights* (the first version of which was produced in 1997) clicked on their laptops. Both *Kind Ness* and *The World in Pictures* embark on an anthropological, historical narrative to undermine it. While the unseen, loudspeaker Narrator in *Kind Ness* has a cool, scientific detachment, Jerry speaks to his images with pathos in a long aside, or hiatus, in a show full of long asides, breakdowns in which meaning is broken down. Jerry's slide-show, like his long set-up at the start and reflection at the end of *The World in Pictures*, has a veneer of sharing, of communality. He thoughtfully suggests, viewing a picture of a pair of shoes: 'here is a gift you might have bought'. A snow-covered, anonymous perspective view of a road is accompanied by the speculation that 'here is a street you might have walked down'. Later in the sequence, Jerry seems to struggle, several images bringing the commentary, 'I don't know'. His palpable effort and vulnerability is pathetic where the Narrator in *Kind Ness* is pompously removed, but in both cases the fixity of the image promises some kind of grounding. Each illustrative lesson promises to solidify our sense of what we are seeing and experiencing in the show 'proper', the acted storytelling performances. Whereas the slide-show in the *Kind Ness* prologue purports to prepare us for what is to follow by teaching us 'what is alike and what is not alike', Jerry's comes after the sack of Rome, during the Dark Ages. As narrator Terry O'Connor tells it, with faltering help from the lighting operator, the Dark Ages are a time of 'forgetting', a time where people 'forget how to read, how to write', a time when 'everything leaves the story', when 'names leave the story'. Making a connection between his present and the so-called Dark Ages, Jerry's slide-show is a plaintively hypothetical reading that, like Chong's *Kind Ness* and *Nosferatu*, locates the spectator in Barthes's 'purgatory of reading'.[1]

Demonstrations that ironize their own authority are hardly new to theatre – not least in theatre that ventures into galleries, lofts, warehouses, parks, streets, and other venues without a red velvet theatre seat to be had. Ironic demonstration is integral to genre descriptors like 'agit-prop' and 'street theatre', and to the work of activist community companies such as Welfare State, Bread and Puppet, and the San Francisco Mime Troupe. It is a key element of much invisible and guerrilla performance, from the AIDS-focused performative activism of ACT UP to the self-styled anarchism of CIRCA (Clandestine Insurgent Rebel Clown Army) to the situationism of the V-Girls holding a 'fake' panel discussion on Manet's Olympia at the CUNY Graduate Center,[2] or Adrian Piper giving out calling cards stating 'Dear Friend, I am black. I am sure you did not realize this when you made/laughed at/agreed with that racist remark'.[3] Alongside these paratheatrical examples, ironic demonstration has an important place in 'proper' theatre, often reflecting an author's desire to undermine conventional propriety: Pirandello's *Six Characters in Search of an Author* (1921), Wilder's *Our Town* (1938) (itself demonstrated by The Wooster Group's 1984 work, *Routes 1 & 9*), and Maria Irene Fornes's *Tango Palace* (1963), all play ironic demonstration against theatrical matrixing.[4]

Twentieth-century performance frequently adopts and/or quotes demonstrative techniques from previous decades, often in ways that go unnoticed until critics elucidate them. Michael Kirby observes in 1965 that 'the Dada distortion of the lecture into a work of art prefigure[s] certain aspects of Cage's lectures' (Sandford, 1995, p. 45). More broadly, Cage's performance pedagogy at Black Mountain College (see Chapter 6) in the 1940s and 1950s, and the Happenings fostered by Cage's teaching, drew on Dada performances in Europe in earlier decades. 'A clear progression', Kirby notes, 'can be traced from Dada activities to the first New York Happening (ibid., p. 19). In the two decades between *Kind Ness* and *The World in Pictures*, 1986–2006, however, experimental theatre has deployed demonstration in a differently quotational fashion, interrogating demonstrative methods and technologies. To cite examples by artists I discuss elsewhere in this book, the United Kingdom has seen the angry farce of Ridiculusmus's 'performative demonstration' of *How to be Funny* (2005),[5] and the acerbic gentility of Bobby Baker teaching us how to cook, *How to Shop* (1993), and *How to Live* (2004). In the United States, George C. Wolfe's *Colored Museum* first displayed itself in 1986, the same year Chong constructed his counter-quotational zoo in *Kind Ness*. Like Chong, the first images Wolfe presents are slides. As air hostess-cum-museum guide Miss Pat invites us to 'Git on Board', images described in Wolfe's stage directions as ones that 'we've all seen before' are projected, slides 'of African slaves being captured, loaded onto ships, tortured'. In 1989, *The Baltimore Waltz* used a slide-show of holiday pictures alongside AIDS-education lessons to alienate the alienation of medical pedagogy, while in *Imperceptible Mutabilities in the Third Kingdom* (*IMTK*) Suzan-Lori Parks showed stills from African-American history in front of which real-life African-Americans 'mutated like hell'. During the 1990s, and into the 2000s, several works pressed scientific and pseudo-scientific discourses through theatrical structures: UK examples include *Here's what I did with my body one day*, *The Receipt*, and *Tangle*[6] (2006) by Unlimited Theatre; US examples include Parks's *Venus*, Skipitares's *Under the Knife: The History of Medicine*, Coco Fusco and Guillermo Gómez-Peña's *Two Undiscovered Amerindians Visit....* (*Pugilist Specialist*, as I discuss in Chapter 7, is framed entirely *as* a demonstration.)

Etymologically, 'demonstration' comprises '*de-*', a Latin prefix denoting of/for, and '*monstrare*', meaning to show, or explain. The 'of'/'for' is crucial here, as it indicates a duality of meanings that haunts, and is exploited by, the theatrical demonstrations I will discuss. To demonstrate is to show, to illustrate; a demonstration is a show, something made for display, *made to be shown*. On paper, the showing of illustration is only subtly different from illustration itself. *The Colored Museum*, *Two Undiscovered Amerindians*, and several of the works of Bobby Baker, show that, theatrically, it can be a vital difference. In their distinct ways, each resists and demands critical response. Play on this paradox is, I will argue, integral to the radical instability of these works, but is habitually *resolved* by critics, whose supplementation artificially settles that instability.

Like *Kind Ness*, *The Colored Museum* is at the cusp of the shift, neatly summarized by Marvin Carlson, from 'the claiming of' to 'ironic commentary on' identity positions. Both works focus on identity, and do so in an anti-hegemonic fashion, but pointedly refuse to follow *any* orthodox line of critique. While both works have been described as 'postmodern' and 'deconstructive', their reaction against theatrical and other representational mechanisms that calcify American and hyphenated American identities is nonetheless polemic and constructive. *Two Undiscovered Amerindians Visit...* (*TUAV*) (versions of which evolved 1992–93), *Under the Knife* (versions of which evolved 1993–95), and Parks's *Venus* (first staged in 1995) focus only implicitly on theatrical spectatorship, and more squarely on the racial and gendered dimensions of relationships between colonialism and the body. On the face of it, this bucks a trend away from identity politics based on binaries and on head-on engagement with race, gender, and class, an engagement often seen as dissipating (in theatre and elsewhere) into and during the 1990s. That *Venus, Under the Knife*, and *TUAV* engage firmly with binaries of race, gender, and class marks them as resistant to such dissipation; but they are also works of their time, reflecting a trend toward the situation of race- and gender-based critiques within a broader, anthropologically informed focus on scholarly traditions and the disciplining of the human.

As its full title suggests, *Two Undiscovered Amerindians Visit...*, is a travelling installation that Marvin Carlson describes as 'probably the best-known performance piece of the 1990s' (Carlson, 2004, p. 202). Coco Fusco and Guillermo Gómez-Peña exhibited themselves in a golden cage (Figure 1) in museums and commemorative civic spaces across four continents, purporting to be Guatinauis, a tribe of 'undiscovered Amerindians' living (if the display of a large map was anything to go by) somewhere or other in the Gulf of Mexico. Barely clad, in grass-skirt fashion, but with ceremonial items (including, in the male's case, what

Figure 1　Two Undiscovered Amerindians visit Covent Garden, London, May 1992 (Photo: Peter Barker)

was actually an Aztec breastplate), the male paced around and babbled away in his native tongue (a made-up combination of, predominantly, nonsense sounds and Spanish words), while the female danced and knitted. Items such as a television, Coca-Cola, and Saltine crackers were introduced into the cage, and they took to these readily. For 50¢, you could step up to the cage and have a photo taken; for $5, you could see the male's genitalia, though the penis was tucked behind the legs to leave a feminine pubic tuft. Guards/docents/educators with 'Ask Me' badges were on hand to answer spectators' questions about the caged couple, about what exactly they were doing and why, what their 'island' back home was like. While Fusco and Gómez-Peña have stated that they intended it as 'a satirical comment on the past', and were surprised how many visitors failed to realize they were professional performance artists, their choice to not print any programme information suggests that they were thinking of the piece, at least in part, as invisible theatre.

Gómez-Peña and Fusco first took their golden cage to Columbus Plaza Colón, in Madrid, as part of an event to commemorate the quincentennial of Columbus's voyage to the New World. The piece had an illustrious two-year exhibition history at various sites, including Covent Garden in London, The National Museum of Natural History at the Smithsonian in Washington DC, The Field Museum in Chicago, the Whitney Museum's Biennial in New York, the Australian Museum of Natural Science, and the Fundación Banco Patricios in Buenos Aires. In *The Archive and the Repertoire*, Diana Taylor locates the piece in 'the museum', which she theorizes through binaries: live/dead; fixity/transience. 'Museums', she notes, 'have long taken the cultural other out of context and isolated it, reducing the live to a dead object behind glass.' In so doing, they 'make spectators discoverers [...] separating the transient visitor from the fixed object of display' (Taylor, 2003, p. 66). Performative treatments of the museum by Wolfe and Skipitares, which I will discuss in this and the following chapter respectively, play against the neatness of these divisions. Their double-voiced theatricality inserts caesuras, alienating and interrupting the spectator's sensation of discovery, bringing the dead to life and animating objects in ways that trouble the traditional boundaries of the museum.[7] Before I discuss in more detail the question of how determinately Wolfe troubles those boundaries in *The Colored Museum*, I want to ask a similar question of *TUAV*.

'Our cage', asserts Fusco, 'became a blank screen onto which audiences projected their fantasies of whom and what we are. As we assumed the stereotypical role of the domesticated savage, many audience members felt entitled to assume the role of colonizer, only to find themselves

uncomfortable with the implications of the game' (Fusco, 1995, p. 45).
Fusco's written reflection on, and explanation of, the piece targets 'a substantial number of intellectuals, artists, and cultural bureaucrats [who]
have sought to deflect attention from the substance of our experiment
to the "moral implications" of our dissimulation, or in their words, our
"misinforming the public" about who we are. The literalism implicit in
the interpretation of our work by individuals representing the "public
interest" bespeaks', she claims, 'their investment in positivist notions
of "truth".' She adds that 'this "reverse ethnography" of our interactions
with the public will, I hope, suggest the culturally specific nature of their
tendency toward the literal and moral interpretation' (ibid., p. 143). The
debate within which Fusco centres herself raises important questions for
the kind of work I am discussing in this chapter, work she describes as
'parodically didactic' (ibid., p. 148). In calling her own critique 'reverse
ethnography', is Fusco claiming that her interpretation is less 'culturally specific'? When does 'ethnography' qualify as a 'reverse' form? Can
criticism of ironic demonstration, including self-critique, do anything
other than disambiguate it in 'positivist' fashion; and is such settling of
instability inherently problematic?

Barbara Kirshenblatt-Gimblett finds no reversal, only a 'restaging'
of 'repudiated modes of ethnographic knowledge and display' (1998,
p. 175). She is angered by the claim that, because the exhibit is contrived
by those in the cage, it turns the tables, reflecting the colonial gaze back
on the spectator and thereby alienating the history of such exhibitions.
She insists that there is no reversal, but rather a *continuity* with what she
calls '"othering" practices'. In using the phrase '"othering" practices',
she links ironic exhibitions such as the couple in the cage to 'certain
recent writing on primitivism more generally (Marianna Torgovnick's
Gone Primitive [1990] is a case in point)' (ibid.). Kirshenblatt-Gimblett
uses the word 'writing' to encompass not just literal writing, but performance itself – that is, not just Fusco's published analysis of the couple
in the cage, but the exhibition itself. In Kirshenblatt-Gimblett's usage,
writing becomes synonymous with a kind of standing-in, a secondary
performance that stands in for a primary one. But, rather than recuper-
ating the 'othering' of the primary exhibition, the secondary exhibition
(Torgovnick's or Fusco's writing, or Fusco and Gómez-Peña's performance) intensifies it, because the putative 'spirit of repudiation' that
accompanies the standing-in is germane to othering practices, 'right
from the start'. In making this argument, Kirshenblatt-Gimblett cites
'foreign villages at world fairs', in which 'not only performers [...] but
also college students, immigrants, and other employees [...] stood in

for Turks, Egyptians, Irish, and Germans. Not always, but not infrequently, those who exhibited and those who were exhibited were one and the same. Repudiation, she argues, is 'constitutive of these othering practices' (ibid., p. 176).

Kirshenblatt-Gimblett's view that the couple in the cage performance works as a form of writing draws attention to the foundational role of writing in making performance mean, making behaviour visible *as* performance. Writing restores. In the context of performance that frames itself as invisible reversal, that restorative role of writing is peculiarly problematic. The frequent quotation of the following passage from Fusco's 'Other History of Intercultural Performance' exemplifies how, in the case of itinerant, concept-rich, variable performances, a maker's description of the work can 'write' the work itself: 'We performed our "traditional tasks", which ranged from sewing voodoo dolls and lifting weights to watching television and working on a laptop computer. A donation box in front of the cage indicated that, for a small fee, I would dance (to rap music), Guillermo would tell authentic Amerindian stories (in a nonsensical language), and we would pose for Polaroids for visitors' (Fusco, 1995, p. 39). Commentary like Fusco's is party to the fraught politics of standing-in and authentic description that the couple in the cage performance analyses. Though notable for the firmness of her opposition to claims (including Fusco's) that the couple in the cage is subversive, Kirshenblatt-Gimblett is certainly not alone in identifying the problematic grounds on which any such claims can be made.

Taylor and Kirshenblatt-Gimblett agree that the filming of the couple in the cage ushers in, or in the latter's view, 'rehearses', the always already assimilating gaze of the camera. They agree that a controlling ideological apparatus adheres to the presence of photography and video cameras in the live performance space, and to the spectatorial conditions of looking at photographic images, and watching the film document, in contexts such as a classroom. In Kirshenblatt-Gimblett's view, the *Couple in the Cage* video takes the so-called 'repudiation' a stage further, the images and the editing lingering on the gaze of the live spectators in ways that make the video-watcher feel superior to the filmed visitors, detached from the danger of the live but doubly able to enjoy the frisson of the so-called duping.[8] An article by film scholar Mary Kate Kelly focuses only on the video. Sharing her experience of screening the video for students, Kelly describes being 'immediately reminded of the 1934 narrative film *Zou Zou*', in which Josephine Baker 'appears on a stage enclosed in a huge decorated bird cage clothed in little more than the few feathers that cover her breasts. Baker (an African-American expatriate) plays the part of Zou Zou, a stage performer originally introduced to the film audience as a Polynesian, who in this particular scene performs the role of an authentic icon of West Indian exoticism' before being 'set free by one of the male stage performers' and leaping 'from the cage into the performer's arms, while the film camera pans back to reveal the applauding Parisian theater audience that has been fixated on her' (Kelly, 1999, p. 113). In comparing it to *Zou Zou*, Kelly writes that *Couple in the Cage* 'reveals' how 'this performance piece staged [Fusco and Gómez-Peña] in an ironic, reflexive gesture to the still widespread allure of native authenticity.' Kelly acknowledges that the methodology and spirit of the performance 'sought, very self-consciously, to critique and interrogate the fascination with primitivism and authenticity that continues to exist in Western culture', but worries that Gómez-Peña and Fusco engage only 'tenuously' with the complexities that haunt any 'process of representing the "primitive Other"' in order to 'engage a history of objectification and dehumanization' (ibid.).

Kelly's statement that the film 'reveals' the performance's staging as 'an ironic, reflexive gesture' is itself revealing. The film, in disambiguating the more cryptic statements made by the performance, establishes itself, in Derridean terms, as a 'supplement'. While the relationship between performance and critical commentary is nearly always slippery, commentaries generally preferring not to name their supplementation of what they critique, a particular kind of slipperiness characterizes the couple in the cage performance/film/artists' written documentation. The French word 'supplément' means both replacement and addition. Derrida is (as usual) acutely conscious of the paradoxical nature of supplementarity: to be an addition means to be added to something complete; but that something cannot be complete if it needs an addition. The film of the couple in the cage is a supplement, extending by repeating the premise of the performance, ultimately usurping that premise in its overwriting. The supplementation of performance by film becomes part of the already charged politics of standing-in that envelop the caged couple.

While Kirshenblatt-Gimblett's earnest, historicized repudiation of Fusco and Gómez-Peña's ironic, 'postmodern' repudiation of colonial exhibition is cogent, the irony of *TUAV* is, as Taylor argues, more seriously considered than Kirshenblatt-Gimblett allows. Calibrating the effectiveness of irony is a tricky thing. My view is that the *difficulty* of deciding whether the ironic demonstration is regressive or subversive is not an unwanted side-effect, but is essential to the effectiveness of late twentieth-century ironic theatrical demonstration. In Bobby Baker performances, the slippage between the naming of an action or list item and her demonstration of that item/action generates a comedic but unsettling ambiguity that Baker exploits to the full. With systematic, idiosyncratic, often sanctifying enthusiasm she ritually performs mundane tasks that bespeak important issues of feminist politics and mental health. In her influential 1991 work, *The Kitchen Show*, for instance, Baker takes us through her Baker's dozen of 13 Actions, some of which meditate on the beautiful order of domestic details ('Action No. 6: Opening a new tub of margarine to see its unsullied perfection') while others make exuberant mess ('Action No. 9: Dancing when inspired by operatic music'). Each Action is accompanied by a 'Mark', a ceremonial adornment such as the pinning of a spinach leaf to the lapel of her white overall. These marks accumulate ridiculously, making Baker an ensign of the struggle between order and chaos that runs throughout the piece. Like most of her work, *The Kitchen Show* is full of both integrity and parody, sincerity and absurdity. Spectators less familiar with Baker's work sometimes find themselves recalibrating the earnestness of her performance as it proceeds.

While Baker's work is strikingly different in tone, and in the identity it performs, from *The Colored Museum* (*CM*) and from the couple in the cage, it operates similar kinds of slippage within performance, and raises similar 'conceptual art' questions about supplementation by commentary and about the disturbing implications and effects of displaying oneself. Like *CM* and *TUAV*, Baker's work practises her interest in archiving and tradition, but does so through demonstrations that exceed the rationality that archiving, even transgressive archiving, calls for. In reading the commentaries on and critiques of Baker's work collected in *Bobby Baker: Redeeming Features of Daily Life* (Barrett and Baker, 2007), I am struck by the particularly contradictory pressures that her work puts on supplementarity. It is not that Baker's *Kitchen Show*, *Drawing on a Mother's Experience* (1988), and *How to ...* pieces are concept-driven, dependent on commentary and critique, not able to stand alone without the support of explanation. It is more that these pieces simultaneously demand and resist critique. They do so because of the exuberance and surety of Baker's performance, for which no taxonomy of matrixed and nonmatrixed performance, or speculation about irony, can account. And then there is the tension between neatness and mess, which the interplay of Baker's performative persona(e) with her script articulates in a way that *is* commentary, establishing a dialogue of ratiocinatory and ambiguous elements for which the work cannot be made to stand. The work is that dialogue.

To an extent, of course, most theatre, most art in general, irrespective of how forthcoming the artist is in explaining their own work, resists criticism. But each work of art resists criticism in its own way, its resistance making particular indications and implications. Given how idiosyncratically and acerbically it invokes how ideas of home, in the sense both of domestic space and of being housed within culture, have failed to accommodate, and have been problematized by the creativity of women, it is deliciously strange (and very Bobby Baker) to see her work assimilated into a reader, within which feminist theorists, art-historians, food critics, and psychoanalysts are all keen to claim her as one of their family.[9] In one of several densely theoretical sentences in an essay included in the booklet accompanying *The Kitchen Show*, feminist art theorist Griselda Pollock argues that the piece presents 'resistances to the domestic as something which threatens women's hold on a singular identity and yet is also the site of its elaboration' (Barrett and Baker, 2007, p. 183). Pollock's identification of the contradictory effects on female identity of 'the domestic' – fragmenting, interpellating, ephemerally fulfilling – is insightful. But I cannot help reading it alongside one of the shortest and pithiest sentences in Pollock's essay: 'Art uses affect cognitively' (ibid., p. 178). Baker's art proves that statement. For me, the joy of reading *Redeeming Features of Daily Life* is seeing how the unmistakeable Bobby Baker 'affect', and the problems it presents to the interpreter, challenges critics as accomplished as Pollock to find a suitable marriage of the affective and cognitive in their criticism of that art.

In an essay on food in performance, Helen Iball suggests that both Baker and Karen Finley 'up-the-staging of' the body in their use of food, but both suffer the vulnerability of being 'upstaged by' the food (Barrett and Baker, 2007, p. 122). Like Finley's personae, many of the exhibits in *CM* display themselves manically, as if unable to digest what they have 'swallowed', their consumption regurgitated as performance.[10] Finley's personae, like Baker's, and like many of those in *CM*, seem to find their voice by participating in an interpellative economy of consumption, raising the question: does their participation allow them to express themselves, or does it masquerade as, or stand in for, self-expression? Unlike Finley's, whose desires, though troubled, are powerful, Wolfe's characters appear to have stashed themselves away so deeply that they cannot access their own impulses: they have sold their individuality to buy relief from the pressure of 'colored contradictions'.

Lala L'Amazing Grace is a Josephine Baker-like performer with a twist of Diana Ross, whose vignette is set in front of the skene, called the 'Closet', of her private life, containing everything (including an embarrassing daughter) that does not fit with her stage persona. In 'Symbiosis', a smartly attired Man decides to subtract the items that make him too black. In 'corporate dress', he throws objects from 'a Saks Fifth Avenue bag' into a trash can, listing the objects as he does so: 'My first pair of Converse All-stars … My first Afro-comb … My first dashiki … My autographed pictures of Stokley Carmichael, Jomo Kenyatta and Donna Summer' (Wolfe, 1987, p. 33). The Kid, the self repressed within this identikit economy of addition and subtraction, is dumped into a large trash can. The Kid stays buried until The Man attempts to discard the final reminder of his former self, a Temptations album. Stage directions indicate that The Man '*pauses, but then crosses to the trash can, lifts the lid, and just as he is about to toss the album in, a hand reaches from inside the can and grabs hold of The Man's arm*' (ibid., p. 37). Throwing away the record is too much for The Man to cope with, and The Kid rises as if from the dead. The rubbish bin motif chimes with Miss Pat's warning in 'Git On Board', the first of *CM*'s vignettes, that 'any baggage you don't claim, we trash'.

Some of the 11 vignettes are sardonic demonstrations, others polemic parody, and others moving monologues. Miss Pat, air hostess trans-planted into a museum guide, is an early sign that this is no ordinary 'museum': it is one that troubles Taylor's binary of fixed exhibit/transient spectator. As opposed to a settled space that fixes what it contains, this museum is a chaotic vessel that flies *through* space. Before we can travel, Miss Pat instructs, we must leave our drums behind. As we fly through time, she points out periods of history following the Middle Passage, including 'the American Revolution, which will give the US of A. exclusive rights to your life', and marked by various wars, whose names ('World War I … World War II … which is not to be confused with the Korean War or the Vietnam War') keep each period separate, as museums traditionally endeavour to do (Wolfe, 1987, pp. 4–5). Miss Pat's induction is ambiguous. Who is the 'you' she addresses? It is possible for readers who are not African-American to read the printed text with a conscious feeling of being an outsider looking in. The play's agit-prop, direct-address style, demanding audience participation, makes that kind of detachment less possible in performance. Analysing the responses of a 'mostly white' audience at the Mark Taper Forum, Itabari Njeri notes that, although both Wolfe and the production team couch the audi-ence participation bits in savage irony, the audience appeared eager to join in.[11] Njeri wonders if some may have missed the irony, or whether they regard it as a duty to join in whenever invited, however ironic the invitation. She watches them 'falter' with the spiritual 'Git On Board' led by Miss Pat (Danitra Vance); 'but when [Vance] gets them started on "Summertime"' – which Njeri sardonically describes as 'Gerschwin's transmutation of black material' – the audience 'practically takes over the show'. And when Vickilyn Reynolds snaps out of her downtrodden Mama-on-the Couch persona to lead the cast in a 'hand-clapping, high-stepping musical number' – the 'audience doesn't miss a beat; they're clapping and swaying with *real* enthusiasm. They are in minstrel heaven'. Several days after the show, says Njeri, 'a very thoughtful black man, not quick to make judgments', asked her: 'There was so much audience participation in that number, do you think it was because they didn't get it?'

Like *TUAV*, and many of Bobby Baker's works, *CM* establishes a particular relationship to the audience that quotes viewing environments other than the theatre. The edginess of all the pieces derives in part from the enigmatic overlaying onto theatre of other performative and spectatorial regimes (such as museums, zoos, self-help seminars, and cookery shows) with their associated codes. The *a priori* imposition of these codes onto 'characters' (again, I am using the word to encompass non-matrixed personae) is a platform on which their authors stage friction between free expression and being driven to perform; or, more accurately and more complexly, they stage paradoxically stationed observation of 'natural' behaviour in which there is a tension between individuality and typicality.

Aware of being widely perceived as non-entity (Jean), expendable (Junie), or freak (Miss Roj), drag queen Miss Roj, Junie 'Soldier with a Secret' Robinson, and pregnant teen Normal Jean Reynolds emerge from cracks between the Museum's other representations, such as Lala, The Man, and the many other exhibits who have assimilated by disconnecting from themselves. Outsiders within, who neither fit nor transcend their environment, they testify quietly, secretly.

'Permutations', the penultimate vignette of *CM*, features Normal Jean Reynolds, a pregnant black teenager who is constantly told how ordinary she is, but who then lays an extraordinary white egg. In explaining the character's name, Wolfe refers to the fact that black children in the South attended what were called Schools for the Normal. The name also evokes Norma Jean, the often forgotten real name of one of the twentieth-century's most iconic celebrities, Marilyn Monroe, who was born Norma Jean Mortenson. Normal Jean Reynolds's mother tells her that God made the exceptional, then the special, then, when he got bored, he made Normal Jean. With her mother at church, however, Jean reveals to the audience her 'sexual relations with the garbage man', who smelled 'of all the good things folks shoulda never thrown away' (Wolfe, 1987, p. 47). When, a few days later, her belly begins to swell, Jean's mother locks her in a dark room, afraid of what the neighbours will think. Uncomfortable at first, Jean gets used to the dark room. A week later, she experiences massive pain and bleeding, passes out, and wakes to find she has laid a large white egg. She notices that 'all 'round this egg were thin lines of blood that I could trace to back between my legs' (ibid., p. 48). When the egg hatches, it is found to contain all the characters we have seen in the previous vignettes.

The 'thin lines of blood' that Jean traces from the egg to between her legs connect her to the array of foregoing exhibits, while the egg itself is an emblem of the extraordinary potential within the ordinary. Wolfe wants to use theatre to incubate new 'permutations' for the representation, and thus formation, of identity. In earlier vignettes, we see characters seizing on packaged forms to bolster their sense of self. Their lack of dimensions indicates that they have relinquished their individuality, swapping it for inclusion by conforming to culturally recognizable, formulaic types. Museums concentrate identity into emblematic clusters of the typical and the special. What is named as 'special' in the Museum is not special in the sense of being different, extraordinary, or the opposite of typical; museums tend to construct the special as the *apotheosis* of the typical.

Like the 'normal' girl who lays an extraordinary egg, Miss Roj and Junie contravene the Museum's laws of typicality. Marginalized in different ways, each sees far beyond their immediate milieu. They communicate their insights using their own gestic forms of expression. Miss Roj's weapon is the 'Snap!', which wipes out all who disrespect her. Roj states that s/he comes to The Bottomless Pit 'to communicate with [her] origins' (Wolfe, 1987, p. 16). The flashing lights, s/he explains, 'are signals from my planet way out there'. Junie, a black soldier killed in Vietnam – yet strangely live, unscathed, and on stage – also hears voices from the beyond:

> God or the Devil one spoke to me and said, 'Junie, these colored boys ain't gonna be the same after this war. They ain't gonna have no kind of happiness.'
>
> (ibid., p. 12)

Junie changes the course of history by taking a small needle and shooting air into the veins of Hubert Humphrey and J.F.K. The 'Pst. Pst' of the needle is his gesture, and a focal point for 'The Soldier With a Secret' vignette, much as the 'Snap!' is for 'The Gospel According to Miss Roj'. Roj's 'Snap!' and Junie's 'Pst' are, on the face of it, innocuous. Meaning nothing particular *in themselves*, they are brought to life in the moment and by their owners' attitude. Junie and Miss Roj are (in Umberto Eco's phrase) 'semiotic guerrillas', perverting conventional lines of discourse from their standpoint. Wolfe's location of Roj in the Bottomless Pit, and of Junie in a limen between life and death, echoes Eco's characterization of the semiotic guerrilla lurking in the margins, but hard to contain within a conventional analytical framework. The 'pst' and the 'Snap!' allow Junie and Roj to go against the grain of convention, and to do so with historical resonance. As well as its connotation of stealth, the 'pst' of Junie's needle resonates, to my mind, with post-Vietnam drug addiction and lethal injections used as a sentence on 'Death Row'. Gay critic and activist Marlon Riggs points out that the snap has a long-standing subcultural significance for black homosexuals. In the mid-1980s, though, the snap, a gesture 'as emotionally and politically charged as a clenched fist', was appropriated by more mainstream black entertainments, such as the television programme *In Living Color*, and thereby 'robbed of its full political and cultural dimension'.[12] Wolfe, via Miss Roj, reappropriates the gesture.

Wolfe often describes *CM* as the play he had to write first, in order to be able to write whatever he wanted to write afterwards. Wolfe refers wryly to 'the guardians of black culture' who raised their eyebrows at *CM* because 'they didn't get it', but came round when they saw positive responses:

> [A] lot of black theater that existed at that time was slogan theater. I understand slogans are very important for movements. *The Colored Museum* is now 'oh oh it's great,' 'it's classic,' and all that sort of stuff, but a lot of the time it was very startling to them because many of the plays that had been done had not dared to self-examine.
>
> (1993a, p. 617)

Theatre, Wolfe suggests, echoes with voices that were once vivaciously idiosyncratic, but have been sanctified, appropriated, rendered reproducible. It is important to remember that it is not the images and icons themselves that Wolfe assaults but the way that, via cultural arenas such as theatre, they are imposed on, and adopted by, African-Americans as badges of identity. He describes Lorraine Hansberry and Ntozake Shange as 'wonderful playwrights' who have become 'dead, stale, empty icons' (Elam, 1992, p.300). Nonetheless, according to reviewer Frank Rich,

'The Last Mama-on-the-Couch Play' left its audience 'devastated', and the 'sacred target' of Lorraine Hansberry's *A Raisin in the Sun* 'in ruins'.[13] 'The Last Mama-on-the-Couch Play' is a parodically taxonomic demonstration. Characters extrapolated from *Raisin* and *for colored girls* are each illustrated by a particular, and particularly parodied, performance style. The parade begins with the earthy realism of the downtrodden Mama; continues with the heightened realism of Walter; rises, with Ruth, to a histrionic, Shange-esque choreopoetic expressionism; and finally, with Beneatha, attains and derides a classical, Attic/Shakespearean Julliard-trained theatricality. The whole 'show' is framed, first, as an episode of *Masterpiece Theatre* (the Sunday night PBS slot hosted by Alistair Cooke in a red leather armchair and usually featuring British actors), then as an Academy Awards-style, show. The Narrator, a tuxedoed Black host, introduces each segment of performance, then prompts the audience to join him in fawning appreciatively:

MAMA: Not in my house, my house, will you ever talk that way again!
(*The NARRATOR, so moved by her performance, erupts in applause and
   encourages the audience to do so.*)
NARRATOR: Beautiful. Just stunning.
(*He reaches into one of the secret compartments of the set and gets an award
   which he ceremoniously gives to MAMA for her performance. She bows
   and then returns to the couch.*)

(Wolfe, 1987, p. 25)

The parading of each style/character is punctuated by the presentation of an Award. When, in the moment discussed by Njeri, Mama comments that she should have 'been born into an all-black musical', a context has been established in which the audience is under scrutiny. What is our role in creating petrified forms, in transmuting black experience into formulaic theatre?

It is an irony not lost on Wolfe that a play attacking the effects of canonicity should itself become canonical. As a Teaching Assistant at the University of Wisconsin-Madison, I taught *CM* on a large undergraduate theatre survey course that was taken as 'Intro to Theatre' not only by all theatre majors, but by students from various other disciplines to fulfil their humanities requirement. Given how frequently it is taught, and how often it has been cited both as a postmodern classic and a landmark of African-American theatre, *CM* has been the subject of extraordinarily little substantial discussion. Harry Elam and Robert Alexander, Jr. introduce their anthology of experimental black playwriting by endorsing Wolfe's view that *CM* paves the way for the expression (as the anthology's title puts it) of *Colored Contradictions* (1996). They take up Wolfe's invitation to 'The Party' which is the endpoint of *CM*. Contradictions cling to the play, and are ultimately embraced in this final scene, hosted – in opposition to the host at the start, Miss Pat, who brooks no contradiction – by Topsy Washington, a young woman whose 'hair and dress are a series of stylistic contradictions which are hip, black and unencumbered' (Wolfe, 1987, p. 50). Topsy, named after the slave child in Harriet Beecher Stowe's *Uncle Tom's Cabin* who Miss Ophelia fails to reform (but who learns instead from her friend Eva), embodies Wolfe's view that African-Americans need to embrace their contradictory feelings about their own history. 'Whereas I can't live inside yesterday's pain', says Topsy, 'I can't live without it' (ibid., p. 52).

'The Party' contrasts with, and throws into relief, the play's more confrontational turns. Stage directions describe Topsy as 'a hurricane of energy'. Capitulating Wolfe's schema, which opposes containment with release of energy, she dances 'to the music of the madness in me', as characters from previous vignettes 'revolve on, frozen like soft sculptures', then unfreeze, echoing Topsy's declaration that she is 'not what [she was] ten years ago or ten minutes ago'. If Topsy recuperates the characters we have seen before, her Party, the opposite of the Museum, recuperates the play itself.

In her reading of *CM*, Una Chaudhuri argues that Wolfe stages 'America as a kind of semiotic machine that generates new forms for old experiences but leaves their core intact', a 'machine [...] that provides new "skins" for old wounds but does nothing to ease their pain' (Chaudhuri, 1995, p. 121). This reading reminds me of the affinity between the characters in *The Colored Museum* and in performance art of the era, in which character is often enacted as a succession of skins.[14] Characters like the Man in 'Symbiosis', who throws away his dashiki and Afro, and dons a business suit from Saks Fifth Avenue, are driven by the desire to hide or reveal themselves as (a particular version of) black. Following Miss Pat, and another kind of hostess, Aunt Ethel 'stands behind a big black pot and wears a reassuring grin' (Figure 2). She concocts the elements of her stew bit by formulaic bit:

> NEXT YA ADD ALL KINDS OF RHYTHMS
> LOTS OF FEELINGS AND PIZZAZ
> THEN HUNNY THROW IN SOME RAGE
> TILL IT CONGEALS AND TURNS TO JAZZ

> (Wolfe, 1987, p. 7)

Figure 2 Vickilyn Reynolds as Aunt Ethel (Photo: Martha Swope)

Aunt Ethel's song is a recipe for black identity. Out of her pot, she pulls (according to the printed text), 'a handful of Negroes, black dolls'. In the renowned 1986 New York Shakespeare Festival production, however, Vickilyn Reynolds' Aunt Ethel pulled a row of white origami cut-out figures. The origami row evokes the entrapping iconicity of formulaic representations of African-Americans – however positive the qualities displayed by those representations may be. The row of dolls is a cautionary symbol, hinting at the iconoclasm to come. In contrast to the fixity and stasis of dolls, or cut-outs, characters like Junie, Jean, and Miss Roj are what Wolfe calls 'silhouettes' (Wolfe, 1993a, p. 605), like multiple outlines of a processual pencil drawing. In dialogue with each other, and susceptible to the pressures of history, geography and aesthetic form, the character 'silhouettes' generate traces and after-images that the museum struggles to contain. Wolfe's use of the word 'silhouette' – a term referring to the eighteenth- and nineteenth-century practice of making cut-out portraits, a practice in which African-American artists participated in the caricaturing of themselves – supports the idea that, contrary to those who would see it as a *break* with historical representations, the play is a dialogue with history.[15]

Wolfe depicts identity-as-acquisition, the packaging of the self in cultural markers of type. But does he do any more than depict it? Do *CM/TUAV/The Kitchen Show* jam the 'semiotic machine'? If they do, it is not by violent anti-critical polemic, but by doing things to received ideas of irony. One such received idea is that the power of irony lies in a lack, or withholding, of explanation to accompany what is said. In terms of allusions and oblique references to people and events, the opposite is also true in Baker's work, in *CM*, and in *TUAV*: they provide too much information. They supplement themselves intensively, not only illustrating and *showing themselves* illustrating, but promising, recapping, summing up, and evaluating, all way beyond the call of demonstrative duty. Encouraging us to enjoy personae objectifying and abjecting themselves, they delight (in ways that owe much to performance artists such as Karen Finley) in 'out-fetishing the fetishist', luring the gaze and mocking it. They are crucially unassimilable: they bristle with impulses that cannot be contained or situated, impulses that are always beyond control. That 'elsewhere' should not be named as the gap between an original and a parody, since all these works complicate ideas, and foreground constructions, of origination and subversion. Neither should it be named as that which is excluded from discourse, as naming necessarily places it within discourse.[16]

While the term 'Brechtian' was, in the late twentieth century, often used loosely to describe a presentational directness and lack of illusionary ornament, I use it here to refer to a foundational aspect of Brecht's epic theatre. Influenced by Piscator's deployment of contemporary technologies in theatre in ways that framed political struggles, Brecht's modelling of epic theatre rests on demonstrative techniques for which the street scene demonstration, in which a bystander acts out an accident for those who want to know what happened, is a blueprint.[17] The key virtue of the street scene as a basis for demonstrative techniques within epic theatre is that it stabilizes spectatorship. By restricting the performer to conveying effects and their immediate causes, the semantic efficiency of the performance, not its aesthetic embellishments or its charisma, is the focus. For Brecht, this is the most reliable way of presenting questions of responsibility and possible answers to those questions, so that interpreters can choose between them. In terms of narrative structuring, the street scene models the dialectic harnessing of representation to commentary, so that acts of interpretation, of choice-making, are foregrounded.

Brecht's street scene is both a reference point and a point of departure for late twentieth-century ironic theatrical demonstration. The pieces I have considered in this chapter are charged by humorous and/or unsettling tension between what is said and what the saying indicates, by a slippage between verbal and physical text, between what is represented and the commentary on what is represented, between the presentation *ipso facto* and its context. Palpably *extracted* representation abrades the commentary that purports to frame it. As a vital corollary, the contract between spectator and audience is ironized. If, for Brecht, the street scene performance stabilizes spectatorship in ways that he wants the epic theatre to do, performances like *Two Undiscovered Amerindians Visit...* foreground, claims Diana Taylor, the 'destabilized postmodern spectator'. I discuss such usage as Taylor's of the word 'postmodern' in my final chapter, but in this one my concern is with the effects and operations of ironic demonstration in particular performances. I do not want to ignore the various strains and complex usage history of the word 'irony',[18] but those delineations and derivations exceed the scope of this discussion of demonstrative theatre of a kind that one could also term satirical, allegorical, haunting, perverse, or, in Fusco's words, 'uncanny' and 'parodically didactic' (1994, p. 148).

Whereas the street scene has an indicative actuality, theatre is always subjunctive: it enacts possible, probable, contingent, conditional scenarios. In Brecht's street scene, the reconstruction is performed by an eye-witness in the location where the event took place, recently. The stage is not the street, nor a European battlefield (*Mother Courage and her Children*), nor the outskirts of a Chinese province (*The Good Person of Szechuan*). Stage performers are not, routinely speaking, eye-witnesses to what they perform. In the particular theatrical demonstrations I have discussed, we get a palpable clash between the subjunctive (which deals with the hypothetical, imagined, or denied) and the indicative (which deals with the factual); and between the presentness of the performance and the histories folded into, and often overwritten by, that performance of presentness.

As Baker establishes in her pauses she pretends to take to recap and assess how things are going, as Njeri notes in her sceptical review of *CM*, and as many spectators of *The Couple in the Cage* relate on the video, these ironic demonstrations immerse themselves conspicuously in the 'now' of performance – its presentness here and for us, and its singularity as an event. They also, though – in the practiced framing of the exhibits by Miss Pat, in Baker's Marks for each of the 13 Actions in *The Kitchen Show* or her enshrining of the 11 Skills in *How to Live*, and in the contextualization by the docents of the couple in the cage that tames eccentric behaviours and deters eccentric interpretations – remove themselves from that singular 'now' to fix themselves as archival, as memorializing. They mark time, but also take performance *out* of time. They use commentary to seal what they say as ceremonial, permanent, inscriptive, but also remove it from inscripting by suggesting that it can *only* be said *through* (in the moment of) demonstration, in the presentness of performance. Without Baker's singular performance of the Actions and Marks, there would be no Actions or Marks. The same is true for the couple in the cage: their individuality is what makes them special, proof that the special is the apotheosis of the typical.

Meaning something other than what they say, presenting ambivalent and/or mundane details with gravitas, mocking authority, marking the instability of subject positions and the fetishization of subjects as exhibited objects, these ironic demonstrations demand to be read as transgressive of dominant/hegemonic traditions of practice, but also resist such readings. Like other forms of theatrical pastiche and palimpsest, they routinely provoke the application of concepts of masquerade, mimicry, and hybridity (terms used in varying, inventive ways between 1986 and 2006 by feminist and post-colonial critics), along with terms like 'queerness', 'cripping', 'signifying', and 'relajo', which mark lineages of transgressive revision from particular identity perspectives (anti-heteronormative, disability-conscious, African-American, Hispanic).[19] Mimicry, mimesis, and masquerade have been productively mined by feminist theorists such as Elin Diamond in *Unmaking Mimesis* (1997) and Geraldine Harris in *Staging Femininities* (1999). Harris's discussion of *How to Shop* vitally illuminates the problems of locating Baker's identity in performance, and of calibrating her work according to feminist ideas of repudiation/redemption/ conformity.[20] In her essay, 'Queering the Crip or Cripping the Queer?', Carrie Sandahl reads four, solo, autobiographical performances in relation to the intersection of the terms 'crip' and 'queer' and their different histories and potentials for 'strategic expansiveness' (Sandahl, 2003, p. 27). Harry Elam applies

The Signifying Monkey by Henry Louis Gates, Jr. to argue that Wolfe brings 'signifyin(g)' into the consciousness of the 'postmodern' spectator. Elam's comparison of *CM* to earlier black plays is insightful, particularly his argument that the resilient Topsy's celebration of 'madness' alludes to, and revises, the conclusions reached in Amiri Baraka's *Dutchman* and Adrienne Kennedy's *Funnyhouse of a Negro* (both 1964), where protagonists (Clay and Sarah respectively) feel able to escape 'the madness of race' only through death (Elam, 1992, p. 296).

While there have been countless insightful applications of terms such as mimesis, masquerade, mimicry, queerness, signifying, and relajo, such readings of parodically didactic work often obscure what is individually and theatrically distinctive about a *particular* work. They do so, partly, because they must resolve much of the instability of tone and signification. Baker's Marks for the Actions in *Kitchen Show*, for example, are signs held up as trophies: they are at once ridiculous and precious. Critical reading risks cashing these trophies in as soon as it succumbs to the temptation of decoding the signs, converting them into a positive explanation.

Because they are perspectively specific, concepts like signifying ultimately risk ghettoizing what they describe, foreclosing its ability to speak beyond the boundaries of marked identities. Habituated application of such terms also risks foreclosing the very dynamism that makes them potentially radical. Establishing terms like 'queer' or 'signifying' as genres, or traditions, can establish credibility; but in doing so, it chains subversion to tradition, shepherding dissident representation into orthodoxy.[21] Such terms are always problematic in relation to notions of universality and cultural specificity, and perhaps can only be useful *by engaging* such problems, as Samir Dayal begins to do in his tendentious definition of 'relajo' as a figuratively diasporic double consciousness, a transnational paradigm of daily life for 'many, if not most' of the world's people (Dayal, 1996, p. 58).

In reference to *TUAV*, Taylor states that 'this kind of "relajo"[...] makes me feel gloriously Latin American' and that 'it is about feeling like they don't get it, and I do' (Taylor, 2003, p. 74). In her more general discussion of 'relajo' elsewhere within *The Archive and the Repertoire* (ibid., pp. 129–31), she describes it as devalorization, a 'blissfully failed performative'. Taylor's use of the word 'relajo' is a reminder that performance is *always* (in Fusco's terms) 'culturally specific': all performances, to greatly varying extents, have particular resonances for particular spectators. I am interested in the questions that terms like 'relajo' raise about 'failure to get it' in relation to works that are very much *about* failure to get it (misrecognition). How does the failure of one spectator to 'get it' impact on the satisfaction – and in that sense, success – of another? Given that the success or failure of a 'performative' is dependent on both producer *and* receiver, isn't the showing, as in signalling, of failure a far less 'failed' performative than *most* performatives, since failure (as Derrida 'shows') is integral to performance? Given that theatre is *always* a signifying form in Gates's terms, because of its subjunctivity – the receiver in theatre is always seeing double, the presented vying with the symbolized – is there not a danger that, in stabilizing what they supplement, applications of concepts such as relajo and signifying can fix the free radicals of the performance of failure?

While perspectively situated readings of demonstration as transgressive have – both cumulatively and in particular applications by the likes of Gates, Elam, and Taylor – usefully framed and claimed subversion, desire to situate meaning has at times obscured what these demonstrations *do to* ideas of meaning and location. The work of Baker, Wolfe, Fusco, and Gómez-Peña should prompt us to recognize how meaning and location in performance can only be accessed through the signs that *pretend to stand* for meaning and location. Subversive irony entails a particular kind of signification, a knowing yet never wholly unknowable insistence by the signifying agents that the signs they are using are problematic, or corrupt. *Naming* any kind of subversive irony is something of a contradiction in terms. Naming arrests the play of possibilities that ironic theatrical demonstrations generate, pinning them in position.

Thinking through the contradictions of ironic demonstration means observing the difference between *framing* those contradictions and *resolving* them. In framing them, all the critic can do is try to recognize our own supplementation, our addition to and replacement of what we critique.[22] What ultimately ties my three examples is that the things they do to and through irony illuminate artistic traditions and ideological orthodoxies, invoking the mechanisms of enunciability within which traditions and orthodoxies – both artistic and critical – operate.

5

Diagnosis: Putting Medical History under the Knife

Diagnosis is the identification of a disease by appearances, or manifestations, which are used to evince causes. Proceeding from the reading of symptoms, and on to treatment, diagnosis is a pivotal act of naming. Like all forms of naming, it operates within, and upholds, systems of enunciability. The pathologies that diagnosis identifies reinforce indices of normality which help to determine who will, and will not, get treated. Diagnosis is teleological: each new diagnosis is informed by previous ones; each diagnostic performance strengthens the cogency of diagnostic logic.

Diagnosis as it developed in medical practice bears more than an accidental resemblance both to theatrical naturalism and to theatre criticism, which bear more than an accidental resemblance to one another. The diagnostic process – reading of symptoms → pronouncement of condition → prescription – is germane to the distillations of Aristotelian dramaturgy performed in the laboratories of Ibsen and Zola. The outlook of both these dramatists, directly informed as each was by the development of modern science and Enlightenment critical discourse, continues to inform theatre criticism and the (still-)evolving set of forms that can be included in the term 'naturalism'. While a constant in medical diagnosis is that symptoms are assessed according to the departure of the patient's symptoms from a perceived normal functioning of the body, a constant across strands and eras of experimental/alternative theatre is that its makers and critics have frequently branded works in terms of their departure from naturalism.[1]

It is a cold Friday night in Iowa City toward the end of 1993. Searching for the University Theatre amidst the charmless blocks of a state campus, I stumble on an ancient medicine man engaged in some kind of ritual in a circle of fire. Wearing very little in the cold, he seems tiny and heroic against the concrete, Brutalist architecture. I enter the institutional warmth of the foyer to join the community of would-be spectators for *Under the Knife: The History of Medicine* (*UtK*), the fruits of a collaboration between feminist puppet-artist Theodora Skipitares and members of the University of Iowa's renowned Playwrights' Workshop.[2] Inside, I am stopped dead by a 12-foot-tall living sculpture, an ancient-looking female, statuesque, huge visage caught in mid-laughter, fluid draining from her arms (Figure 3). (I couldn't confirm it at the time as I had no reference guide, but I have since consulted and can tell you for sure that this was Medusa.) Her giant skirt opening to create a pathway for our entrance, we were instructed to progress while she chanted in cautionary fashion: 'He who takes the blood from the veins of my left can heal the sick. He who takes the blood from the veins of my right can cause disease and bring destruction.' A precarious binary to be sure, I thought, as I passed through her legs to begin the journey.

I would like to present the symptoms as I saw them that November night; I should then be able to give you my diagnosis, informed by a case history of Skipitares; after referring to authorities, I could offer treatment options. I would like to, but, the thing is, I'm not a real Doctor. I'm just a Doctor of Drama. The night I walked through Medusa's legs, I had already read about Skipitares's performance in the late 1970s, the 'enigmatic but affecting' episode in which she 'mounted on a wall 75 masks of her own face in a wide range of expressions, cover[ing] her actual face with different masks as she chanted, moaned, and intoned' (Orloff, 1984, p. 40). I knew she had moved from using masks to motorized mechanical bodies while she herself appeared in her performances less and less. Variously grotesque and exquisite, the array of mechanical bodies in this Iowa incarnation of *UtK* and its three resurrections at La Mama, was dazzling. And yet, despite their variety, scaling the miniature to the monumental, they had a ghostly similarity, a universal resemblance that appears and disappears.

There were 23 scenes in the final version performed at La Mama in 1996. They took place in all kinds of setting: from operating theatres where legs are removed and dissections performed to a cabaret room featuring the Gyno Gals (singing female forms with theatres inside their transparent torsos) to a so-called Garden of Germs, as unlike a 'Garden' as one could imagine, in which bacteria, made from large plastic bubbles and what look like recycled household items, drop suddenly from the ceiling amidst smoke and gaudy lighting. En route between these scenes, we are shown public information films, invited

Figure 3 Spectators pass through the enormous skirt of a 12-foot-tall Medusa to begin their journey through the history of medicine (Photo: Nancy Chu)

to listen on headphones to stories excluded from visual presentation, and dared to peer into glass cases in which gothic-horror meets interactive museum. Along with the many high- and low-tech visual elements representing the body – including actors, mannequins, manipulators, prostheses, skeletons, radiographic images, slides, video, anatomical charts – sonic elements play a key role. A plangent soundtrack by Virgil Moorefield underscores the entire show, working in eerie tandem with a guide whose narration manages to be both hushed and booming at the same time. In an irony as savage as any within *UtK* itself, Tom Costello, narrator in this and many of Skipitares's previous works, died of pancreatic cancer two weeks after the last of many nights spent telling the story of medicine. Mediated voiceovers by Costello and other actors recite facts and quotations. On the face of it, these voices from elsewhere explain the physical action, framing it with historical facts, adding footnotes to the body of what is enacted. As in Laurie Anderson's work, though, the authority of the digital voice is ironized. Skipitares frequently uses the layering of voices to enact two characters becoming one, their individuality dissolving as they become objects of treatment.

While we tend to use the word 'scene' to refer to a unit of dramatic action, scenes in *UtK* really are spatio-temporal worlds. Introducing a script published in *PAJ*, Skipitares states that the scenes are 'connected by chronology' (Skipitares, 1996, p. 93). After the medicine man and the birthing ritual of the Medusa, we are held in a waiting-room, then visit an 'Egyptian Underworld' before going to Mesopotamia for a Medical Match performed in the style of the board-game *Operation*. At the end of the show, a mourning ritual staged in Washington DC in 1993 is reconstructed. In it, an AIDS activist and victim speaks from beyond the grave while his body is processed in a clear, plastic body bag by fellow members of ACT-UP, who read his final request to have his body paraded around and dumped on the lawn of the White House in protest against his government's treatment of AIDS. The last scene is set in the future: two posthuman bodies, constructed from beads of light, look back nostalgically on diagnosis that involved actual human-to-human contact.

Costello wondrously en-scenes the performance space with his majestic pronouncements: 'You've seen what the nineteenth century can do, now [...]'; 'This way to the Renaissance. This way to the Operating Theatre'. His shaping of the spectators' promenade makes audience members subject to, and can make them feel complicit in, and/or victims of, his en-scening. The disconcerting other-worldly gravitas of Costello's tone, like the Wizard of Oz speaking as if behind his illusory machinery yet right there before us, prevents us from settling into genuine appreciation of the march of science that is described. That march is not without its perils. In our promenade, we rehearse science's difficult navigation of space and time, the need to bridge and traverse potentially treacherous dead zones that threaten to leave us behind. The diagnostic pronouncement of scene names (by Costello and other voices emanating from seen and unseen bodies) provides literal and metaphorical grounding, telling us where to stand and where we are, ordering time, space, and us, in ways that divide the flow of the narrative, like the division into parts of the body that the narrative charts. Scene names dissect the space. Like medical dissection in accounts of medical history, the narratorial announcement of the name confers existence, as if the scene only materializes, only exists, once it is named ('The Garden of Germs').

The scenes at the core of the show are those frequently used in histories of medicine to chart the momentum of history as a story of incremental but unstoppable progress: the Church lifting its ban on dissection, the discovery of bacteria by Louis Pasteur, of x-rays by Roentgen. These scenes, in Bahktinian terms, invoke chronology, pointing to their own chronological impact, their epoch-making situation. In Bordieu's terms, these moments *font date* and their protagonists *fait date*: they make a name for themselves by making history.[3] Unchaining these 'names' – Roentgen, Pasteur, Harvey – from their self-historicizing narratives, Skipitares and her collaborators threaten their scenic aspirations, wresting each narrative bead from its place as an originary moment, a 'now' in a string of bygone nows. If the history of medicine is a history of the en-scening of originary moments, Skipitares's techniques de- and re-scene them. Her fondness for uneasy conjunctions, and for naming sacrifices made (but usually unnamed) in the name of progress, removes the 'eureka' from eureka moments.

Bodily phenomena (functions and diseases) are named according to their discoverer – who is named as if s/he were their creator – and the date they were discovered or 'created'. Through such naming, bodies are mapped as territory to be colonized. Roentgen rays and Crooke's tubes insulate discovery from the ravages of time, patenting creativity as originality. Patenting each story of discovery maintains not only the maker's name, but the tradition of making: making the name of the discoverer maintains the centrality of origination within medicine. *UtK*'s stream of unstably individual replications plays against the purity of origination on which medicine's constructions – of the body, and of itself – are predicated. The mechanical actants are stand-ins for, and mutations of, bodies, each neither-same-nor-different. Puppets stand in for doctors as they operate on puppet-bodies, but behind the puppet doctors are human manipulators, pulling the strings but overshadowed. Behind the puppet-patients are other manipulators, usually unseen. The strange ontology of the puppets seeps into the mystical medical drama of the patient's status. As spectators, we are never allowed to forget that we are in the awkward position of standing in for those previous spectators who were unable to watch, even as we are cast in the privileged role of participating in diagnosis.

Much of our time in the show is spent in promissory spaces: waiting-rooms, entrance-ways, pitch sites. Those addicted to *ER*, where healing, or calamitous failure to heal, is always in the present, might suffer an adrenaline drop as we journey through spaces in which healing is promised, delayed, deferred, foreshortened and foreshadowed, but never in the present. In 'The Waiting Room of the Future', 'a 1950s puppet resembling a futuristic flight attendant' asserts that 'history-taking will be painless'. Reversing the old joke that 'nostalgia ain't what it used to be', Skipitares mocks the claim that deferral will, eventually, be worth waiting for. With laborious effort, the performing bodies strive puppet-fully toward a 'proper' rendering of bodies, a rendering needed for the history of medicine to be demonstrated. But they are, in the end, just puppets. What they cannot do, how they do not work, is as significant as what they can. Rita Charon and Maura Spiegel observe that 'objects become things when they don't work properly'. If a 'thing' is constructed as unmediated nature, and an 'object' as scripted materiality, a thing is that which must be incorporated into a symbolic order, coerced into an object position. The puppet that isn't quite a real actor can, as Charon and Spiegel say of 'the sick body', 'achieve a thingness of tremendous force' (2003, p. 135).

While the objectification of the body is crucial to medical science and its documentation, there must always be more raw nature ready to be discovered and objectified. The need to deny nature, to recuperate its thingness, is at odds with the dependence on, and constructions of, its unmediability. Before the body can be available for (theatrical or medical) diagnosis, its materiality must be called up, it cannot just 'be there', it must be summoned, captured, released or precipitated for diagnosis to retain its power. What theatre, not least in the hands of Skipitares, has in common with medicine – and, as Rebecca Herzig observes, with critical theory after Judith Butler's *Bodies that Matter* – is its equivocation with raw material presence. Opposing drives to assert the existence of materiality and to tame, and thereby annihilate it are as much a reality of medicine as they are of performance, and performance theory. The centrality of the body in contemporary theory is inextricably tied to how consumed analysis of culture is with and by reducibility and irreducibility to the material. Introducing *Bodies that Matter*, Butler considers the idea that the materiality of the body is that which essentialism clings to in the face of deconstruction. It is not that the body is not material, she reflects, but the very fact that it is so material that we have to be able to think, to conceive it, to express what it is and what it feels, that makes it the site of construction par excellence (Butler, 1993, p. xi). 'Are certain constructions of the body constitutive in this sense: that we could not operate without them, that without them there would be no "I", no "we"?' In playing the authority of discursive systems against the body's efficacy as an agent of excess/transcendence/resistance, *UtK* estranges constructions of the body's materiality.

In *Arts de Faire* (*The Practice of Everyday Life*), Michel de Certeau states that: 'From birth to mourning after death, law takes hold of bodies in order to make them its text' (de Certeau, 1984, p. 139). While medicine has historically constructed its practice as symptom → diagnosis → treatment, for Skipitares, as for de Certeau, medical practice might more accurately be characterized as:

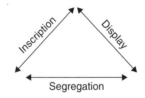

Like all good cultural binaries, the opposition of sick/well – and its correlatives clean/dirty, healthy/toxic, and safe/dangerous – restricts social mobility. Skipitares shows how leprosy and the plague known as the Black Death are opportunities to normalize segregation. After passing through Medusa, we enter 'The Waiting Room', a holding-scene in which a leper recites the decrees that control his walking: 'I forbid you to enter the church or monastery, fair, mill, or market-place...' (Skipitares, 1996, p. 96). A parallel is established between the leper – whose entire existence is defined by, and becomes a metaphor for, prohibition against roaming – and the spectator. In a scene set in a sanatorium, we are advised: 'Keep in mind, ladies and gentlemen, that several very contagious patients will be walking down this aisle.' In the mourning ritual for AIDS victims, we are told that ACT UP 'had a permit for the procession, but Washington ushered them to the city limits' (ibid., p. 114). Where *we* can and can't promenade, what we are and aren't allowed to see, is repeatedly indicated. At times, we are encouraged to meander like 'free radicals'; at times we are carefully controlled, either by the 'natural' patterns of crowd behaviour (like the movement of blood around the heart as described in a scene about William Harvey), or by coercion from a god-like director who is only semi-visible, like a chemical intervention.

Segregation of people from one another is never just about the in- and exclusion of particular individuals from particular treatment options. Segregation is necessary for tight control of the relationship between individual bodies and the social body. The long birth of modern medicine – from the fifteenth to the eighteenth centuries – is a gradual process of the body's individuation. Medicine, in the modern sense is, to quote de Certeau, 'the representation, administration, and well-being of individuals [...]. After having long been only a "member" – arm, leg, or head – of the social unit or a place in which cosmic forces or "spirits" intersected, it has slowly emerged as a whole, with its *own* illnesses, equilibriums, deviations and abnormalities [...so that we can] isolate the body as one isolates an element in chemistry or microphysics' (1984, p. 142). As Skipitares notes in a scene about Renaissance Italy, the isolation of the body operates alongside the separation of the body into parts, which was itself driven by emerging forms of capitalism. The notion of 'specialization' is tied to the maintenance of cities like Rome, in which, 'because of its size', and unlike rural areas, 'all doctors can find a living'. In addition to these three kinds of isolation that work sympathetically – the isolation of the personal from the social body; the separation of individual bodies from one another; and the separation of the body into parts – *UtK* mimics a fourth kind. In as much as it involves isolating the body for treatment, segregation means cutting off the body from the spaces that penetrate it and which it penetrates. Medicine must treat what borders the body before it can treat the body itself. Just as writing develops towards a condition in which 'there is nothing outside the text', medicine constructs the illusion that 'there is nothing outside the body'. Evoking de Lauretis's idea of the space-off, Skipitares repeatedly shrouds her bodies in darkness, then points to what we cannot see, confining our gaze inside the frame before re-directing it outside.

Born in San Francisco to Greek-Orthodox parents in the 1950s, Skipitares often stages purity tussling with promiscuity that threatens its exclusionary sanctions. In a scene about polio, a nuclear family of black-and-white puppets is lined up neatly while behind them is a public information film about the March of Dimes, the charity set up at the start of World War II for the protection of American children. The Father, his sleeves rolled up like a lumberjack, declares: 'No one can predict just when the victory will come', while the mother fearfully exhorts us to 'keep a sharp eye on our children', 'watch them closely'. Father explains, as if we are all his children: 'Polio-myelitis is a strange, unfamiliar house down one road in the fast-building neighbourhood of medical knowledge. In the outside darkness, we cannot quite make out its shape and design. Inside, only a few rooms are lighted. One room with dim light is Cause. We make our way through the room of Symptoms. Next – much better lighted now – is Treatment. And nearby is a room, Financial Cost, so brilliantly lighted by the generosity of Americans that it holds no fear.' Uncannily on-message, the boy and girl puppets pipe up: 'The dimes and dollars given by the American people [...] finance the search for the bullets of drugs to end the insidious career of an unseen enemy' (Skipitares, 1996, p. 113). It's all here: domesticity articulated with America, capitalism, scientific conquest and normality; foreign bodies as shady military adversaries. As the 'strange, unfamiliar' new neighbour, polio is like the Youngers in *A Raisin in the Sun*, moving into Clybourne Park only to be driven out by the generosity of Mr Lindner and his all-American tenants association.

Metaphors of patrilineal productivity sketch the development of medicine as a function of the development of capitalism, which builds on and supplants earlier ideologies centred on religious belief. Grubbe states: 'I have lived long enough to see the child that I fathered develop into a sturdy, mature, and worthwhile product' (Skipitares, 1996, p. 112). A cured patient rejoices that he 'can do a good man's work in the mines'. In the wake of a scene of George Washington dying after being bled, the Pitchman, dubiously clad in Native American garb, describes as 'the dark ages' those days when medicine was about purgation (ibid., p. 106). He heralds a new dawn, where tonics can make us thrive. From the recuperation of race to the evolution of capitalism, the Pitchman is at the cusp of a shift described by de Certeau from 'a therapeutics of extraction' (in which disorder is identified as excess, something superfluous which must be drained from the body) to 'a therapeutics of addition' in which the consumer can compensate for a lack, or deficit, by drugs and supports.

While death is the enemy of capitalism, robbing it of consumers, the enemy of medical progress, as figured in *UtK*, is not death but invisibility and discontinuity. Skipitares shows science continually naming progress as a logical sequence of 'nows', each of which makes both the body and threats to it more visible. The present time of performance retrospectively organizes the past, but, crucially, also points toward the constructedness of its own presence, showing how each bygone 'now' garnered presentness performatively by attaching itself to previous nows whose limitations it promised to surpass. Skipitares's 'molecular chaining' (her phrase) of bygone nows wrests scenes that want to be historically deterministic (1984, p. 93). By turns, she permits and frustrates their working to make history.

The documents of modern medicine from which Skipitares quotes are saturated with visual metaphors that equate the knowable with the seeable. *'Framed on either side by 8-foot-high illuminated towers made of X-ray images'*, Dr Grubbe, one of the first to use Crooke's tubes to develop x-ray imaging, eulogizes the freedom it provides for 'the mind to walk in among the tissues themselves'. A slide of van Leeuwenhoek looking through his microscope in 1676 silhouettes an actor clad in white who recites his diary: when old ladies see what he sees, confides the great visual interpreter, they see what they think are 'eels in vinegar'. Because he is a medical scientist, he knows that this is 'a microscopic world': for the medical scientist, the natural world is named after, and constituted by, the instruments of seeing. In van Leeuwenhoek, Skipitares seems to argue, we see the true birth of modern medicine, a world in which it is not just the body, but *seeing itself* that must continually be intextuated.

The identification of a disease by its symptoms, diagnosis springs from a view of nature as the external manifestation of internal causes. Inherently vague and notoriously contested as it has been for many centuries, 'nature' has often been conceived in modernity as routinely invisible life force, perennial possibility that must be brought forth. This conception is continuous with patriarchal ideas of woman/femaleness as interior, bed, potential, and masculinity with technology that mines and realizes. The Gyno Gals, with miniature theatres inside their bellies, are Skipitares's feminist palimpsest of anatomy lectures purporting to unlock the secrets of nature that lie within woman's reproductive organs, shielded vainly from the prying instruments of men. Galen, the Gyno Gals cheekily recount in a cabaret number co-scripted by Diana Son, declared that while men proudly expose themselves, women need to be revealed, their insides made available to view, surrendered to the domain of the visual. Colonists of 'the microscopic world', like Van Leeuwenhoek, help to do just that.

In one of several neat reminders of the connectedness of visual pleasure, patriarchy, and the growth of modern capitalism, two tubercular

Victorian girls are kept in confinement, but when their chest exam results show signs of improvement, they are rewarded by being allowed to see moving pictures (Skipitares, 1996, p. 111). The world of medicine animated by Skipitares is a world in pictures, a 'microscopic world' defined by instruments of seeing, instruments which turn 'an undetermined something' into 'a tangible parasite'. *UtK* suggests that, while seeing is continually constructed as innocent, it is always intending, and always scripted. Amidst the panoply of resources used to animate this world in pictures, one of the most powerful scenes is, in terms of theatrical technology, the poorest: a monologue in which a seated actress plays Madame D'Arblay, aka the writer Fanny Burney. She describes, in the words of an actual letter to her sister, the mastectomy performed on her in 1812. In minutely observed detail, she recounts having her entire breast removed with a steel blade without anaesthetic: 'I began a scream that lasted during the whole incision' (ibid., p. 104). Her unflinching rendition of the excruciating pain is chilling and claustrophobic. Tellingly, it is the failure of a device intended to prevent her from seeing that allows Burney to view every stage in the performance of the operation: a cambric handkerchief placed over her eyes proves an inadequate barrier to her observation. Burney's doctors insist that the watching Nurses leave while the operation is performed, but the patient vigorously insists that they remain.

Skipitares stresses the fact that Burney is a woman and writer resourceful enough to be able to control, at least in part, the conditions of spectatorship and documentation of her surgery. In exercising that power, Burney refuses to exclude the cries of her body's pain from her writing. She represents, in Kristeva's formulation, that memory of being to which the music of the body brings testimony.

For centuries, the music of the body – from oral reading to cries of pain – has been steadily excluded from language. Orality, argues de Certeau, is precisely that 'from which a legitimate practice – whether in science, politics, or the classroom – must differentiate itself'. In Skipitares's schema, Burney and her writing are a stand-in for all the testimonies absent from histories of medicine. The desire to recuperate absence haunts *UtK*. In a scene (scripted by Erik Ehn) depicting a legendary transplant operation in the sixth century, we are told that the sister of the African man whose leg was chopped off and grafted onto a white patient does not fit in the picture but was watching at the side. While *UtK* traverses millennia, continents, and belief systems, the firmest continuities it traces are the raced and gendered dynamics of inclusion and exclusion. From the waiting-room to the die-in to the personal testimony, Skipitares and her collaborators draw attention to deferral, lack, loss, and exclusion.

De Certeau writes of the cry of the body as the repressed within increasingly mechanized medical science, refusing to go away but existing as a trace that cannot be assimilated into machinic forms of intextuation. He describes how the sounds of the body are cleaned up in the transition from oral to written culture, from speech to text, and argues that the evolution of medical science is coterminous with that process. Throughout *UtK*, we are reminded of the relationship between tools and words, of 'the instrumentality of language' in 'the incarnation of knowledge'. For Skipitares, as for de Certeau, the conduit for the shaping and moulding of the body is writing. We may not imprison and display offenders by their wrists and ankles in the stocks or by their neck in the pillory, but violators of moral codes are 'pilloried' or are 'a laughing-stock', today's phrases bearing the traces of forgotten bodily treatment. In Skipitares's portrayal of capitalism gradually taking hold of the body through medicine, motifs of writing oppose images of reparation. In his medicine show, the Pitchman cites the inscription of our doom: 'From the instant you are born you begin to die and the calendar is your executioner. Is there some way you can delay [...] that final moment before your name is written down by a bony hand in the cold diary of death? Of course, there is, ladies and gentlemen, and that is why I am here' (Skipitares, 1996, pp. 106–7). His speech is littered with images of saving the body from writing, his miracle cure guaranteed to release 'bile from the system [...] as black as any ink you have seen come from a bottle' (ibid., p. 108). Writing is again portrayed as lethal in a scene in which errors of translation are held responsible for the suffering of asthma patients in the Bronx in the mid-1990s. In Spanish, 'asthma' translates as 'fatiga'. Confusion between the written diagnosis 'fatiga' and the English word 'fatigue' led to scores of desperate kids being treated as hypochondriacs (ibid., p. 115).

The shift narrated by de Certeau (at his most Baudrillardian) is toward a contemporary state in which 'writing and machinery, no longer distinct, are themselves becoming the chance modalizations of programmatic matrices determined by a genetic code, and in which, of the "carnal" reality formerly subjected to writing there perhaps remains no more than the cry – of pain or pleasure – an incongruous voice in the indefinite combative system of simulations' (de Certeau, 1984, p.146). The narrative of *UtK* tells a similar story. As it proceeds, there are an increasing number of automatic-sounding command prompts, gnomic en-scening instructions, and scene-cappers such as: 'The system makes its full diagnosis.' The cry of the body is never suppressed, but remains as a trace within medical practice that marries scriptural immanence with machinic efficiency. Listening to the body's cry becomes superfluous in a diagnostic economy that devalorizes sensory and intuitive signifiers because they undermine efficient intextuation. *UtK*'s final scene, 'Auscultation', is disarmingly short, simple, and touching in more than one sense. It takes place entirely in a dark lit only by post-human subjects 'made of pulsing lights'. They pulse, first only faintly and infrequently, and then more excitedly, as they converse:

> FEMALE: Sir, can you tell me the meaning of an obsolete word? [...]
> MALE: I'll try. What word?
> FEMALE: Auscultation. It meant listening.
> MALE: Listening to what?
> FEMALE: Sounds made by the human body [...] Doctors used to listen to patients' bodies, and palpate them directly, too.
> MALE: Directly? You mean they used some simpler kind of palpating machine than ours?
> FEMALE: [...] I'll have to demonstrate. Come here. Put your hand on my wrist – right on it, skin to skin.
> MALE: May I really?
> FEMALE: Yes, yes. No one's looking.
> (*When the two bodies touch, the lights pulse faster and faster.*)
> (Skipitares, 1996, p. 116)

Listening to the patient is conventionally seen to be the foundation on which diagnostic systems are built. Echoing Cixous's famous insistence on 'lessening dependence on the visual, stressing the auditory' (Cixous, 1984, p. 546), 'Auscultation' is a nostalgic 'suffering back' to the era of individuated humans in direct contact.

Skipitares reminds us that, at the root of medical discourse lies an animating agon: chance, wonder, the need to believe in a natural world beyond our ability to comprehend versus the need for certainty, for the mastery of doubt. *UtK* begins with a birthing-ritual (passing through the skirt of the Medusa) that predicts the treatment of those (us) who take part by subjecting them to the curse, less disturbing than it should be as we have no context, no acculturation at this point into the lore behind the curse. At the end of the evening, the ritual procession of the AIDS victim's corpse brought theatrically back to life is far more uncanny than it should be, as it slips us back into a present that should feel distinct from the past, but which is now disorientingly imbued with strange superstition and ruthless rationality. Seemingly attempting to shore up these

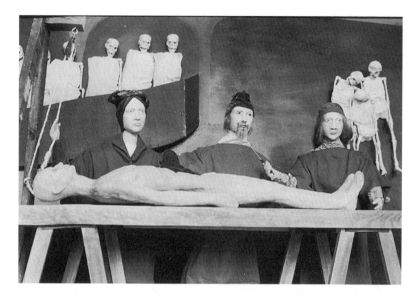

Figure 4   The Church lifts its 1400 year ban on Dissection (Photo: Valerie Arias)

haunting rituals with ordered practice, demonstrations of rational procedure follow hot on the heels of ritual. The trouble is, the more rational
the rules of practice become, the more arbitrary and dependent on symbolization they seem, and thus the more they resemble myth and curse.
After passing through Medusa, we are introduced to the Mesopotamian
Medical Code, 1950 BCE, which states that a Doctor will be paid according to the class of the man he cures, and will lose his hands if he kills a
man. It quickly becomes clear that the history of medicine is a history
of rationality pretending to *ward off* superstition by means of the very
symbolization that creates it. Skipitares narrates the treatment of the
fourteenth-century 'Black Plague', during which millions, unable to be
helped bodily, were taken to churches. In those days, before the birth of
modern medicine, there is both a ritual cleansing and literal pragmatism
to the segregation – spiritually protecting the segregated and preventing
the spread of disease beyond the walls of the church. The claim that forms
of seeing break the boundaries of the body is countered by references to
the Church's 1400-year ban on dissection, a ban that demonstrates how
powerfully bound forms of seeing are by cultural sanctions (Figure 4).

Thanks in some part to her Greek Orthodox upbringing and in some
part to her interest in Foucault, Skipitares is particularly attuned to

baptismal, birthing, and other rituals of induction whose genealogy consecrates myths of origin; and to the ways in which these myths resemble scientific accounts of origin that underpin traditional histories of medicine. Modern medicine may be unthinkable without the separation of Church and State, but the language of medicine today bears strong traces of the Scriptural, the language of prophecy, revelation, and the immanence of diagnostic practice. It is not just in the act of diagnosis itself, but in the discursive framework in which diagnosis lodges that the connection of medicine to religion inheres. Every diagnosis is a religious act, a baptism, that attaches the named individual to a tradition, a community, and a belief system. It is a theistic ritual at the heart of subjectivity: becoming a subject means becoming an individual, which means *being* subject. The moment of becoming recognizable as an individual is the moment of becoming officially, or symbolically, subject to laws that largely proscribe individuality.

There is so much I have failed to fit in to my diagnosis, overwhelmed by an abundance of symptoms. I must let the system make its full diagnosis.

6
Programming: The Designated Blueprint

A Forced Entertainment (FE) piece always frames itself, the tone, manner, and duration of that framing saturating the piece. Unlike *First Night* and *The World in Pictures* (where the framing is intent but ironically blocked, undermined, and long-winded), *Instructions for Forgetting, Exquisite Pain,* and *The Travels* establish themselves with surety and economy. *The Travels* 'starts with a list of street names. A list concocted from UK A–Zs and from internet map sites. These are streets with literal names. Streets that seem directly or indirectly to promise adventure, or at least metaphor and allegory' (Forced Entertainment, 2002, p. 5). So Claire Marshall tells us a few minutes in. She sits alongside the five other participants as they report their experiment. They are all behind long, plain, rectangular desks, scripts in front of them, on a stage free of adornment, under theatre lighting, designed to look utilitarian, that is neither brutal nor lush (Figure 5). They proceed to describe the terms of the experiment: reciting some of the names they drew from a hat, alluding sketchily to the rules of the game that the piece promises to review. They begin to tell stories about the places they visit, but they are stories about the suitability of the street name, and the gaps they perceive between the street name and the place/the other visitors they encounter/trace evidence of local life. While the text tells of the travellers' meandering, their wandering, the text itself has a carefully controlled rhythm and delights in its own structural rigour. Momentum is generated by alternation of monologues with montaged sound-bites, but the whole has been tightly arranged into sections, each full of juxtapositions that highlight coincidences between individual journeys only visible in the 'meet back to compare notes' phase. The orchestration of coincidence generates a second process of writing, a collective one, in which the script develops larger themes and ideas. Toward the end, when dozens of stories have been told, Marshall

Figure 5   *The Travels* (Photo: Hugo Glendinning)

reflects again on the process. In a library in Story Street in Broadstone (Dorset), 'I read something on the early map makers. The time before triangulation, the time before the aerial view, before satellites. Back then a map was made from stories – the certain ones and the rumours too. Some guy comes back from a journey and tells the stuff he's seen. All that gets added to the map. Each map a new mix of stories, each mix a new version of the world. I'm thinking that's how we are working. On the ground. Building space out of rumours' (ibid., p. 20).

'Building space out of rumours' sums up a late twentieth-/early twenty-first century branch of performance to which *The Travels*, along with work by the likes of Lone Twin and Graeme Miller, belongs. These works are performance experiments in which movements are regulated in and by a particular space, but write themselves onto space, revealing personal geographies and hidden histories. Miller's *The Desire Paths* 'is a stage work about walking in a city. The title derives from a term used in town planning – a desire path being the route that people choose to take, the path worn across a green by use that bears no correlation to the concrete one provided. These unpredictable routes make a hidden pattern marking human lives on the landscape'.[1] A review in *The Guardian* sees this as 'no ordinary A–Z of a city […] a metaphor for our memories, for the complexity of things we know, the vast amounts of material which we organize in our own heads and which, when exchanged with others, become part of a shared reality'. *Desire Paths* might be seen as a precursor of FE's 1995 *Nights in This City*, a guided bus tour of Sheffield with the emphasis more on the guiding than the tour; and *Nights in This City* as a forerunner to *The Travels*.

FE make performance about negotiating the space of theatrical performance. They dwell on the context of address, the venue and imagined setting, the interpersonal relationships that shape and are shaped by the performance. Marshall's observation of *The Travels* as cartography in which 'each map' is a 'new mix of stories [...b]uilding space out of rumours' evocatively describes how the performers' decisions and musings exploit the experimental framework, how their navigation of the heuristic environment unearths and remoulds memories. The work of the performer in travelling, observing, recording, and reflecting is stationed by, but presses against and remaps, space. The ongoing friction between work and space – from conceiving the experiment through drawing the names out of a hat to the journey to the location to the execution of tasks discussed in advance to contemporaneous and extemporaneous scripting of the travels to the performance of the script for a theatre audience – entails a continual refiguring of both work and space, a continual remapping that constitutes the piece. By the time she and her collaborators present their work on stage (I saw it at the Contact in Manchester), four kinds of space play off one another: the image of the place, based on its name and depiction on the A–Z map; the physical actuality of the place visited; the perceptual space, or mental geography, of the performer; the here-and-now space of performance. The first three of these are repeatedly nominated in the script: indeed, the discrepancies between them *generate* the script. The fourth kind of space, the here-and-now of the performance, is curiously ex-nominated, excluded from discussion. It is designed to not look designed, to not draw attention to itself. It is theatrically dressed down, dematrixed, resembling a press conference or committee report – a resemblance that is constructed in its asceticism.

A programmed performance about movement in space that nominates chance elements as a driver and finds richness in everyday behaviour: in describing *The Travels*, these characteristics situate it in the tradition of the 'Happening'. I want to read *The Travels* against US Happenings of the 1950s and 1960s. It is perhaps useful to note that the idea of the Happenings as a coherent tradition or practice is very much open to debate; and that a separate, sometimes contiguous, body of work made in various European countries, including Germany and the United

Kingdom, is often thought of as a separate, but also often as part of the same genre as US Happenings.[2] When I say I want to read *The Travels* 'against' Happenings, I mean, in part, that *The Travels* contravenes most of the (notoriously varied) definitional criteria of the term 'Happening': it is a presentation of a full-length, carefully prepared script with a narrative structure that maintains full separation of audience/auditorium from performers/stage. Before reading *The Travels* as a development or extension of Happenings, I want to consider the extent to which Happenings are programmatic; and what Happenings, and later Forced Entertainment, tried to do, have done, and might do, to ideas about programming in relation to performance.

Experimental performance of the twentieth century often foregrounded and manipulated the relationship of blueprint to actualization. The Dada and Futurist performance experiments, with their (anti-)art manifestos and processual interventions, are often cited (including by Cage himself) as an influence on the father of the American Happenings. John Cage's *Theatre Piece*, first produced in 1960 but harking back to a 1952 Black Mountain event often seen as a prototypical Happening, offers future performances an elaborate textual blueprint in the form of plastic overlays that proffer individual scores for one to eight musicians. The actor, explains Cage, can read the words and numbers and 'be able to make a program of action just as I made one' (Sandford, 1995, p. 62).

A program, according to the Chambers dictionary, is the provision of an outline of proceedings arranged for an entertainment, conference, or course, with relevant details highlighted. It is a plan of things to be done; a presentation for broadcast singly or as part of a series; a series of actions to be performed by a computer in dealing with data of a certain kind; a series of encoded instructions to fulfil a task or series of actions; a course of instruction by book or teaching machine in which subject-matter is broken down into a logical sequence of short items of information, so a student can check immediately the suitability of their responses. The word 'program' has Greek roots, *pro-* and *gramma*, or *graphein*, literally translating as to 'to put forth a letter' or 'to write publicly'. The idea of Happenings as public writing, a letter 'put forth', is key to my reading of them in relation to programming, a reading that is informed by Michel de Certeau's idea of writing as inscription (introduced in my previous chapter) – the process by which cultural laws inscribe themselves on the individual and the social body. The transitive verb, programming, has an additional meaning: to program is to create a certain kind of thought pattern or reaction.

Figure 6   Cage performs at Harvard University (1990) (Photo: Betty Freeman, courtesy of John Cage Trust)

Many of the most renowned works made in America in the late 1950s and early 1960s, and labelled Happenings by their creators and by critics – works like Dick Higgins's *Graphis* series (which began in 1958), Allan Kaprow's *18 Happenings in Six Parts* (1959), and Alison Knowles's event scores such as *Child Piece* (1962) and *String Piece* (1964) – fit most, but not all, aspects of the Chambers definition of programming remarkably closely.[3] They provide an outline of proceedings arranged for an entertainment; a plan of things to be done within a work to be presented singly or as part of a series; a series of actions to be performed in dealing with data of a certain kind; a series of encoded instructions to fulfil a task or series of actions; an instruction by book or teaching machine in which subject-matter is broken down into a logical sequence of short items of information, so a participant can check immediately the suitability of their responses. What they don't do, on the whole, is create a certain kind of thought pattern or reaction: they don't do this because, while these works are programmatic, they also, as Mike Sell insightfully theorizes in regard to US Happenings, want to 'jam the programming machinery' (2005, pp. 133–213).

Jon McKenzie identifies as 'the organizational theory of the new information economy' a wide-ranging model of performance, arising in the late 1950s and early 1960s, that encompasses physical and cognitive activities: that model is IPDM (information processing and decision management). One of its most influential proponents is Herbert Simon, who conceptualized decision-making as a four-phase process: 'finding occasions for making a decision; finding possible courses of action; choosing amongst courses of action; and evaluating past choices'. In the crucial third phase, 'choosing amongst courses of action', Simon distinguishes between programmed and unprogrammed decisions. Programmed decisions involve routine situations with well-defined criteria and information channels; they rely upon rules and uniform processing. Unprogrammed decisions involve novel situations with unknown criteria and undefined information channels. They rely upon judgement, creativity and heuristics. As diagrammed by the organizational charts of traditional machine bureaucracies, only top management makes unprogrammed decisions, with programmed decisions being handled by lower and middle management. According to Simon, however, computer technologies upset this division of labour by opening all levels to unprogrammed decision-making. As 'decision processes' and 'their components become more and more embedded in computer programs, decisions and the analyses that underlie them become more and more transportable' (Simon quoted in McKenzie, 2001, p. 75).

While McKenzie's account of programming and performance does not address Happenings, and none of the accounts of Happenings I have read address programming in relation to decision-making, the link is a compelling one. In chronological terms, Simon's analysis of the changing nature of decision-making in organizational performance contexts are published at exactly the time that Happenings-makers such as Kaprow, Higgins, George Brecht, and Al Hansen are working with John Cage at the New School for Social Research and beginning to produce work recognized as their own. Parallel to the self-rationalizations of IPDM by the likes of Herbert Simon, the work of these Happenings-makers is accompanied by essays and proclamations that assert the desire to model new kinds of participatory decision-making as a response to a rapidly changing economy of production. Both contemporaneous accounts of Kaprow's *18 Happenings in Six Parts* by participants like Samuel Delaney, and subsequent analyses by Mike Sell, Sally Banes, and others, have situated the participatory ethos of the Happenings as a reaction to the shift, particularly after World War II, from a physical to a cognitive locus for decision-making as the preponderance of employment shifts from blue- to white-collar work (see Banes, 1993; Sell, 2005). Models like IPDM, as McKenzie points out, are a reaction against 'Taylorism's strict distinction between management and worker functions' (McKenzie, 2001, p. 77).

Happenings and IPDM attempt to conceive decision-making in ways other than solely top-down and solely rational. To that end, great attention is paid in both Happenings and IPDM to interplay within decision-making processes between the rational and the intuitive; and (on a structural level) to the dialectic of centralization and diffusion. Both Happenings and IPDM promote an organic, participatory ethos via a scientific rationale that wants to be both ludic and efficient. The claim that in the shift from Taylorism to IPDM, the 'judgement, creativity and heuristics' of unprogrammed decision-making is devolved to workers chimes with the idea that Happenings are a reaction against an economy in which art is cultural capital subject to massive inflationary pressure. In an era, according to Frederic Jameson, in which there is a frantic printing-up of increasingly valueless signifiers, decisions about the production and distribution of art are regulated by managers, while those who make and those who consume it are relatively passive. Like the workers envisaged by Simon (1977), Happenings construct spectators as participants whose interpretations – their 'judgement, creativity and heuristics' (to quote Simon of his workers) – animate and give integrity to the work.

As Jameson and others, have pointed out, the co-opting of creativity is a hallmark of late capitalism. From the late 1950s on, the word 'creativity' is such a resilient positive term in business models and organizational theories of management that it can be seen as a marker of positivity. McKenzie charts a shift in theories of production since the mid-1950s from controlled efficiency to liberated creativity, citing the work of Douglas McGregor – published, like that of Herbert Simon, between 1957 and 1960. In McGregor's theory of Performance Management, creativity is the means by which capitalism absorbs the energy, and re-stages the rhetoric, of emancipation. Creativity is not just that which offsets an emphasis on efficiency: it valorizes models of performance designed to yield greater efficiency.

Valorization, as defined by Marx in *Das Kapital*, is the final, cementing phase of the process of commodification, a process that he describes as alienation → transformation → valorization. I am intrigued by the parallels between Marx's commodification, de Certeau's writing as inscription, and the processes that constitute Happenings. As it is to Herbert Simon, and to the Happenings-makers, it is the commodification of labour that is of particular interest to Marx. Commodification renders bodily labour, labour that organically emerges from the body, separate from the body. It disconnects labour from bodies. That separation enables the refiguring of labour as a commodity, a thing with an illusory autonomy, a thing that can be circulated and celebrated.

The process of commodification outlined by Marx (alienation→ transformation→ valorization) is contiguous with de Certeau's own three-phase model, as expounded in *The Practice of Everyday Life*: segregation → inscription → display. For de Certeau (as discussed in the previous chapter), the shift from oral to written communication between the fifteenth and eighteenth centuries is firmly tied to the privatization of the body – the marking out of individual bodies from the social body followed by the breaking-up of the individual body into parts, each with its own specialist doctor and specialist tools. The privatization of the body is conceived by de Certeau as a three-phase process of segregation → inscription → display, in which bodies are segregated from one another; laws are inscribed onto bodies and their parts; and the inscribed bodies and their behaviours are exhibited as texts. During the twentieth century, as de Certeau suggests, and Herbert Simon's analysis of computerized decision-making also elucidates, the ingenuity of written communication is inexhaustible, the tools of writing increasingly inscrutable, dynamic, machinic. Nonetheless, as de Certeau argues, the dazzling changes in forms of writing are indicative of a powerful continuity: writing, the process by which culture inscribes its laws on bodies, always adapts in such a way that it can continue to intextuate and commodify bodies, however behaviour might re- and deconstruct, might perform and liberate them.

Happenings-makers and theorists, while valorizing programmed performance, present their work, its performers, and themselves, as struggling to resist intextuation and commodification. To that end, it is vital that the strips of behaviour their programs process are seen to derive from quotidian behaviour. That indication of the quotidian is essential to the Happenings' branding of themselves as a craft that admits living, breathing, organic nature. It is the impulses of the individual who is performing, and the instinctive reactions of spectators and other performers to what happens during the performance, that drive Happenings. For makers such as Dick Higgins, these impulses bring the spontaneity of the everyday into the artwork. In Higgins's *Graphis* series, of which there are over 100 pieces, improvised speech and gesture contend with notation.[4]

Action in *Graphis 82* is bound by a web of words, a kind of free-form lexical version of the game *Twister*. Players in *Graphis* move across the web, using it as a map, performing actions suggested by the words, using their own personal cueing system to move on to another point. In the trial and error of various versions of the map, Higgins was keen to avoid the 'literary'. 'Notice', he explains of the series including *Graphis 82*, 'that the location of material is arbitrary. You cannot walk from "lock" to "locksmith" without "macaroni" there in between.' The more I read about Happenings, the more I am struck by the work that words like 'arbitrary' are made to do. It is no accident that Higgins opposes 'arbitrary' to 'literary'. Works like *Graphis*, or Cage's *Theatre Piece*, are often referred to, because of their apparent valorization of chance elements, as aleatory performance. Such names can lead us to forget how chance is *made to work*. It is fitting that the catalytic figure of aleatory performance is a man whose deployment of chance is so intensely controlled. For someone often described as 'an anarchist artist', John Cage is as rule-bound as they come. For Cage, nothing is so strict a law as the law of chance operations: it is *only* the intense level of detailed control and planning that allows chance to make sense. What critics name 'chance' in Cage's work is often really 'found', which can be a very different thing. While Kaprow famously (and repeatedly) declared himself sick of the fetishizing of the artwork, he fetishizes the 'foundness' of the artwork, the experimental assembly of found, banal elements so that unprimed performer-participants could 'organically', and unrepeatably, actualize the work as they performed it. But the 'found' is always a selection of what is available, and very rarely a random selection, whoever is elected to make the selection, and wherever they decide to look for it. In a somewhat torturous, typically self-conscious description of his own manipulation of found material, Cage describes his painstaking 'intention to relinquish control of my ego'. Anxious to exclude (and be seen to exclude) 'ego' from his work, Cage asserts that 'the Happenings makers came to be interested in themselves. I came to be interested in anything but myself' (Sandford, 1995, p. 69).

As in *Graphis* and *Theatre Piece*, *The Travels* foregrounds the interplay of its own experimental actualization of a blueprint, or program, for performance dictated not by the ego of an author but by a combination of chance and planning. Randomization in *The Travels* lies in the random sequencing of names by straw-drawing to create an itinerary, a patina of chance layered over names that have been previously, deliberately, consciously *selected* from the A–Z. But there is no 'intention to relinquish control of one's ego', rather, like Higgins's performers moving around his map, an enjoyment of what the ego does to get around the rules of the experiment.

Having himself made Happenings over several decades, Higgins reflects on how the Happenings grew up in opposition to the charisma of the individual artist in the 1950s and 1960s art market. By the 1980s, he suggests, impersonal, non-charismatic art commanded top dollar, and art that was passionate, political, and testimonial was once again ignored or appropriated into and recuperated by gallery culture, so that Higgins himself felt the desire to *restore* ego, raw personality to art. In FE's work, and specifically *The Travels*, ego is both celebrated and mocked. Action in *The Travels*, as in Happenings, is driven programmatically by instructions, but invite actions that deploy those instructions as a point of departure. Happenings programs such as *Graphis*, *Theatre Piece*, and shorter, Fluxus-style invitational works by the likes of George Brecht and La Monte Young, textualize the space, laying down grids, maps, templates, and other symbolic frameworks, and they thereby station the movement of the body through space; but the movements of the bodies in the space perform their own counter-inscription that reconceives the maps and grids, dislocating the logic of the program. While the actors write performance onto textuality, the structure of the piece as a whole folds the intextuation of the performing body back on itself within an environment that is all text, but in which textuality is always becoming performance. In *The Travels*, a thick top-layer of self-consciousness dominates the script, a layer in which the performers analyse their own counter-inscription, their own *writing onto the experimental program*, their *failure to follow its rules*.

Many early Happenings, most influentially Kaprow's *18 Happenings in Six Parts*, took place in gallery, warehouse, and workshop spaces similar to those at Black Mountain College – where Kaprow and so many other subsequent Happenings-makers witnessed and took part in the prototypical events led by Cage. Such spaces lent themselves to the kind of compartmentalization often invoked in early definitions of Happenings. *The Travels* features no such obvious control or segmentation of space. It recalls *Instructions for Forgetting* (2001), in which Etchells sits at a utilitarian desk with a microphone in a 1970s-style football shirt, flanked by television monitors, while Richard Lowdon, a visible technician, sits unceremoniously downstage left, with a casually arranged stack of video recorders (on another utilitarian desk) next to which is whatever he happens to be drinking. *Instructions* anticipates *Exquisite Pain* (2005), the staged reading of Sophie Calle's wry calendar of bitterness following the break-up of a romantic relationship. FE would be the first to acknowledge that a lack of representational decor does not equate to an absence of connotation. Everything on stage signifies; everything is aesthetic. Consciously or not, the presentation space of *The Travels* reads as a presentation of non-space, a staging of a despatialized zone. The idea of the performance space as a blank slate, an erased tablet or physicalized mind-space from which knowledge has been wiped clean, has intriguing connotations for both the Happenings and *The Travels*. For the Happenings-makers it is the space of experimentation itself that is a kind of empty, neutral space, allowing the scripted, spontaneous play of action and reaction to register without the distraction of ornamental decor. For FE, the presentation space is emptied, but that space is not the space of the experiment's actualization, only of its *reporting*. In *The Travels*, the presentation space is not so much an empty as a utopian space, in the true sense of the word 'utopia': non-place. It resolves, in a way, the tension between the actual spaces visited, and the imagined spaces conjured, prior to visiting, by names. The scientifically decluttered space of performative reportage allows mental and physical geography to coexist, both appropriated to the utopian space of the performance game, a space free from geography of any kind. In this space free from geography, subjectivity can flourish, writing onto everything that stands in its way.

This sense of a space free from geography that subjectivity freely intextuates is explicitly invoked at the end of *The Travels*: 'I'm nearly home', writes Claire, 'but I don't want my journey to end. I text Cathy. I send her the start of a story.' What she actually sends, or at least what she reports sending, is not just any 'story', but a story about *space becoming story*:

> There were times when the landscape at night seemed more bearable than the too vivid landscape of the day. At night the country was inked out, edited, transformed by an absence of its own detail [...] At night the views were reduced to the glowing icons of lit windows in houses and towerblocks, the luminous rectangles of street signs and billboards, the fake orange supernova stars of streetlamps, the trailing lights of the tail lamps of cars and lorries, and the endless glow of tarmac rippling under headlamps, its surface like that of a sea.
>
> (Forced Entertainment, 2002, p. 26)

A view of the world as organic and found, existing prior to or outside the reading of it, underpins the valorization of 'nature' in Happenings. By the turn of the century, the time of *The Travels*, no such 'real' world is evident. Intextuated geography is comforting to Cathy, or at least to the

'I' whose story she 'texts' to Claire. This 'story' of space becoming story reminds me of how, for Higgins, everything, including the actors bodies, become a score, becomes something to be decoded. In both his and FE's experiments, there is a valorization of the body's ability to counter the inscription of the program, to exceed its performance parameters, but a delight in the fact that, in their performance, the performers render themselves readable, scoreable as elements in relation to the parameters of the program.

Happenings like Kaprow's are a would-be bracketing of 'culture', a creating of space outside culture in which the 'natural' instincts of the performer, impulses perceived to be deeper than acculturation, can organically process elements that, because they are found rather than constructed, are viewed as natural or raw material. In the era of FE, uncomplicated use of the words 'culture' and 'nature' tends to meet with derision. There is, however, something of the same sense of authenticity of raw material, the fetishizing of foundness, in FE's work, or framing of their work, as in Kaprow's, albeit somewhat etiolated. Many Happenings were designed to allow, as Schechner describes it, the kind of complexity one might encounter at a busy city intersection (Sandford, 1995, pp. 53–70). In FE's DVD, *Making Performance* (2008), and in his similarly reflective book *Certain Fragments* (1999), Etchells describes the desire to take the sound at a busy city crossroads at night as music from three different directions meets, or fails to properly meet, and put that sound on stage. But in FE's work, there is a stronger sense that the street is already theatre, that there is no 'nature' extricable from 'culture'. In *Instructions for Forgetting*, Etchells invites those who send in their videos to 'send what you have' rather than 'anything special'. The ones he selects, however, and the stories he tells around them, evince an everyday life that is nothing but found culture that has already been processed, quilted not from bits of a 'real' but of a kind of dead theatre, full of competing textual encodings and spectatorial investments, needing to be unpicked and recoded by the storyteller. These stories include a tale of musical theatre auditionees dancing across a busy highway, unaware that they have been framed in a reality television set-up. And that many-versioned tale about George Best on a hotel bed with Miss World, loads of money and champagne: a long-time hotel employee bringing something to the room sees the scene, shakes his head and sighs 'George, George, George, where did it all go wrong?'

In *The Travels*, Claire describes arriving at her designated locations with 'the feeling that yesterday, even five minutes ago, might have been a better time to arrive'. Her sense that she should be there at a different time, that this time of arrival is not the right one, is very FE. In *First Night* and *Spectacular*, it is the spectator who is made to feel as if something has happened on a previous night that will not be repeated for our benefit. In *The Travels*, it is Claire and her company colleagues, performing their own spectatorship, who report a sense that the time of the spectacle is out of joint. Repeated claims of unrepeatability are essential both to FE's work and to the particular brand of commodification that characterizes Happenings. While I have participated spectatorially in the odd revival or reconstruction of Fluxus work, and have seen films and other documentation, reading Happenings, for me, means reading scores and imagining the performances they (might have) yielded, with the aid of accounts by makers and participants. While I cannot pretend to have anything like the same experience as some of those who participated in or were at a performance of, say, *Graphis* in 1962, 'reading' Happenings is always about reading the score. I often feel, when I see Happenings-makers present their scores at exhibitions, in books, or on internet sites, that my reading is both authentic and degraded, as if that feeling of degradation is somehow part of the authentic Happenings experience. When I read contemporaneous accounts of Happenings, a sense of not being in the right place at the right time seems to be inherent in Happenings from their inception.

The claim of unrepeatability combines, in the rhetoric of Happenings, with the keyword, or 'Kirbyword', 'de-matrixing'. The combination of de-matrixing and unrepeatability is the USP (Unique Selling Point) of Happenings as a brand of performance. In broad terms, de-matrixing resembles what Marx calls alienation. More specifically, when Knowles, Kaprow, Claes Oldenberg, or Jill Johnston cut off strips of ordinary, repetitious experience from their context in everyday life and rework them within the context of purportedly unrepeatable performance, their performative re-matrixing endows those strips with value. In reacting to what Jameson calls the printing up of ever-more devalued signifiers, Happenings are an attempt to create value. In the language of Marx, Happenings alienate, transform, and valorize everyday life, all the while asserting (with a paradoxically canny idealism) that what is valuable within everyday life is its unstructured, uncommodified spontaneity.

The thousands of scores for Happenings and Fluxus events that have been published and exhibited individually, and especially collectively, constitute programs, but equivocate with programming machinery, enjoying its power to release creative potential but writing randomness into logic, neutralizing the program's teleology. The following, which are amongst Alison Knowles's most notorious pieces, were first performed in

1963 (a breakthrough year for Fluxus in New York and at European Fluxus festivals in cities such as Dusseldorf). *Street Piece* (conceived in 1962, but, fantastically, not premiered until August 1963) instructs: 'Make something in the street and give it away.' *Color Music #1* (1963) directs: 'List your problems from one to five. For each problem list the best solution you can think of. For each problem also list a color. Whenever the problem arises in your mind, think first of the best solution, and if you cannot act upon it immediately, switch to concentration on the color until an absolute necessity intervenes.' In *Child Art Piece* (which was altered for performance in New York after it upset the Society for the Preservation of Cruelty to Children), 'the performer is a single child, two or three years old. One or both parents may be present to assist him with a pail of water or a banana etc. When a child leaves the stage the performance is over.' Reading these Knowles scores alongside the dictionary definition of a program as 'a course of instruction by book or teaching machine in which subject-matter is broken down into a logical sequence of short items of information, so a student can check immediately the suitability of their responses', it is clear that Knowles deploys but disrupts programmatic logic. She appropriates the logic of the program to a scheme not of goal-oriented, objective efficiency but of subjective distraction. In the flow of carefully programmed events, 'subject matter is broken down into a logical sequence' but one that explores rather than resolves a 'problem'. Spectators are left with the unassimilable elements of a 'teaching-machine' with nothing to teach, and a child, 'the suitability of their responses', for once in their lives, '[un]checked'.

What is most potent about the event scores of Alison Knowles is that they precipitate the peculiar mixture of programming with randomness and spontaneity that hovers around longer Happenings like Higgins's *Graphis* and Kaprow's *18 Happenings in Six Parts*. In performing programming that scores resistance to programming, Knowles's works de-matrix the program from various possible actualizations, and in doing so, commodify it. In their troubling of the separation of programmed and unprogrammed decisions maintained by IPDM and by Performance Management, they might be seen to jam the programming machinery even as they lubricate it.

Happenings strive to bring the everyday into the theatre, using theatre to unlock the creativity of the everyday without, in Marx's terms, alienating and transforming it. The problem, of course, is how the everyday can assert its place *as* art without being valorized *by* art, which entails alienation and transformation. In the privileging insertion into Happenings (and Fluxus scores like Knowles's) of quotidian real life – what Cage calls 'banal elements' – there is a desire to assert *both* that there is such a thing as real life that, *and* that there are traditions of art, of the *representation* of real life. Affirming a historical tradition of representation as 'real', in the sense of consensually identifiable and autonomous from other traditions, is not as paradoxical an aim for Happenings as it might sound: it bespeaks a desire to prove that there is a real, separate from representation.

While Happenings-makers invest in tradition and in the intrinsic value of the everyday with a remarkably uncomplicated fervour hinting at desperation, the makers of *The Travels* display desire to identify a real, separate from traditions of representation, but the everyday they encounter is pathetically empty, degraded. They frequently turn to alcohol, seemingly unclear in themselves whether this is to relax, to block out the place they find themselves in (perhaps joining in with the locals in doing so), or to block out themselves, the too many thoughts that prevent them from blending in. *The Travels* typifies Forced Entertainment's nostalgia for history, evident also in *The World in Pictures*. Whereas the structural coolness of Happenings is warmed by the idealism of 1950s and 1960s counterculture that suffuses their work and the framing of it (which, I would argue, is part of the work), idealism in Forced Entertainment pieces is always touching, suffused with irony. In contrast to the eschewing of the 'literary' in *Graphis*, the street-names selected to generate performance in *The Travels* are literary, macabre, exotic, and emotive. In reflecting on these names, several of the accounts convey nostalgia for, and ironizing of, the lack of grandeur of the place named by the literary name. Cathy Naden, for example, reflects wryly on the opposition of classical to modern offered up by the names Oracle and Delphi: 'getting all this to happen in Salford is going to be hard' (Forced Entertainment, 2002, p. 15).

De Certeau contrasts the aspirational naming and grand planning of civic spaces with their actual usage, which produces the desire paths that fascinate Miller. While de Certeau figures desire paths as evidence of guerrilla tactics subverting hegemonic control, Miller, and particularly Forced Entertainment, sound a more plaintive, nostalgic note. While the names selected from the A–Z convey a sense of tradition, the places themselves feel unmoored, out of kilter. Finding himself in Hiroshima Promenade and Nagasaki Walk, names that not even the locals have heard of, Jerry Killick is disturbed by the gap between what the map says and what the locals know – it is a gap that, for Jerry, points, like Cathy's comments on Salford, to a lack of memory (Forced Entertainment, 2002, p. 10). Jerry's account conveys the loneliness of the exotic name, a pathetically forgotten memorial. As the report of *The Travels* progresses, even the recent past is erased, demands archaeology. A postman tells John Rowley that Story Road, Chichester, 'does not exist anymore'. As he looks amongst its potential 'ruins', he finds a local who tells him 'they moved it a little and rebuilt it but its here and on a map he shows me' (ibid., p. 18). While *The Travels* frames itself as a quest, this is wishful thinking.

Pathetically pastiching explorers of previous centuries returning to lecture to enthralled audiences back home, the reporters are wistfully aware of how hard they have to work to inject romanticism into their contemporary travel narrative. Their wistful reflection on the gap between the august and the banal evidences, also, a peculiar national attitude to celebrity. It is with a very British perversity that FE valorize the ordinary, even the dour, enjoying the idea of faded grandeur. This morbidly comedic fascination with dullness is akin to, though more comforting than, nostalgia, and for many Brits is a vehicle for bonding.[5]

If de-matrixing and unrepeatability are the USPs of Happenings as a brand of performance, it is a brand that spawned various niche brands of solo performance and performance art in the 1970s and 1980s, particularly those which explored personality and issues of identity politics on stage. In the 1990s and 2000s, the first generations of internet users made performance about shifting ideas of community and about the excitement and anxieties engendered by those forms. In what is sometimes referred to as 'new media art', for example, there is a blurring of solo and group work and a shift toward the exploration of new forms of communication, of new ways of being solo and of being a group. Happenings give us models, leaving the actualization of the program open. Accounts of particular actualizations are the telling void, the ex-nominated element, in the documentation of Happenings. *The Travels*, in contrast, gives a particular account of a particular actualization, focusing on the actants' choices, the way they bend the rules of the game, the way their subjectivity exploits the program. The onus is on the individual to make something happen that can contribute to the group exercise; whereas in Happenings, things happen all around the individual, who is as much part of the group when they are paused as when they are active. In the course of a Happening, individuals' performances are there to observe, but are not spotlit by monologues or arranged by script-editing. In *Graphis*, the emphasis is on fleeting patterns, the interplay of interpretations within a group exercise, on picking out individual moments; in *Travels*, the emphasis is on the individual's perceptions, and about different ways to *make* the individuals *into* a group by picking out aspects of each individual journey that can be tied together to form a moment of communality. New media art often plays with, and refigures, the relationship between a blueprint for action and action itself. As hinted by its title, Philip Auslander's article 'The Performativity of Performance Documentation' offers a range of examples of documentation of performances that never, in any concrete sense, 'happened'. Auslander defends Amelia Jones's assertion of 'performance's dependence on documentation to attain symbolic status within the realm of culture' (Jones quoted in Auslander, 2006, p. 3). Amongst the several aspects of Dada and Futurism that Cage and his protégés developed were the performance manifesto and the performative lecture. Lecture and manifesto forms lend themselves to the interrogation of the relationship between statement and proof, blueprint and actualization, script and execution that (as I argue across the chapters of this book) remains a driving preoccupation of experimental performance. While lecture-like performance proliferates in the (problematically termed 'absurd') playwriting of Ionesco, Beckett, Fornes, McNally, and Durang, and in devised theatre and performance art (by Bobby Baker and Ping Chong to name but two), the manifesto finds its apotheosis in Happenings and the related Fluxus movement. Fluxus is littered with new forms of manifesto, arguably Happenings in themselves. George Maciunas's *Fluxiosity* is a block of capitalized text consisting of qualities, neologisms, names, and information, valorizing through a parody of valorization in a manner that mocks, illuminates, and exploits the aestheticization of capital that characterizes post-war consumer culture (Figure 7). It might be seen as a suitably ironic brand statement for Fluxus.

In Happenings, we see the roots of the auto-telic artwork, and in FE the fruits. By 'auto-telic', I mean a work that forms its own territory, makes its own rules and its own methodology. I also want to invoke the associations of the word 'auto-telic' in psychology, where it is often used to describe rewarding engagement with everyday life in and for its own sake, rather than as a means to a promised end such as monetary gain. In the hands of FE, however, the auto-telic artwork is a method of insulation against an everyday which is the opposite of auto-telic, in which there is always already a strong sense of not being there at the right time, of there being a reality that is just out of reach. The anxiety of the Happenings-makers of the 1950s and 1960s – that capitalism ensnares desire by constantly deferring its object – is borne out by the end of the century in FE's irony-suffused, advanced-capitalist world. FE's response is more knowingly, wilfully pathetic than that of

```
FLUXUS  HQ  P.O.  BOX  180  NEW  YORK  10013
FLUXSHOPS  AND  FLUXFESTS  IN  NEW  YORK
AMSTERDAM  NICE  ROME  MONTREAL  TOKYO
V  TRE  -  FLUXMACHINES  -  FLUXMUSICBOXES
FLUXKITS  -  FLUXAUTOMOBILES  -  FLUXPOST
FLUXMEDICINES  -  FLUXFILMS  -  FLUXMENUS
FLUXRADIOS  -  FLUXCARDS  -  FLUXPUZZLES
FLUXCLOTHES  -  FLUXORGANS  -  FLUXSHIRTS
FLUXBOXES  -  FLUXORCHESTRA  -  FLUXJOKES
FLUXGAMES  -  FLUXHOLES  -  FLUXHARDWARE
FLUXSUITCASES  -  FLUXCHESS  -  FLUXFLAGS
FLUXTOURS  -  FLUXWATER  -  FLUXCONCERTS
FLUXMYSTERIES  -  FLUXBOOKS  -  FLUXSIGNS
FLUXCLOCKS  -  FLUXCIRCUS  -  FLUXANIMALS
FLUXQUIZZES  -  FLUXROCKS  -  FLUXMEDALS
FLUXDUST  -  FLUXCANS  -  FLUXTABLECLOTH
FLUXVAUDEVILLE  -  FLUXTAPE  -  FLUXSPORT
BY  ERIC  ANDERSEN  -  AYO  -  JEFF  BERNER
GEORGE  BRECHT  -  GIUSEPPE  CHIARI  -  ANT-
HONY  COX  -  CHRISTO  -  WALTER  DE  MARIA
WILLEM  DE  RIDDER  -  ROBERT  FILLIOU
ALBERT  FINE  -  HI  RED  CENTER  -  JOE  JONES
H.  KAPPLOW  -  ALISON  KNOWLES  -  JIRI  KOLAR
ARTHUR  KØPCKE  -  TAKEHISA  KOSUGI  -  SHIGE-
KO  KUBOTA  -  FREDRIC  LIEBERMAN  -  GYORGI
LIGETI  -  GEORGE  MACIUNAS  -  YOKO  ONO  -  BEN-
JAMIN  PATTERSON  -  JAMES  RIDDLE  -  DITER
ROT  -  TAKATO  SAITO  -  TOMAS  SCHMIT  -  CHIEKO
SHIOMI  -  DANIEL  SPOERRI  -  STAN  VANDER-
BEEK  -  BEN  VAUTIER  -  ROBERT  M.  WATTS
EMMETT  O.  WILLIAMS  -  LA  MONTE  YOUNG
FLUX  -  ART  -  NONART  -  AMUSEMENT  FORGOES
DISTINCTION  BETWEEN  ART  AND  NONART,
FORGOES  ARTIST'S  IND ISPENSABILITY,
EXCLUSIVENESS,  INDIVIDUALITY,  AMBITION,
FORGOES  ALL  PRETENSION  TOWARDS  SIG-
NIFICANCE,  RARITY,  INSPIRATION,  SKILL,
COMPLEXITY,  PR OFUNDITY,  G REATNESS,
INSTITUTIONAL  AND  COMMODITY  VALUE.
IT  STRIVES  FOR  MONOSTRUCTURAL,  NON-
THEATRICAL,  NONBARO QUE,  IMPERSONAL
QUALITIES  OF  A  GAME,  A  PUZZLE  OR  A  GAG.  IT
IS  A  FUSION  OF  SPIKE  JONES,  GAGS,
GAMES,  VAUDEVILLE,  CAGE  AND  DUCHAMP
```

Figure 7 George Maciunas, *Fluxiosity* (Permission courtesy of Ken Friedman)

their performative precursors. As Terry tries to narrate the history of *The World in Pictures*, she suffers waves of interruption, performers getting carried away, periods of deflation in which nothing happens. This undercutting *is* the performance. Whatever the message of the group's failure to tell the story, a thing, as demonstrated by Richard's constant warming of his bare arse on the portable heater meant to show the invention of fire, is just a thing. Like and unlike the Happenings-makers, FE program to de-program, refreshing experimental performance by reading the parameters of experimentation in ways that reflect on theatricality.

7
Disclosure: Transcript and Testimony

Actors in the company Recorded Delivery listen to recorded interviews on a headset while they are on stage and repeat what they hear. Blythe sees herself as following in the footsteps of 'Anna Deavere Smith, who first combined the journalistic technique of interviewing subjects from all walks of life with the art of recreating their exact words in performance'.[1] Blythe and her company aim to 'bring the language of the street into the theatre in an unmediated form, giving voice to a huge range of characters, never heard on stage before'. She speaks of the need to avoid 'reminding' her subjects 'that they are being recorded and making them self conscious', explaining: 'I try to make the microphone as unobtrusive as possible' (Soans, 2005, p. 102). Blythe's portrayal of herself as an anthropologist hiding her fly, making her 'microphone as unobtrusive as possible', contrasts ironically with the image of her actors, who, in *Come Out Eli* (2003),[2] wore mini-disc players and earpieces connected to the players with wires that spectators were hardly likely not to notice. Clearly, 'unmediated' does not mean face-to-face, but rather an instant replay. 'Giving voice' means recording, rehearing, and copying the voice.

Comparing the deployment of recording and playback devices in *Come Out Eli* and in the Riot Group's *Pugilist Specialist* (2003) raises questions about documentary theatre that I will explore in this chapter. Three of the characters in *Pugilist Specialist* (*PS*) – Lieutenants Emma Stein (an explosives specialist, idealist, and poster girl for women in the army), Harpo Studdard (an earnest, humourless, communications specialist), and Travis Freud (uncouth and wilfully ignorant, but, it turns out, a crack sniper) – await mission instructions from the fourth, Colonel Johns, who accuses Stein and Studdard of having a 'fetish for evidence'

(Shaplin, 2003, p. 43). The character names bespeak a different kind of communication game. Surnames Freud and Stein roughly correspond to their (respectively patriarchal and feminist) psychoanalyst namesakes. Freud's first name (Travis) points to Travis Bickle in *Taxi Driver*; Stein's (Emma) perhaps to Emma Goldman, or to the (anti-)heroine of whom her author Jane Austen suspected 'no-one will like her very much'. Harpo, like Studdard, was the Marx Brother that said almost nothing; the last name, equally ironically for a character who wishes to remain *incognito*, is shared with Ruben Studdard, who won 2003's *American Idol* television show a few months before *PS* premiered in Edinburgh.

Shaplin seems to want us to know that naming is a game, and as the pugilists discuss their mission, the seriousness of the game is grotesquely muddy. Their mission is to take out a Saddam-like leader, referred to as Big Stache, in the kind of palace coup that US forces frequently tried to execute prior to their eventual capture of the Iraqi dictator. The set is minimal: it consists only of '*two wooden benches, each approximately twelve feet long. Hanging directly above the benches is a plain microphone*' (Shaplin, 2003, p. 13). It becomes apparent – more gradually and eerily in performance than in reading the script – that the microphone is diegetic. Many spectators will begin to surmise this when it becomes clear that there is no relay, no whisper of amplified sound through speakers. As references are made to 'communications', 'tapes', and a 'briefing', spectators might, along with the characters, become more aware of the presence of the microphone. They certainly do so later on, when 'the microphone' is explicitly mentioned, or when Studdard nods toward it and reminds his colleagues: 'We're live' (ibid., p. 19).

As in *Imperceptible Mutabilities in the Third Kingdom* (*IMTK*), the characters are aligned according to their attitude to the record. Studdard, the manager of the record, is painstaking to the point of paranoid. He sees the record as a beautiful, dormant volcano of 'careless conversation [...] a kingdom of sound bites and transcripts' over which he presides, taking 'care of words when they lose their bodies' (Shaplin, 2003, p. 43). Outlining Lt Studdard's responsibilities, it is clear that Colonel Johns sees the record in more pragmatic terms: 'Primarily you'll be responsible for recording and editing an hour-by-hour audio document detailing the mission. This will be used as a training tool for black-op procedure and, in the event that this document is misinterpreted, or becomes the subject of misinterpretation, you will be expected to toilet this particular document. Alternately, if our actions are celebrated, you will prepare excerpts for distribution' (ibid., p. 27). Johns finds Studdard more than up to the job, mocking his 'fetish for evidence', which he sees as a 'kinky ritual'. It is hard, though, to know exactly what Johns thinks: he forbids empathy and desire 'to be sure our passions don't dilute our focus' (ibid., p. 34). The problem for Johns is Lt Stein, whose gender, heroism, and idealism have scored her too much publicity. Johns, who likes to do things behind closed doors through off-the-record chats, is concerned to 'keep this mission off the cover of the *New York Times*', while Stein wants everything to be done properly, and declares that she 'refuse[s] 'to exist off the record' (ibid., p. 61). In her old-fashioned way, she sees recording and playback devices as a vital tool in attaining information and proving veracity. When Johns tries to get her on-message – 'I don't like honesty. I like loyalty' – Stein holds firm (ibid.). Something, as we will discover, has to give.

PS bears provocatively upon documentary theatre: so-called 'verbatim' pieces like those of Recorded Delivery, Anna Deavere Smith (*Twilight: Los Angeles, 1992; Fires in the Mirror: Crown Heights, Brooklyn, and Other Identities*), Tricycle Theatre (*The Colour of Justice; Bloody Sunday; Guantanamo*), and Robin Soans (*Talking to Terrorists*), in which all words performed are re-performances of words spoken, or written (in the case of *My Name is Rachel Corrie*, in emails), by actual people impersonated by actors; and plays like David Hare's *The Permanent Way*, Peter Morgan's *Frost/Nixon*, and Gregory Burke (for the National Theatre of Scotland)'s *Black Watch*, that meld direct quotation of words spoken by actual people with invented action. Like all of these works, *PS* goes behind closed doors to expose institutional procedures in the wake of real events. It presents itself as a reconstruction of those procedures for investigative purposes. It is in significant part about the politics of nomination, of the significance of the private leaking into the public, of confidential utterances flashed by the glare of publicity – a theme enshrined in docudrama titles such as *My Name is Rachel Corrie, Talking to Terrorists*, and *The Vagina Monologues*.

It is the ways in which *PS* is at odds with what we usually take to be documentary theatre, though, that make it most informative *about* documentary theatre. I will argue that both the authors of and characters within *PS*, their speech highly contrived and palpably 'self-conscious', invent reality in ways that raise vital questions about the premises and preoccupations of documentary theatre.

When Anna Deavere Smith started out *On the Road* in her '*Search for American Character*' in the early 1980s,[3] one of the few examples of documentary-style writing making an impact on the US stage was Emily Mann's work. Mann's *Still Life* (1980), about the Vietnam War, and *Execution of Justice* (1983), about the murder by San Francisco Supervisor

Dan White of gay colleagues Supervisor Harvey Milk and Mayor George Moscone, were an influence on Smith. *Execution of Justice* re-enacts the court case and public statements, drawing on testimony derived from interviews. Despite visual and aural devices that arrest and frame it, the narrative has a strong and emotive momentum. Mann homes in on the time-line in the build up to the event; the psychology that might have led White to shoot his fellow officials; and the effect it had on those involved. In comparison with *Execution of Justice*, documentary theatre since 1990 seems meditative. While it takes catalytic events, it consistently works more with the catalysis than the event, focusing on the discourses and processes that emerge from events.

Blythe is right to cite Smith's method of transposing closely studied speech performance into theatre as groundbreaking. The event that sparked the 1991 Crown Heights riots is dealt with extensively in footnotes and introductory material to *Fires in the Mirror*, but in performance the magnifying-glass is on the contrasting tonalities and argots of those who emerged as spokespeople. Though there has been a stylistic return to playwriting and ensemble work more in line with Mann's than with Smith's work, the force of attention of documentary theatre during the 1990s has continued to shift from the depiction of events as discrete to the interrogation of the procedures that the mediation of events brings to light. To take the example of an act of violence as a catalytic event, the management of that event (in temporal terms) begins not with a journalist reporting a story, but with a perpetrator, and continues with witnesses or those who arrive at the scene of a crime (a friend of the victim, a passer-by, or police officer), each of whom has a backstory to trace. But in what I will call the 'docudoc', the specific circumstances of perpetrators, victims, and other figures centrally involved is summarily incorporated into the rustle of reactions that is the centre of the drama. In Tricycle's *The Colour of Justice* (1999), which is an edited, verbatim replication of the Inquiry into the police response following the murder of Stephen Lawrence, that rustle consists of how the police communicate with one another and with the Lawrence family; and how they defend their conduct to teams of lawyers in a meticulously restored Inquiry room full of computers and notebooks, a courtroom that is a semiosis of procedural machinery.

'Documentary' is often used as a genre term synonymous with 'nonfiction' and 'issue-based'. Stressing the non-fictive and issue-based qualities of 'documentary theatre', however, occludes the great extent to which documentary theatre, from the mid-1990s onwards, is increasingly *about documentary processes*, including those of theatre. It is the mixing, or mosaic, of processes of documentation that characterizes the docudoc. As Carol Martin suggests, modern documentary theatre, unlike the contiguous body of work 'historical fiction', is 'created from a specific body of archival material: interviews, documents, hearings, records, video, film, photographs, etc.' (Martin, 2006, p. 9). While many docudocs have certainly contributed to debate around particular issues, the less celebrated but equally important contribution lies in what, as a body of work, they tell us about the changing nature of mediation. Ways of making news, and shifting relationships between media outlets and institutions of government, are thematically key to *Fires in the Mirror, The Colour of Justice, The Laramie Project, The Permanent Way, Talking to Terrorists, Black Watch*, and *Frost/Nixon*. The procedures that events within these works reveal are a tangle of the juridical (involving legal, and usually medical and parliamentary law-making bodies) and journalistic (involving outlets including television, newspapers, and magazines): the dependence of forms of government on forms of information is *the* defining feature of documentary theatre of the 1990s and 2000s.

These docudocs feature interplay between ceremonies of documentation, and should remind us that theatrical works are themselves ceremonies of documentation, each of which has its own reflexivity. The historically specific self-awareness of training documents or codes of conduct for prison officers, police, or soldiers bristles against reflexive theatrical devices. In no small part, *The Laramie Project* (2000) portrays the entry of members of Tectonic Theatre into Laramie, their experiences in becoming involved in the mediation of the events following the murder of Matthew Shepard. It also *features* theatre in portraying both a theatre student (Jebadiah Schultz) and a theatre professor (Rebecca Hilliker) at the University of Wyoming. In *Black Watch* (2006), the playwriting process is presented within the product, in the form of the Writer figure (based on the play's author Gregory Burke) interviewing members of the regiment. While the Writer attempts to glean information about the Black Watch, the tension between his self-presentation and that of the soldiers, the banter between them, gives the play its compelling, offbeat intensity.

Docudocs situate themselves in counterpoint to other accounts of the subject they represent. Representations of the Black Watch regiment are handed down via 'the Golden Thread', stories and images passed from one generation to another within families from the Scottish 'heartland' of Perthshire, Fife, Angus, and Dundee. These images and stories are powerful identity-shaping and recruitment tools. In stark contrast to these community-driven representations, the image-machine world of television looms large in *Frost/Nixon*. A television interview is the 'central' event within Morgan's play, but as in the other works I have discussed, that event occupies little stage time relative to the debate about television and politics that the event occasions. It is James Reston, Jr. – the historian and advisor who furnishes Frost with the document he uses to pin Nixon to his mendacity – whose commentary drives the play. While Frost fends off jibes that he is not up to engagement in serious politics because he is a talk show host (and, in America, a failed one), Nixon bemoans that he is not cut out to be a politician because he sweats when he is on television. As we reach the crucial moment of the final interview, in which Nixon's resistance gives way to ceremonial remorse, the screen at the back of the stage is explicitly addressed for the first time:

> NIXON: I let them down. I let down my friends. I let down the coun-
> try. Worst of all, I let down our system of government and the
> dreams of all those young people that ought to get into govern-
> ment but now think it's too corrupt. I let the American people
> down, and I have to carry that burden with me for the rest of my
> life. My political life is over.
> *Jim Reston walks on stage.*
> RESTON: The first and greatest sin of television is that it simplifies.
> Diminishes. Great, complex ideas, tranches of time, whole careers,
> become reduced to a single snapshot. At first I couldn't understand
> why Bob Zelnick was quite as euphoric as he was after the inter-
> views. Or why John Birt felt moved to strip off and run into the
> ocean to celebrate. But that was before I understood the reductive
> power of the close-up.
> (Morgan, 2006, pp. 77–8)

The outcome Morgan dwells on is not that Frost finally gets the better of Nixon, but that Reston is led to recognize television's growing power to write and rewrite history.

Five streams feed the river of procedure that runs through the docudoc: preparation of the play; practices within the institution(s) featured in the play; enquiry into one or more critical incident(s); reporting in media outlets on the incident(s) and attendant enquiry; reactions to the play. In chronological terms, these can be listed as follows:

1. **Preparation of the Play** – The conducting of interviews and other research sources, and the textual and performative deployment of that research.

2. **Institution-Specific Practice** – Procedural methods and codes of behaviour practiced within an institution, such as training procedures and structures of decision-making.
3. **Enquiry** – Either a public investigation is shadowed, in which different parties/institutions meet to process one or more critical incident(s), as exemplified by the interview of Nixon by Frost (*Frost/Nixon*), the Macpherson Inquiry (*The Colour of Justice*), the trial of Henderson and McKinney (*The Laramie Project*), and the first trial of the officers who beat Rodney King (*Twilight*); or the play creates its own mode of investigation, as in *Black Watch, Unprotected, My Name is Rachel Corrie*, and *Talking to Terrorists*.
4. **Reporting** – Media and other coverage of (2) and (3) (above), including analysis and debate at conferences and other gatherings, in newspapers/magazines/journals, on radio and television, on blogs and other websites.
5. **Critique of the Play** – Assessments of and reactions to performance/publication of the play (in the outlets mentioned in (4), above).

Docudocs rely on chronology to make sense of events, but not everything is forward momentum: there are strong ebbs and counter-currents as the streams of activity cross and buffet one another. In more intending terms than a river metaphor alone can convey, each processual domain anticipates and echoes, reacts to and against, second-guesses and casts shadows upon one or more of the others. Synchronistic, vertical reactions play against chronological, horizontal ones. Characters are treated as witnesses, their statements made available to be assessed, their claims to validity methodically tested. Scrutiny is visual as well as verbal, camera close-ups and slide projections are used along with the weighing and counter-weighing of pieces of testimony. These pieces include utterances made in the heat of a moment, jotted in semi-personal notes or emails, or composed in more carefully scripted public statements: each is likely to be pored over; and the context of the utterance is itself worthy of scrutiny.

In the finished dramatic work, the five processes form an internal combustion system within which their are various dialogues, or feedback loops: (2) is acutely, but usually covertly, aware of (4); (4) refers explicitly to, and attempts to excavate (2). As in the production and reception of all theatre, but with an emphasis on the ethics of process, (5) looks for evidence of (1) and (1) anticipates (5). Everything points to the centre (1, 2 → 3 ← 4, 5): the docudoc examines, but also doubles by reassembling, enquiry into the critical incident.

The predominantly inward-facing nature of this flow of attention raises the spectre of solipsism. If the ethos of the docudoc is to excavate material to uncover the truth, isn't an inward-facing examination of mediation counter-productive? Like an enquiry, a documentary play must sequester itself from the rawness of the event; in so doing, both an enquiry and a documentary play are necessarily, paradoxically insular. To get at the event, they must stand outside the spontaneity, the feeling, the uncertainty that is the eventness of the event.

Different authors use different strategies to distance the materiality of feeling and experience while bringing it closer, to pull the materiality of the human from the dematerializing effects of (whilst, of course, adding to) mediation. *My Name is Rachel Corrie*'s reliance on email enables Alan Rickman and Katharine Viner to capture some of the randomness, subjective feeling, and physicality, as well as the analytical distance that Corrie's emails to her parents convey. How physicality and subjectivity come across depends, of course, on the skill and interpretative choices of the performer who stands in for Corrie. Other pieces exploit the inward-facing predisposition of the docudoc form to give characters something to kick against, to assert the materiality of what it is to be human even as they are swaddled in mediation and bureaucracy. Smith uses juxtapositions based on universal human concerns such as 'Hair' to fashion links, and ghost dialogues, between people who might normally appear oppositional. Morgan evokes the loneliness of Nixon and of Frost, not only in the build-up to the interview where they are holed up with their advisors, but as figures who feel tortured in the public eye despite continually fighting to be there. *Talking to Terrorists* goes further down the universalizing track, emphasising bodily desires and functions to establish, albeit thinly, a cross-identification between disparate voices. Presumably, Soans feels that the audience will relate more easily to what seem to be presented as 'typical terrorists' if they talk about ordinary things that anyone might talk about, such as fancying boys or girls, liking certain kinds of biscuit, or needing to go to the toilet.

Docudocs, then, seek to rescue the humble human being from the warring hyperbole of mediation while keeping analytical sight of the issue in hand. But there is another qualification that needs to be made regarding the 'issue-based' nature of the docudoc: it concerns the word 'based'. On the face of it, a burning issue, debate of which is precipitated by a fatal incident, is what occasions a work of documentary theatre: the killing of a Black teenager in London highlighting racism in the police force and the local community; of a Guyanese child in Brooklyn highlighting Jewish privilege in relation to their Black neighbours; of a gay student

highlighting homophobia and hypocrisy in a small town; of a local pros-
titute, highlighting the levels of danger to which law-makers continue to
subject all women, including female sex workers. Dig a little at makers'
accounts, however, and it becomes evident that the impetus for creating
documentary theatre is not always the desire to find a form to do justice
to a particular event or even issue. The four Liverpool-based writers of
Unprotected sat down not because of their desire to address the issue of
prostitution, but – at the invitation of the Everyman Theatre, with whom
all the writers were already working – to do a piece of verbatim theatre.[4]
Blythe states in regard to *Come Out Eli* that she wanted to do a piece about
fear, so 'a gun-siege seemed a good starting point' (Soans, 2005, p. 101).
Like Smith before her, Blythe wanted to find a form of theatre to suit her
talents, and to transpose experiences from workshops into a performance
situation.[5] I do not mean to suggest that there is anything heinous about
a priori desire to do a piece of documentary theatre. Much of the pleasure and political potency of Tricycle's work comes from a commitment
to a particular documentary method. Watching certain pieces (such as
Fires in the Mirror, Talking to Terrorists, and *Unprotected*) however, I have
found myself feeling uncomfortable – despite, but also because of, the
serious subject matter presented, and the palpable evidence of extensive
interview research – that the issues were not only addressed, but were
appropriated, by a bankable artistic technique.

Makers and critical champions of docudoc claim it as recuperative of
other forms of mediation. Katie Laris, in *Theatre Journal*, declares that *Twilight* 'offered insights into LA's violent conflagration unmatched by any
of the myriad newscasters, psychologists and politicians pontificating
nightly'.[6] Reviewing a Tricycle production, Michael Billington eulogizes:
'the great merit of this kind of tribunal drama is that it takes us behind
closed doors and exposes the way in which a cataclysmic event like
Bloody Sunday occurred. It also shows that in theatre nothing is as hypnotic as fact. You emerge from the event, after two hours, not only better
informed, but feeling that, at its best, theatre is a vital part of a democratic
society.'[7] Problematically, though, eagerness to adopt a recuperative role
can lead, as Alisa Solomon has opined, toward sentimentality and self-
aggrandisement.[8] Perhaps this is also a legacy of the stir caused by Anna
Deavere Smith's work. One of the many ironies attendant upon the reception of Smith's work was that, while she spoke against the idea that actors
should see themselves as 'special vehicles', she was herself often endowed
with shamanic/voodun/preternatural powers.[9]

Titles of docudoc are emblematic: the title *Fires in the Mirror* promises
a spiritual calm in the heat of crisis. One set of binaries, violence

between opposing groups (Blacks/Jews; rioters/riot police) is recuperated by another set (performer/ audience) redemptively provided by the (mirroring function of) the theatrical work. Something very similar is conveyed by Robin Soans in his opposition of *Talking to Terrorists*. The conjunction of binary structures with a cool, analytical approach – a conjunction also exemplified by the tone and title of *Frost/Nixon* – constitutes the branding of docudoc as a redemptive form.

* * *

Three characters are led to a windowless room, not knowing precisely why they are there. They test each other out, each digging at the others' pasts and their desires. They seem to be driven in equal (and entwined) proportion by a desire to glean information that may be useful for their own survival, and by habitual cruelty. They are temporarily joined by a fourth character, who has more knowledge of why they are there but releases that knowledge carefully. Decidedly dark, the drama is faintly allegorical and comic, though the joke seems to be on us. What exactly is happening here, who is making it happen, and what does it mean?

The preceding description suits Sartre's *Huis Clos* and the Riot Group's *Pugilist Specialist* equally well. Like *Huis Clos*, *PS* broadly resembles a murder mystery, in which each of those gathered together is suspect, witness, and would-be sleuth. No god-like detective arrives to provide a satisfactory interpretation. The overhead microphone, however, is a god-machine ruling over the action, authoritative and inscrutable. It is a presence that holds sway over all that can be made present. The stage direction at the start of the printed text states:

> *With the exception of scenes at the end, the action is expressed as audio, suggesting a transcript or taped conversation. No naturalistic movement accompanies the entrances, exits, or travel. Actors face forward. There is a measure of gestured movement including head turns, nods, and hand movement. Imagine actors in a studio recording a live radio play.*
>
> (Shaplin, 2003, p. 13)

These important notes on staging only hint at what is not named by the restoration. They begin to nominate the restoration's selectivity by identifying what is theatrically missing: 'naturalistic' rendition of 'entrances, exits, or travel', and of people turning to look at one another or around the space. The performances are, like the web pages of so many organizations, outward-facing: passionately presentational but economical, discrete, efficient. There is a palpable sense that, for all the trappings of a precise reconstruction, we are not seeing the inward-facing version. The entreaty to 'imagine actors in a studio recording a live radio play' indicates that the events happen in a duplicitous (or triplicitous) tense, as (a performance of) a reconstruction of something that has already happened. Or has it? Is it merely the veneer of forensic scienticity painted by the microphone and the outward-facing performance style that figures this performance as a reconstruction. Are we supposed to take this as a reconstruction or a specious show of dissection that dissembles what occurred? Did the event, even within the parameters of fiction, happen at all, or is this a painstaking autopsy of an event that never happened?

For me, the Riot Group offer more 'complex pleasure', in Brecht's terms (Willett, 1964, p. 181), than the average docudoc, engendering in the spectator that state of 'suspicious inquiry' and 'detached eye' that Brecht attributed to Galileo (ibid., p. 192). Unlike Brecht's Galileo, however, the marines in *PS* betray very little through gesture. They test their world with words, weighing one another up that way rather than with the exploratory movement of stone in hand. Shaplin is an acute analyst of the role of linguistic manoeuvres in the science of information management so crucial, the play asserts, to the operations of the US military. The soldiers flex their linguistic muscles through semantic drills. Every exchange of fire is an attempt at killer phrasing, a manoeuvre to go on or avoid going 'on record'. It is a kind of colonization of language, a scramble to gain semantic territory, as that is what meaning is, territory to be gained and traded. The three lieutenants test and hone their command of the rules of engagement by lobbing situation reports at one another, each peppered with official euphemisms: civilians killed in battle are 'collateral' or 'consistent obstructions', while a marine uncomfortable with the terms of a mission has FTA (Failure to Adapt). Until the final stages, by which point the linguistic preparation is complete, this *is* the action of the play, a continual striving to assert status through linguistic prowess, using descriptions of past missions to build a language with which to construct the present mission.

While the lieutenants grapple to identify the subject of the mission so that they can eliminate the target, Colonel Johns, not as stupid as he first seems, points out that the mission is not to eliminate but to maintain the target while continuing to practice grappling to identify it. Slavoj Žižek has argued that for the perpetrators of the attacks on the Oklahoma City Federal Building and the World Trade Center, these buildings were not the real targets, merely obstacles that lay in the way of their 'true objects'. The attackers, argues Žižek, were consumed by a hatred that led them to become more obsessed with 'the obstacle [...] than with the object they try to reach' (2008, p. 78). *PS* suggests that for many aggressors, including the United States, obstacles must remain, or appear to remain, *as* obstacles. As Johns puts it: 'No more targets, no more history' (Shaplin, 2003, p. 80).

Johns informs his marines that they must 'shape the target', and, by extension, shape history. Historical context means recent missions: to get up to speed the lieutenants share what they know of recent missions in the expositionary phase of the play. It is clear that none of them have the same knowledge, which makes them hungry to overcome their lack, to consume more knowledge, and in so doing bolster the commodification of history that is their job. Their Colonel obliges by informing them that his brief will last 'fifteen minutes, during which time you will be rewarded with all knowledge relevant to this mission' (Shaplin, 2003, p. 25).

Having done too good a job of locating and preparing to eliminate the quarry, Stein becomes the quarry herself. Killing two birds with one stone, Johns directs Freud and Studdard to take out the over-zealous heroine so as to maintain the target. For most of the play, Stein is a sharp-shooting subject who continually makes statements, always ready to swiftly nail any objects of conversation that arise. In the end, she becomes the object, sentenced to elimination; Johns, who appears to have barely a basic grasp of language, triumphs. The spin quartet in *PS* offer interesting parallels with Presidents Bush senior and junior and their respective sidekicks Quayle and Cheney. Some of Johns's lines – 'Koran is Arabic code for Bible. Right?' (Shaplin, 2003, p. 56) – could have come from the mouths of Quayle or Dubya, whose inattention to linguistic and philosophical nuance led to fervent speculation about the correspondence between quotable idiocy and genuine ignorance.

Throughout docudocs such as *Fires*, *Frost/Nixon*, *Rachel Corrie*, *Colour of Justice*, *Talking to Terrorists*, and *Black Watch*, chronology and causality are a refuge from uncertainty. They simplify the chaos of layered and conflicting accounts and are relied on to forge objectivity from the partiality and emotiveness of subjective experience. The grid that chronology and causality enforce seems to possess agency beyond that of the characters, as if the grid can explain events better than the people whose actions are arranged along it. In *PS*, the construction of spatio-temporal logic is enacted:

> JOHNS: I want you to be my eyes and ears on this mission.
> STUDDARD: Why not refer to the instant replay? (*Indicating the microphone.*)

JOHNS: I've got to misplace my trust somewhere, why can't it be with you?

(Shaplin, 2003, p. 62)

While Studdard's response may seem like a sardonic riposte, he is merely asserting what is always true but rarely nominated: chronology and causality can only be seen as reliable when they are artificially removed from the realm of subjective experience that is needed to construct them. Playing tricks with temporality, including its own, the pugilist specialists shelter themselves from a historical gaze. As betrayed by another uncannily quotable linguistic twist ('I've got to misplace my trust somewhere, why can't it be with you?'), Johns is already preparing to deter that gaze by setting Studdard up as his fall guy.

For all their reflexivity, there is a danger that, in adding more layers of reportage, docudocs strengthen the impression that news events transcend or deny agency by establishing a life of their own. If the news event is controlled by layers of interpretation and counter-interpretation, each layer qualifying others, in ways that are interdependent, how strong is the agency of those whose actions are the subject of the perpetual interpretation that the docudoc seems to facilitate? Whereas much of the time in docudocs is spent naming people who made statements and recounting precisely what they said, *PS* dwells on the deliberate obfuscation of identification and attribution by individuals, contextualizing obfuscation within institutional practices. While docudoc-makers routinely claim to go 'behind closed doors' of propaganda, none do so as mordantly as the Riot Group. *PS* reverses the valence of Billington's admiring comment that 'nothing is as hypnotic as fact'. Eschewing the hypnotizing effect of factual delineation, the Riot Group's enigmatically savage satire remind us that the mediation of the event does not follow the event but provides the conditions of the event's ordered enunciability.

A favoured word to describe the process of creating a docudoc is the word 'distillation'. 'In the edit', reports Blythe, 'I try to distil the characters and the key moments for dramatic effect'. Echoing Norton-Taylor, who states in the Foreword to *Colour of Justice* that 'the transcripts of the [Stephen Lawrence] inquiry amount to more than 11,000 pages which I have distilled into about 100', Everyman Literary Manager Suzanne Bell describes how 'over 1,000 pages of transcripts were brought together and distilled, through meetings with the writers, director and dramaturges, to a 60 page script' for *Unprotected*.[10] Distillation is not just a reduction in size, but a purification. In processing information, the distillers clean up the mess that information makes. That dimension of refining is nominated in forewords to printed texts and other extra-textual commentary rather than within the text 'proper'. In *PS*, we are made uncomfortably aware of how much is left out of purported reconstruction.

Though it is not documentary theatre in the way that term is generally defined, *PS* unsettles in ways that documentary theatre should. The play constructs history in ways that make me continually wonder where allegory ends and realism begins. While it is a raid on the territory of documentary theatre, a *coup de théâtre* that throws the docudoc into ironic relief, I do not want to posit the play as a corrective to the problems inherent in the docudoc, not least because it brings new problems of its own. However one interprets the Group's self-presentation vis-à-vis their work, there is certainly a continuity between the play and their framing of it: a reluctance to be pinned down to a definitive record. The Group's framing adds to the sense that this is a paradoxical text: an agentless restoration. The insistence that the 'text' offered here 'is just one unfixed, unfinished component of a dialogue between author and ensemble, performance and audience' is at odds with the fact that the 'text' performed is presented as automatic, pre-scripted, complete. Whether deliberately or not, the disclaimer highlights a tension between the openness of a dialogic process, in which the audience and ensemble work collectively, and the branding of the Riot Group as auratically anonymous and close-knit, unwilling to be pinned down to a particular performance or script which the quartet, or writer Adriano Shaplin, is willing to present as authoritative. An intriguing comparison is invited between the guerrilla tactics of the American military's advanced guard and those of the European-inflected, theatrical avant-garde.

8
Monstrosity: Branding the Phatic

'For most of us', writes poet Michael Pollick, 'an average day is filled with phatic communication and we never even notice':

> We may call it small talk, but in reality we would be lost without [the] phatic [...] Sociologists suggest that phatic communication, such as discussing the weather, opens up a social channel. This, in turn, can lead to more substantial or factual communication. Very few people start and end conversations with straight facts – phatic communication such as a handshake helps set the stage first. Some people are simply not comfortable with the idea of making meaningless 'small talk'. Others seem to embrace the social ritual of phatic communication, even to the point of avoiding much factual conversation with others. Communication experts suggest finding a middle ground, using phatic communication as a means to open up more substantial conversation. Too much emphasis on small talk can make a person seem unfocused or chatty, while too little can make someone appear stern or unapproachable. The trick lies in finding a proper balance between factual and phatic communication.[1]

Behind the idea that effective talk consists of 'a proper balance between factual and phatic' lies an abiding linguistic orthodoxy that speech consists of kernels of information surrounded by a variety of other tonal and lexical elements that indicate relationships between and attitudes of speaker and listener. 'Finding a proper balance between factual and phatic' implies that the serious business is the passing of the kernel of information from speaker to listener, while the role of the phatic is to 'open up a social channel' through which the kernel may be passed. And behind this view lies a binary between serious and trivial that continues to hold sway over all kinds of communication, including theatre.

In reference to a group of works performed at the 2006 Edinburgh Festival Fringe, Joyce McMillan applauds their serious engagement with the apparently trivial:

> As cities burn and displaced children run through shell-shattered streets, it's hard to give a damn about people who feel oppressed because the office equipment's not working, they can't get a boyfriend, or they're not famous by the time they're 25. So it's all the more impressive, against this backdrop, to find a clutch of fine Fringe writers and performers who have discovered ways of reflecting on yuppie misery and alienation that give these tales a wider meaning, and a sense of connection to the bigger story of our times.[2]

Like Pollick's description of the phatic, McMillan's view of 'yuppie misery and alienation' (that it becomes serious only when its 'connection' is marked 'to the bigger story of our times') invokes a binary of serious/trivial content. Her observations are made in a glowing review of a show called *The Receipt*, which went on to win a Fringe First.[3] If *The Receipt* needs to be defended against the charge that it is an amusing tale of 'yuppie misery', some would say that *Say Nothing* (1999), by Ridiculusmus – an irreverently satirical romp about life in Derry, a hot-spot of 'the Troubles' in Northern Ireland – needs to be defended against the opposite charge: making light of the horrific. In my comparative reading of these two devised pieces, I will argue that *Say Nothing* and *The Receipt* draw on double-act comedy and absurd theatre to 'out' the contingencies of censorship in the build-up to and start of the twenty-first century. I read the pieces comparatively to show how they challenge the traditional linguistic/sociological characterization of the phatic, and the binary of serious/trivial as mapped by Pollick and by McMillan. In mounting their assault on those binaries, they uncover common ground in terms of the operation of censorship across two differently charged arenas: Irish/British relations and globalized corporations.

The notion of 'common ground' is key to *Say Nothing*, a response to what its maker-performers Ridiculusmus (Jon Hough and David Woods) call 'the circulations of the Peace Process' in Northern Ireland.[4] It is a description that, like the piece itself, plays on various senses of the word 'circulations': the maddening circumlocution that seems, to protagonist Kevin, to have replaced elocution in the troubled areas of Derry and Donegal; and the demonic currents of ire and angst that are as strong as ever when forced underground by the demands of having to keep the surface peace. As field work for his PhD in Peace and Conflict Studies at a (fictional) university in the (real) town Goole in England, Kevin goes to Derry, but is forced to escape to Donegal after upsetting the locals during a sing-along. He tries to open a channel of communication with Sally, who 'runs' the guest-house in which Kevin is attempting to stay (see Figure 8 below), by enthusing about Donegal, which he describes as Derry's 'huge, vast, raw back garden'.[5] Kevin says he feels 'drawn to' Donegal: 'it's, like, my spiritual home'. Emboldened by Sally's phatic nodding, he enthuses that Inishowen 'is like a macrocosm of Donegal'. A mumble of assent encourages him further: 'Of the world, even'. Still, though, no real dialogue is taking place.

To draw Sally out, and avoid the embarrassment of silence, Kevin begins to list names of places in Donegal, as if to indicate his credibility as something more substantial than a tourist. Kevin and Sally slowly begin to trade in nouns: names of places with which they are both familiar, an attempt to literally and metaphorically locate common ground. Sally indicates little recognition of the places named, and chips in other names that are not in Donegal, either not understanding the rules of the list or not very familiar with Donegal. Bemused, but without any hint of

Figure 8   Jon Hough (left) as Sally and David Woods as Kevin (Photo: Chris Tait)

openly questioning Sally's apparent lack of knowledge, as that would be impolite, Kevin asks how long she has been there:

SALLY: 15 years. Before that I was in Birmingham.
KEVIN: Oh right, I've just come from England myself, from Goole.
SALLY: Oh yes, Goole, lovely place. [*Pause*]. Where is that exactly?
KEVIN [*attempting to map it with his hands*]: It's in the North, sort of, here.
SALLY: Ah, Bronte country.
KEVIN: No, no, Bronte's [*busily adjusting his hand-map*] more ... here.

Sally begins to spout names she associates with the part of the country he is indicating, each wrong association causing Kevin to redraw the increasingly complex map, his hands struggling to keep all the points on the imagined map in place. Sally's proffered cultural landmarks shift from literary to televisual and from high-brow to popular, including James Herriot, Catherine Cookson, Melvyn Bragg, *Brookside*, *Queer as Folk*, *Hollyoaks*, *Last of the Summer Wine*, *Coronation Street*, *Eastenders*. Once Kevin has completed the map, neither one knows what to say for a while. 'Originally I'm from Craigavon' offers Kevin, switching the focus back across the water. 'Oh yes, Craigavon, lovely place'. 'Yeah, yeah, it's, er, got great, er ... roads'.

If 'phatic communication' is positively genteel in Pollick's analysis, in *Say Nothing* – a title that quotes a line from a Seamus Heaney poem about the Troubles, 'Whatever you say, say nothing' (Heaney, 1975, p. 59) – it is decidedly monstrous. On the back of their successful adaptation of Flann O'Brien's *At Swim-Two-Birds* (1994), Woods and Hough were invited to become the resident theatre company at the Playhouse Theatre in Derry, a city keen to celebrate its links to O'Brien. The duo both had Irish ancestry, and were proud to regard themselves as part-Irish; since London was proving an impossibly expensive place to run a small theatre company, they decided to take up the offer. Though they remained in Derry from 1994 to 1999, they found the city's embrace to be less than wholehearted. During this five-year residency, they felt a thinly veiled hatred toward Brits and British accents from many quarters, compounded by a widespread suspicion of theatre's, and particularly new theatre's, propensity to express feelings and ideas. It wasn't until they left Derry in 1999 that Woods and Hough felt settled enough to reflect on what they had experienced there.

The 1998 Belfast Agreement (the Good Friday Agreement) was heralded as a new dawn for peace in Northern Ireland. It was a sun, felt Woods and Hough, that drove bitterness further below ground. Throughout *Say*

Nothing – which toured the United Kingdom and Ireland at the dawn of the twenty-first century – Woods plays 30-something Kevin, born in Ireland but resident in England since boyhood. The other characters are all played by Hough: Sally, the 'guest' house proprietor; Frank, the explosive manager of the dubious 'centre' where Kevin is working on a conflict-resolution project called Hands Across the Barricades; and fellow project worker, the excruciatingly fey Dan, with whom Kevin (as practice-based field work for his doctorate in PhD Peace and Conflict Studies) attempts to jointly facilitate a forum to allow border residents space in which to heal and reflect.

Space, as a metaphor for openness, is always invoked sardonically in *Say Nothing*. The action, though it might better be described as inaction, takes place on a sizeable playing area, but only a small, obsessively neat rectangle in the centre is used. The duo perform the play's many episodes on this tiny strip of turf. The grass seems to have spewed from an open suitcase that forms the border of this tight inner stage. Kevin's 'conversations' with both Frank at the centre and Sally at the guest-house take place in uncomfortably liminal spaces: draughty corridors, hallways, and doorways. Feeling at home is a luxury Kevin is never able to attain, despite the overbearing welcome he receives from Sally, Frank, and Dan – all of whom restrict, and intrude on, his personal space, while accusing him of trespassing on theirs. Sally, the guest-house owner, insists that Kevin sleeps outside in his car until the completion of work on his room, the exact nature of which is only vaguely explained. In one of the play's many sardonic allusions to the guarding of personal space, Sally forces Kevin to pay rent for six weeks to retain the room, compensating him by bringing to his car, early each morning, a huge, 'traditional' cooked breakfast. The combination of disingenuous tourist-board rhetoric and life-threatening burnt offerings threatens to send the normally mild-mannered Kevin over the edge.

Craving room to breathe, meaningful work, and escape from the monotony of compulsory small-talk with Sally, Kevin goes to the venue where the conflict-resolution forum is to take place. Emerging from the sanctuary of the toilet, he tries in vain to explain to Frank, the centre's irate proprietor, that it is kids and not Kevin responsible for flicking shit around the bathroom. Sounding like a vitriolic preacher stung by a bee, Frank claims to know nothing about any conference and attacks Kevin for leaving his car in the car-park, making him pay an arbitrary charge, which they then negotiate. Asking for 50 pounds but quickly settling for 50 pence, even Frank himself seems unsure what he's after in the negotiations, just whatever he can get that feels like a good deal.

Something theatrically strange happens when the above encounter – like the one in which Kevin tries to find common ground by identifying places Sally might know – is enacted for a second, and then a third time. Laughter wanes with repetition. A reflective atmosphere seems to fill the theatre as the audience feels the force of being stuck in a demonic groove. Audience members may find themselves dwelling on the significance of small textual variations and differences in tempo and gesture. There is something sinister about the repetition; or, more precisely, about the cyclical, circular, counter-active structure of the action in which repetitions play a part. Mirroring Woods and Hough's feelings about the peace process, Kevin's stay begins with an initial period of euphoria, is followed by pragmatic adjustments, then sinks into a destructive phase where differences are not just unresolved but wearingly reaffirmed. This is not the progressive, jazz-like repetition and revision of, say, a Suzan-Lori Parks play: *Say Nothing* is repetition and entrenchment. Its rhythms are hilariously vitriolic. Whereas Parks's characters grapple with realization, their myopia gradually lifting, breakthroughs in *Say Nothing* are violent purgations of sedimented anger. That vitriol is unleashed on romanticism, sentimentality, and hypocrisy – all of which help to maintain the habits that paper over entrenched divisions. Sally continues to press Kevin to have a nice cup of tea. After she does so for the twenty-sixth time, he finally unloads a torrent of rhetorical bile, waxing demented about 'traditional Irish cups of tea, traditional Irish Bailey's, traditional Irish Jameson's, traditional Irish Bushmills, traditional Irish hatred, traditional Irish kneecapping, traditional Irish punishment beating [...]'.

Say Nothing is partly a riposte to Marie Jones's plays *A Night in November* and, in particular, the multi-award winning *Stones in his Pockets* (directed by Pam Brighton) which played in the United Kingdom to packed houses and great acclaim before returning to Derry.[6] According to Woods, Jones's jovial account of tensions within an Irish village was loudly booed by those angry at what they saw as (at best) the play's liberal guilt and (at worst) a desire to cash in on a romanticized view of Ireland by pretending that even Protestants are really nationalists at heart. In his MA thesis, Woods describes Jones and Brighton as 'a breed of non-native catholic-protestant more passionately Irish than the Irish, more nationalist than the nationalists'.[7] He suggests that such contradictory identities permeate the borderlands, where descriptors such as 'West-Brit', 'native German Irish', and 'Pinko-Provo' struggle to name contorted allegiances. Being ethnically in transit while pretending to be settled is the norm, with many German, American, and British visitors making intense effort to speak in local accents. Woods reports: 'In the six years of our residency in the province we were followed by the IRA who suspected our giveaway accents as possible SAS integrators – stories of SAS (pronounced 'sass' in Derry) [...although] death threats in the end came from the Loyalist faction the LVF, who gave a blanket 'get out or be shot' warning to anyone engaged in peace and reconciliation work in 1997.'[8]

It is through this quagmire of suspicion, hostility, and disguise that Kevin attempts to move. I first saw *Say Nothing* in 2001, fresh from my own PhD, and wondering whether the ground-clearing, future-oriented, epistemologically recentring discourse of the 1990s had done more than plaster over cracks between realities of difference. Watching *Say Nothing* made me think of Anna Deavere Smith: while Smith directed her audiences to 'search for American character' in the 'gap between' the 'real person' and her 'attempt to seem like them', other gaps identified in her work caused controversy, such as the gap between the vaunted transparency of 'verbatim' and the contingencies of interviewing, editing, and staging within which Smith's performance of speech was bound. Whereas Smith's *On the Road* project presents itself as open, *Say Nothing* presents itself as bitterly cynical. And yet the stylized but coruscating attack on closure and hypocrisy in *Say Nothing* left me more optimistic about theatre as a seeing-place than Smith's performance of empathetic listening.

A different site of dysfunction was scoured in Woods and Hough's next show, *Ideas* Men (2003), about two 'creatives' under pressure to come up with 'the next big thing'.[9] The office in which they work is the hub of the only department in a factory-based corporation that is left in the United Kingdom once the entire manufacturing operation has been exported to the Far East. *Ideas Men* taps into the dark side of role-play, an activity highly valued in the corporate world as a conduit for creativity. Mike and Liam are sick to death of their role-playing and in desperate need of real inspiration. They cannot do without the games because they cannot face the possibility that there is nothing but the game. As in *Say Nothing*, dysfunction is a cycle that drives and is driven by denial: the games *make* them 'frazzled, overworked, dried up', but allow them to avoid *confronting* the fact that they are 'frazzled, overworked, dried up'. Also as in *Say Nothing*, the devising process is layered with the product, the fictional with the autobiographical. Research found them 'hanging out in the City and with business students on an MBA course', wearing 'suits so we didn't look like outsiders, and becoming fluent in office slang' such as 'EBITDA: Earnings Before Interest Taxation Depreciation

Amortisation [...] Then we made up a few ourselves, such as ICARUS: I Can Achieve Real Unparalleled Success', useful when they presented their ideas at a Unilever-sponsored creativity contest.

A similar pitting of theatrical against corporate role-play underlies *The Receipt*, in which actor/deviser/stand-up comedian Will Adamsdale narrates and plays protagonist Alan Wiley, while sonic artist Chris Branch produces a battery of sound effects from a Moog synthesizer and a couple of filing cabinets. Wiley works for a company called RotoPlas, though what they actually do is not clear. As well as being the name of the corporation, RotoPlas is also the name of the building in which a range of other, apparently unrelated, companies are housed. Who is pulling whose strings is difficult to determine. It is a world of pseudo-transparency, full of rules, protocols and agendas that purportedly systematize communication and prescribe the navigation of space. To pass through one arbitrarily demarcated area to the next, Wiley is asked to present 'an entry docket' or 'an exit docket' before being buzzed in. Things begin to go wrong for Wiley when he is sent to NeuCom to get a portable presentation surface called a BusiWall. Arriving at NeuCom, he presses the intercom and a voice answers, 'NeuCom':

> WILEY: I've come to pick up the BusiWall.
> INTERCOM: No, mate, this is DivertEntry:HerenotHere.
> WILEY: Yeah, I've come to pick up the BusiWall.
> INTERCOM: No, the building's closed, mate; this is DivertEntry: HerenotHere.
> [*Pause*]. I'm not here.[10]

NeuCom's intercom system meets the needs of the visitor to the closed building by connecting them to someone hundreds of miles away who tells them when the building will be open. The someone that greets Wiley is, as they converse, also rearing chickens in a farm near the coast. Ironically, it is with the intercom chicken farmer that Wiley enjoys the deepest encounter he has in the entire play. Explaining his career choice to Wiley in avuncular fashion, DivertEntry:HerenotHere tells him: 'It doesn't matter what you do, mate, just find something and stick to it.'

Having gained access to the BusiWall, Wiley finds he cannot move it in one piece despite the assistance of the BusiHandle, a BusiWall product designed to make the BusiWall more portable. Returning to RotoPlas with only the base, which he intends to take upstairs before returning to NeuCom to pick up the other segments, he is told he cannot leave it in the lobby as he doesn't have an object docket. As he wonders how he will ever get the whole of the BusiWall up to his office, Wiley's boss informs him that RotoPlas are to go into business with BusiWall, the people who make the BusiWall. 'You know what this means don't you, mate? We're going to do the BusiWall presentation *to* BusiWall! And you know what that means, don't you, Wiley? I'm going to need you to take the BusiWall to the BusiWall building, mate'.

Other than moving BusiWalls, Wiley's work consists largely of answering phone calls asking what RotoPlas does. He seems well drilled:

> Hello RotoPlas; space up. Well, you've probably heard of us from the space management stuff? OK. Let me play a little game with you. When you think of 'space' what do you think of? No, no, you can't be wrong. Well: people talk about space to work, space to live; here at RotoPlas, we like to talk about space to dream. That's what we do.

Wiley's dreams come to an end when he fails to master the subtleties of the RotoPlas switchboard, inadvertently hanging up on a client, who, unbeknown to him, is Alain Fête. (Who Alain Fête is remains a mystery; hanging up on him, though, is clearly a sacking offence.) Wiley's boss (barely distinguishable from Branch's many other roles) dismisses him with the rationale: 'You can't hang up on someone like Alain Fête, Wiley. It's a busy time for us, mate, what with the re-branding.'

After being let go by RotoPlas, Wiley begins a new and, to everyone except him, disturbingly random line of work: the search for the rightful owner of a crumpled piece of paper he finds in the street – a receipt for a glass of chardonnay. Wiley hopes that if he can reach the first target, the bartender noted on the receipt as Server 8, this will lead him to the actual purchaser behind the encrypted credit-card information – customer 241482. The quest is both a surrender to irrational personal obsession and a symbolic rite of passage that takes Wiley beneath the veil of consumer culture. Coming home from his first day of work on the receipt, though, he suffers a setback when he finds himself evicted from his flat, which, it turns out, is owned by RotoPlas. He resolves to live in the self-storage locker in which all his possessions have been crammed. Unphased by being cooped into a tiny space with no amenities, he appears liberated by self-employment as he recalls the advice of the chicken farmer – 'just find something and stick to it'.

Wiley's quest takes him to (as Branch insists it is pronounced) *drincoffee*, the running-together of the two words integral to the aura of the brand. It is a cheeky merger that leads Adamsdale to ponder other consumer items, which, on the contrary, are one thing impishly disguised as two – such as a shirt with a false layer that appears to be two shirts. After *drincoffee*, he realizes he must go to a branch of another bar chain owned by the same company, Indel. bar_*space*_bar is a collocation of estate agency, café and nightclub, catering ingeniously to the previously unrecognized needs of those searching for property and a drink at the same time while saving space and maximizing mood possibilities. Wiley, who just wants to wait until Server 8 comes in, struggles to master bar_*space*_bar's esoteric policies about which piece of paper, or 'space tab', will enable him to buy the kind of drink necessary to allow him to sit in the daytime. Just as he seems to be defeated by Indel bureaucracy, he remembers to utter the name of Alain Fête and doors magically open.

The Receipt, like *Ideas Men* and *Say Nothing*, is an enterprise in which the handling of language and of space pits theatrical solutions against business solutions. From the start, unwanted sonic contributions by Branch impede Adamsdale's attempts to progress – a dynamic reminiscent of double acts such as Abbot and Costello, Laurel and Hardy, Morecambe and Wise. Branch's undermining of Adamsdale takes us into territory that devised theatre so frequently visits these days: the labour-intensive telling of a story about the impossibility of telling a story. But *The Receipt*, like *Ideas Men*, exemplifies another brand of contemporary storytelling: the anthropological study of life in workplaces in which no meaningful work is actually done. Whereas *The Office* (BBC, 2001–03)[11] was television that parodically quoted television documentary, and *Nathan Barley* (Channel 4, 2005)[12] was television infected by, and satirical of, new media art platforms, *The Receipt* is very much a piece for the stage. Adamsdale's Wiley is mobile, animated, and demonstrative. Using direct address, and switching with felicity between narratorial and actantional modes, he enjoys an empathetic complicity with his audience, his innocent, Martianist tone posing insights as questions for spectators: 'Why is technology increasingly named after fruit? Are you on Apple? I mean, I'm on Apple too, but it works better if you're on Orange as well.' Struck by the volume of paper that supports and surrounds office machinery, he asks whether machines weren't supposed to limit the need for paper, rather than generate it? Branch, in contrast, is physically static, always seated and side-on to the audience, always largely shielded by his keyboard stack. He occasionally chips in but mostly remains detached. As Adamsdale's stress levels climb, Branch remains irritatingly untroubled by the beeps, buzzers, alarms, and bits of muzak that are the soundtrack to Wiley's alienation, his mundane tone and side-on efficiency the perfect foil.

The playing by one performer of multiple, luridly antagonistic roles is a common feature of political satire on stage and on film. Kubrick's deployment of Peter Sellers in *Dr Strangelove, or How I Learned to Stop Worrying and Love the Bomb*,[13] draws on a theatrical tradition referenced, in the form of the Third Man, in Vogel's *Baltimore Waltz*. What is different about *The Receipt*, is that, rather than going for vivid signification of type, as Hough's performance of Frank, Sally, and Dan does in *Say Nothing*, Branch's performance is strikingly mild-mannered and not (in Kirby's terms) matrixed. At the same time, it is not non-matrixed, but closer to what Kirby calls the 'symbolized matrix', in which 'the referential elements' of a world are applied to, but not acted by the performer (Kirby, 1995, pp. 45–53).

Ambiguity about the matrixing of Branch's performance creates the image of the corporation as impalpably demonic. While having one person play an entire corporation seems like a flight of theatrical fancy, it should be remembered that corporations have, for centuries, been masquerading as individuals – a point made in *The Corporation*,[14] a film documentary which shows how laws designed to help freed slaves counter discrimination were exploited by nascent corporations. To this day, a system that allows corporations to function legally as individuals limits responsibility by masking power. *The Receipt* parodies the personification of the corporation that enables actual individuals to mask themselves as they carry out corporate work.

In *The Philosophy of Horror*, Noël Carroll conceives the horrific in a way that resonates with Wiley's journey through the corporate world. Though one barely has time to notice if the monster does its job properly, monsters (claims Carroll) are monstrous by virtue of their structurally transgressive ontology, what he calls their 'fantastic biology'. His two main types of fantastic biology are fusion and fission. Fusion monsters are individual entities in which categories normally opposite and exclusive, such as living/dead, are unified in figures like zombies, vampires, or mummies. The prototypical fusion monster is what Freud calls the collective figure or condensation, frequently found in dreams. In *The Baltimore Waltz*, it is in the extended daydream that the condensation figure appears, and when the playwright's alter ego wakes up, we glimpse a more mundane reality but one infused by the consciousness of the dream. In *The Receipt*, as the RotoPlas slogan promises, there is space to dream, but it is not a dream we are ever fully immersed in or suddenly wake up from: the condensation figure remains throughout, in the person of Branch, uncannily singular and multiple, real and fantastic.

Whereas fusion monsters unify opposing categories, fission distributes them. If fusion is about collapsing, fission is about splitting. It can be temporal, dividing characters over time within one body, as in Dr Jekyll/ Mr Hyde or a werewolf; or it can be spatial, as in the doppelgänger or alter ego, in which one, self-contradictory entity is distributed over different bodies. While fusion and fission create the underlying logical deviance needed to make a monster, monstrosity is intensified and specularized by operations that include self-replication and extreme changes of scale (cloning and massification), along with startling changes in demeanour.

Fusion, fission, cloning, and massification thrive in the corporation-governed world depicted in *The Receipt*. It is a world in which many companies, some invisibly incorporated, can share, or appear to share, the same space; a world in which estate agency can merge with binge drinking; in which outlets of different natures can be controlled by the same corporate body; and in which previously exclusive categories of human and machine merge to create an intercom chicken-farmer.

Though Carroll's focus is on horror, the structural logic he describes bears more than a surface resemblance to what I will call the 'genealogies of takeover' that can be found in Naomi Klein's analyses of branding, analyses which – in a lexicon as structural and as formalist as Carroll's in *The Philosophy of Horror* – parse mergers, acquisitions, incorporations, lateral monopolies, and multi-platform synergy.[15]

Carroll focuses on how, in philosophical terms, monsters work. But what makes monsters charming are the ways in which, in practical terms, they *don't* work. Zombies, for example, being both living and dead, tend to move incredibly slowly. Confusion and bluntness are the decoys that make corporate schemes seem more innocent. When it comes to creating a brand like RotoPlas, a job like space management, and a system governed by 'dockets', evacuation of substance passes as provision. The non-communicative language and non-servile services alienated in *The Receipt* are potent ways for corporations to restrict social channels.

Like the BusiHandle, the Baudrillard is a tool that tends to evade the grasp, but we should persevere, as it is useful for portability. In *The Transparency of Evil*, Baudrillard examines the stealthy evacuation of substance satirized in *The Receipt*. He describes a world in which 'every individual category is subject to contamination, substitution possible between any sphere and any other […] Politics is no longer restricted to the political sphere, but infects every sphere – economics, science, art, sport, which is no longer located in sport as such, but in business, in sex, in politics, in the general style of *performance*' [his italics] (Baudrillard, 1996, p. 8).

For Baudrillard, performance is a 'style' that supersedes substance. Thanks to this supersession, 'value' is allowed to roam free of structures used to contain it. Historically, he states, objects had a natural or use-value; then, in the commodity stage of culture, they had exchange value, which could be determined by reference to a logic, or system, of commodification; later, they had structural value as signs, determinable by reference to a set of codes. In the fourth stage, which Baudrillard calls fractal, viral, or radiant, there is no law of value, but a dispersal or haphazard proliferation of value. As Wiley is reminded during his detective work by several employees of Indel (perhaps Indel is short for Indelible?), the receipt has no natural value, no commodity value, and no structural value. The receipt is a valuable project precisely because it is just another discarded piece of paper. It is as if value, for Wiley, can only be determined by escaping the values of a world in which value itself refuses to be quantified. In such a world, the chicken-farmer's advice makes sense to Wiley: 'it doesn't matter what you do, just find something and stick to it'.

For Wiley, as for Baudrillard, contamination between spheres like estate agency and clubbing is alarming. He is perplexed by the 'obscure origin and questionable utility' of haphazard mergers, since the corporations seem helpfully to be reminding us, as if we have forgotten, exactly what should happen where. 'Eat this', they tell us, offering pointers like brown bags that say 'E.A.T.' or 'Medium Brown Bag'. Showing us the sections of the Saturday *Guardian* newspaper one after another, he wonders if we need to be told what a 'Family', 'Work', and 'Travel' are.[16] Such supplements convince us that we have lost our memory, that we can't do without their aid. At its most, as it were, 'evacuous', corporate culture is both phatic *and* factual.

In satirizing commodified creativity and vitriolic vacuity, the double-acts I have re-presented take severe theatrical issue with the idea that genuine communication 'lies in finding a proper balance between factual and phatic', between information and the padding that seals the channels along which value-rich information flows.

9
Graphting: Plotting the Body as Puzzle

It was 2006, on that day named after St Valentine (which of several Roman 'Valentines' the Day is named after is debated amongst historians of theology). I was in the wrong place (not that there is anything inherently wrong with Alsager) as I watched Lightwork's *Voici ce que j'ai fait un jour de mon corps* (*Here's what I did with my body one day: A genetic detective story*).[1] I bought tickets to see a band called the Concretes, then realized that it was the same day I was taking my Multimedia class to see that Lightwork show. To make matters worse, my girlfriend decided to pass on the gig – she liked the band, and liked dancing, but hated standing up and being hot. I'd have to go to another city to see Lightwork, and compare notes with my students. Since I was seeing it first, I would be able to tell them things to look out for, perhaps tease them with red herrings. The only problem was it was Valentine's Day, and my girlfriend didn't want to go to the theatre – she liked theatre, but she hated sitting down. I went on my own, grumbling that my viewing of this show was cursed from start to finish.

As the positively life-changing piece of theatre ensued, I soon forgot about the apparent curse. If only its protagonist had forgotten about *his* apparent curse: if only he had scrutinized appearances more sensibly. Lightwork's *genetic detective story* finds commonalities between three historical figures: symbolist composer Ernest Chausson (1855–1899), discoverer of radium Pierre Curie (1859–1906), and ardent semiotician Roland Barthes (1915–1980). In different fields, these three Frenchmen strove to perfect a means of reading the body, of capturing its movement and its music in words, pictures, symbols. All three died in traffic accidents. Onto this real-life coincidence, *Here's what I did* (*HWID*)grafts fictional ones, centring on protagonist David Rée, who tells us early on that the accidents in which Curie, Chausson, and Barthes perished all involved members of the Rée family.

David is a French-born genome researcher who has always lived in England. He is en route to Paris to speak at a conference on non-coding or 'junk' DNA, accompanied by his father, a translator, who is French but (scared by the curse) has not been to France since before David was born. Knowing that he has a 50/50 chance of inheriting Huntington's Chorea from his father, David has chosen not to take the simple DNA test that would tell him one way or the other. The disease causes uncontrollable muscular movements, memory loss, mood changes, and lapses in concentration. When his father goes missing at the hotel having, according to the Concierge, hired a car, David panics: should he do his presentation or look for his dad?

Like the three intellectuals his family may or may not have killed, David is himself a professional plotter, a participant in the Human Genome Project. Just as David is about to start his presentation on the subject, the conference organizer (Ernest) announces that another programmed speaker, David's friend Pierre, will not be able to speak as there has been a minor traffic accident. As David's thoughts unravel – (has his Dad gone and killed another French intellectual, or is he merely a danger to himself?), he begins to discursively fix strands of DNA, trying to stave off distractions:

> Greg Hillwell wrote in 1997 that you are as likely to unlock the secrets of the human genome by studying Junk DNA as you are to solve a detective story by studying the red herrings [...] I want to show how recent advances in our understanding of non-coding DNA have proved Hillwell to be mistaken. In thrillers, a red herring is an element that seems important but turns out not to be. But thriller writers are also adept at the opposite; making vital clues seem unimportant. A casual mention of a twin, some play on words, a jokey reference to a family curse. At Ashford we spent the best part of 1995–99 sequencing Junk DNA in chromosome 4. The data has revealed a number of suggestive patterns. In particular, human DNA at 4q33 showed identical strings of nucleotide pairs with rat DNA at – Did you say Pierre was in a road accident at Pont Neuf?
>
> (Lightwork, 2006, p. 25)

As David implies in refuting the claim that 'junk' DNA is just a 'red herring' in the genome story, the key to solving a mystery is defining the object of enquiry, or deciding which quest to pursue. This involves a discipline, a concentration, that is intensely, paradoxically solipsistic. Concentration, by definition, distracts the mind from potentially significant details, filing them as 'junk' or 'red herrings' so it can nurture the potential of other details. The concentration of Chausson, Curie, and Barthes, the concentration to which David aspires, is akin to magic. Magic dazzles by focusing attention and distracting it: a fundamental principle that, as *HWID* seems designed to remind us, underlies both naming and theatre. In drawing attention, concentrating the gaze, naming trains seeing to a logic of figure and ground, a perceptual geography in which meaning itself appears to fall naturally into clusters, nodes marked by names. The magical deployment of projections in *HWID* – images of rain projected onto umbrellas, photographs projected onto canvases that are reversed and unfolded, daring us to deconstruct the image – takes our perceptual geography to task.

Signs can help to orient and explain, but they are treacherous. Who better to explain the spectral properties of signification than Barthes, who, every time he tasted coffee, could not re-create the pleasurable sensation of the first time he smelled coffee as a child, not realizing until later that it is actually the smell of cognac added to and emanating from the coffee which he found so alluring. Like crack cocaine, the first hit of which corrals the synapses in ways that demand repetition but can never quite be repeated, that first experience of the coffee forms a semiotic link that can be neither forgotten nor resolved. The story of the cognac-infused coffee is a cautionary tale to David, and by extension to the spectator, to question what we see, and what we think (of what) we see.

Like the would-be radiographer trying to fix radium long enough to capture an image of the human body, like the composer trying to arrange music, like the semiotician ordering chaos as signification, and like the DNA researcher trying to piece together the codes of life, we must find ways to tie the story down even as its strands of narrative cross, and our assumptions prove unfounded. We are made to look to names (landmarks, canonical figures) to hold the story in place, to tie it down, but names refuse to settle as we hurtle through a ghost-train in which history dances with the future. The play's exploration of coincidence, misreading, and superstition hinges on duplicitous naming, the actors doubling as both actual historical figures and modern-day characters who share the names Ernest (Chausson/the President of cross-domain corporation GenTechnica), Roland (Barthes/a map-seller), and Pierre (Curie/David's scientist friend). These doublings are audaciously schematic, fittingly so in a narrative that continually reminds us of the ingenious efforts and magical results of plotting and transcription. Palimpsestic, coincidental naming grafts the imagined present onto the imagined past, the fictional onto the factual.

Going way beyond the boundaries of their disciplines, Curie, Chausson, and Barthes strive to perfect the plotting of information: sign systems; musical notation; imaging the human body. In their ground-breaking endeavour, they, like the spectator of the play, get caught up in the pleasures of reading, transcendent and purgatorial, escape and trap. Our interpretation is keyed by Lightwork's projection of words, images, and patterns of light onto bodies and objects, which under-scores thematic development of the entrancing but distracting pleasure afforded by visual technologies – a pleasure that preoccupies the dead intellectuals.

Our interpretation is further keyed by several episodes in the play that are about deixis. When David flees the scene of the conference, he arrives at a busy Parisian intersection to find gendarmes noncha-lantly channelling traffic, directing what David experiences as chaos with authoritative aplomb (Figure 9). As Brecht's street-scene exercises

Figure 9 'Directing chaos with authoritative aplomb' (Photo: Pau Ros)

were designed to show, busy intersections are paradigmatic sites for the training of spectatorship and an inspiration to Barthes – who pops up when needed to remind us of the importance of orientation in semiotics, expounding on the stage right/audience left orientation conventional to theatrical reading. Barthes' modern-day namesake in the play is a bouquiniste, Roland, who David asks for directions while looking for his dad. This modern Roland is one of those entertaining cameo figures often mistaken for red herrings in detective fiction. Clutching the free map provided by his hotel, David asks the bookseller whether he has seen the man in the photo he has found in his father's notebook, a photo of two men, one of them his father, and a woman:

ROLAND: He look like you.
DAVID: I don't see it but okay.
ROLAND: What does 'Find the bitter' mean?
DAVID: I don't know, why?
ROLAND: I think you will find it on the back of the photograph.
DAVID: Huh. Yes. 'Find the Bitter'. [...] It's probably an old note he scribbled down. Meant something once. You haven't seen him then?
ROLAND: No.
DAVID: Well, thank you for your help.
ROLAND: You sure you not want to buy this excellent map? A man with a bad map is a prisoner. With a good map you are free.
DAVID: I'll be okay with this one.

(Lightwork, 2006, p. 21)

By the time of the late-night pile-up at a Parisian junction that ends the play, David's lack of an appropriate map has proved far from 'okay'.

If Lightwork are fond of leaving clues, so too is David's dad. When he goes missing, he leaves behind the aforementioned notebook containing the aforementioned photograph. Though he has looked and looked at the photo left for him by the man he has always called 'dad', David cannot see what is obvious to the book-seller: that it is the other man in the picture who looks like David, while his 'father' does not.

The play's figuring out of answers to the various questions raised – whether David has Huntington's, what's happened to his father, whether there really is a family curse – is a treatise on the signifying systems on which epistemologies rest. It is a show that interrogates reading, that reflects on how different fields, over successive generations, test the philosophical and technological limits of interpretation.

David cannot help but assemble the pieces because he is bound to see a connection between the accident and his missing dad. Given his illness and, of course, the curse, his father should not be driving. What if his dad has killed Pierre? As David pursues his father, spectres of the past fog a present haunted by absence. Who is the other man in the picture? Who is the woman? Why is David's mother not in the photo? A ghost, Pierre Curie, is on hand with a reflection on the viewing of images that cautions against the assumptions that naming engenders:

> PIERRE: Fifteen years after my death the first microscopes got power-ful enough to look into the nucleus of the cell and the first man in history looked at a chromosome but and you can't blame him he's seeing this pile of string pieces and maybe the slide's badly prepared the lenses got fogged in the old glass and he was tired late in the laboratory because the hours but he looks and counts forty-eight chromosomes. Forty-eight? But there are forty-six...for nearly forty years they stopped looking and they just see forty-eight in the books even big photographic plates and underneath it says forty-eight chromosomes and you just have to look and count but no one does but if you don't really look you don't see. No one can say that in our search for radium Marie and I didn't look we did nothing *but* look.
>
> (Lightwork, 2006, p. 24)

Once chromosomes or fathers have been named, no-one really looks at them properly: naming is recognition, but also decognition.

Despite the warnings of the map-seller, who interprets the photo-graphic evidence with fresh eyes, David continues to accept his named genetic inheritance. Like Chausson, Curie, and Barthes, who appear intermittently to reflect from beyond the grave on their own deaths and legacies in ways that frame David's problems and our viewing of them, David is something of an idiot savant, obsessively attentive to detail but with a dangerous propensity for wondrous dreaming. It is a power-fully creative combination, but one not without peril. Engrossed in the particulars of their sensual, intellectual quests, they fail to recognize dan-ger right in front of them. We are told that Curie's party-piece involved turning off the lights and dazzling guests with a bottle of radium that he produced from his breast pocket, oblivious to the fact that the magic-trick was creating 'a permanent lesion over [his] heart'. Chausson's mission to connect himself purely to music finally succeeds when his bicycle skids fatally ('It takes me only a minute to die and all the while I feel music, sticky hot music, pouring out of me onto the road'). Barthes, it is surmised, is considering the famously dense semiotics of the city street when a laundry truck hits him.

The epic, international Human Genome Project in which David participates is a finite puzzle,[2] but raises as many questions as it answers. Traits previously seen as socially constructed and mutable are genetically programmed, while biology that we thought was immutable can be altered with increasing ease. A kind of microcosmic theatrical equivalent of the Genome Project, *HWID* figures history in the way that DNA research figures the body. *HWID*'s graphting 'makes' history in ways that raise similar ethical and ontological questions to those about the manipulation of bodies that attend upon the Genome Project. In the Genome Project, the possibilities afforded to intervention in the workings of the body expand as more and more organic material becomes coded. Do histories – personal, disciplinary, institutional, and national – become similarly manipulable as a result? Are the codes of history reducible to the codes of the human, the codes that create humanity; in other words, are the codes of history controlled by intervention at the level of the individual body?

In Lightwork's heuristic 'graphting', a mixture of graphing and grafting, history functions as the host onto which the play grafts (or 'writes', the word 'graft' deriving from 'graphos' and 'graphein', the etymological roots of writing) the foreign body of its fiction. But the idea of history as a host is problematized. Conceptions of specific histories – be they family, national, institutional, or disciplinary – as a home, a repository of domesticity, are integral to the establishment of personal and cultural identities. Collectively, these conceptions construct history itself as a host, and foreignness as that which does not belong within it. As David plots his personal choices and career moves, and navigates a country he feels he should belong in, he encounters, and we encounter along with him, history contaminated by previously hidden pre-existing conditions. David's history is an unsafe host: grafting onto it leads to what scientists refer to as GVHR (graft versus host reaction). He wants to graft new experience, but is haunted by a past that he doesn't fully know, and which proceeds to write and unwrite itself.

Motifs of writing and unwriting abound in the play, words forming on a screen behind the characters as they are said, and then dissolving. This formation and dissipation of words is just one aspect of the play's continual detachment of sign from effect, which alienates processes of encoding and decoding. Proper names, like Curie, not only make a name for those who lend their name, they 'make history' as time that is marked by names. It is possible to make history – or *fait date*, in Bordieu's thinking of it – only if history is constructed as the marking of time with names. Lightwork construct a theatrical narrative that conspicuously depends on a making of history and of geography by signs that cannot hold.

HWID interrogates the role of naming practices – specifically, the practices of 'naming after' and 'naming across' – in branding and historicizing human endeavour. Interrogation of the practice of 'naming after' – a son after his father, a disease or a technology after its discover or developer – binds the play's exploration of personal identity and of vocational creativity, and is underscored by character naming that trades on duplicity. Though it works in specific ways in particular contexts (differently, for instance, in religious than in secular families, in royal families than in others), naming after within families has always been a peculiar practice, marking repetition and continuity but inviting direct comparisons, inviting observations of difference. In contrast, naming after within art or science constructs singularity, working by synecdoche to fit individuals to particular attributes or phenomena. *HWID* suggests that naming after (both personal and vocational) has been superseded by 'naming across'. By 'naming across', I mean extensions of 'naming after' that entail naming across domains. The conference that David attends (a conferring, or coming together, of plot strands as well as of DNA scientists) is sponsored by multi-national corporation GenTechnica, whose business ranges 'from genetic engineering to music sales'. GenTechnica, to paraphrase Baudrillard, represents the trans-apparency of branding. In familial naming after, the logic is of continuity, and in vocational naming after it is one of attribution: in both cases, naming works to fix the named individual to a particular achievement or family line. In naming across, naming works to unfix the named entity from achievement or family line. For corporations, naming distinguishes paradoxically – by positioning the named entity as generic and anonymous, an unlimited company.

The struggle of names to hold the play's framework in place draws attention to the ways in which naming itself draws our attention, creates perceptual nodes that focus the gaze by distracting it. *HWID* weaves a discursive web of languages from various domains: semiotics, radiography, music, forensics, theatre, DNA research, French and English language, branding, and ICT (information and computer technology). Names, their referentiality overdetermined, struggle to hold that web in place as the play explores the ways in which conventions of 'naming after' and 'naming across' work within and between domains.

Naming in the play makes visible, but is exceeded, transcended, and resisted by the mysteries it works to coalesce. The structure for which names are the glue barely manages to define the inchoate, unassimilable domains of bodily memory, death, and creativity that the play invokes. Naming is palpably elliptical: behind each name, there is a story, the unfolding of which reveals a lost presence behind the past of the name. David is driving along, relating to his companion Ernest the story of his father's illness as they search for him, when he remembers another car journey, taken by Huntington himself, in which he first discovered the illness that bears his name:

> DAVID: He was driving with his father through a wood on Long Island.
> And it's dark, the sky is dark blue with high trees silhouetted against it.
> And they turn a wide sweeping bend in the road
> And the car headlights catch something in their beams.
> It's two women; a mother and daughter. Tall, thin, cadaverous.
> And they're both twitching, grimacing, bowing.
> Huntington was terrified.
> What were they doing? What did it mean?
> ERNEST: What did it mean?
> DAVID: He found that this disease was localized to this particular area.
> He identified it as a specific, inherited disorder.
>
> (Lightwork, 2006, p. 47)

Huntington's fascination with and compassion for these seemingly undead 'cadaverous' women leads to his own strange afterlife as a name for a disease.

Distinguishing the name Barthes from the person, *HWID* suggests that 'Barthes' may be seen as an over-familiar sign. Because everything in semiotics is a sign, there is a tendency to see the semiotician as someone in love with signs. I found myself wondering whether Barthes's appearances in the performance are themselves a red herring, tricking us into seeing everything as semiosis. Movingly, Barthes reminds us that he is not in love with signs, as we often assume, but one who experiences semiosis as 'a purgatory of reading': 'no signs or symbols, isn't that the very definition of desire?' (Figure 10).

Whether they like it or not, it is the fate of Barthes, Chausson, and Curie to become, like Huntington, names, signs. They become subject to the operations of transcription and encrypting, the magic of code-breaking, that so fascinates them. *HWID* switches between the perceptual

Figure 10   David Annen as Roland Barthes (Photo: Pau Ros)

questing of the intellectuals and their assimilation by future generations, whose history-writing will continually recode their efforts. It is part of the curse of communication that the harder we try to name, the more we become subjects, and the more we become subject to the naming we perform. Driven to use (and driven by our use of) signs, we are destined not so much to die but to become signs ourselves. In 'becoming a name', the named subject lives and dies.

If you haven't guessed it already, David discovers that the man he always *called* 'father' is not. Freedom from worry about whether he has Huntington's, not to mention freedom from the family curse, is short-lived. Though you wouldn't know it from the appallingly bad French that causes waiters, map-sellers, and gendarmes to laugh at him, David was born in France. This, as he angrily tells those 'real' French workers who crack jokes about the English, makes David French. And he is an intellectual – who soon dies in a traffic accident, along with the man he has always called father.

The deaths of Chausson (whose bicycle skidded on loose slate in 1899), Curie (struck and killed by a munitions lorry in 1906), and Barthes (hit by a laundry van in 1980) animate and haunt proceedings, their resurrection pulling us, as ghosts tend to, both back in time and forward, to the final fatal scene. In its exploration of the prevalence of death in life, the play can be seen as a contemporary twist on an age-old form: the *danse macabre*. Dan Rebellato's text begins as follows:

> *Waterloo International Eurostar Terminal; Platform 20; Eurostar RG6743; Coach 14; Seat 31; Friday, 28 May 2004, 6.34pm. Enter David, with laptop bag. An image of a male dancer, waltzing alone in a ballroom. David sits and sets up his laptop.*
>
> (Lightwork, 2006, p. 4)

The opening stage directions, ridiculously precise, play with particularity as if desperately trying to frame singularity amidst the ineluctable dancing of duplicates, sound-alikes, simulations. In the course of the narrative, David, armed with his laptop, will try to still the chaotic images that bombard him so that he can piece together the puzzle of his father's disappearance, like delineating the puzzles of genetics. A few pages/minutes in, Curie, Barthes, and Chausson are introduced, waltzing 'behind a screen', their movements becoming ominously grotesque, linking them to David via Huntington's disease by anticipating the story told later of how Huntington 'discovered' the disease that bears his name when he encountered a mother and daughter in the involuntary throes of what struck him as a dance of death.

The stark reality of death – which science measures and tries to explain, to manage, to stave off – contends with the romantic escape of dancing. The play's images of dancing are bound by death(s). Dancing is that which allows the characters to transcend their lives, and their deaths, to transcend their characterhood and become deconstructive. As in *The Baltimore Waltz*, death is a reality that demands to be confronted and dancing evokes the ephemerality of escape, usefully entrancing but ultimately impractical.

Shortly before dying, Barthes finds a locked ballroom, 'the last ballroom of the twentieth century'. He *'dances with death, then unwrites his scene title'*. The link between semiosis and the death drive is underscored as Chausson is depicted reflecting on his own death from beyond the grave:

> All art aspires to the condition of music.
> All music aspires to the condition of silence
> And this silence
> All silence aspires
> Come, come, we know this.
> All silence aspires to the condition of death.
>
> (Lightwork, 2006, p. 36)

The moment of Chausson's termination is also an apotheosis, in which he feels 'the music pour out of him'. As he dies in the car crash that ends the plot, David becomes the fourth in the play's line of intellectuals whose quest to decode ends in his own annihilation. True to type, he is analysing 'what he's done to his body' in the moment of impact, a moment, as for Chausson, of tragic release:

> My ribs are crushed and my lungs are punctured.
> From somewhere, deep somewhere I remember being told:
> In a car crash there are three collisions:
> The first is between two cars
> The second is between you and your car
> The third is between your organs and the walls of your body.
> It is the third collision that kills you.
> My father's chest hits the bonnet of the car
> There are constellations of glass in the air
> Droplets of blood from my father's broken arms and legs
> Slowly splashing into my face.
> And stars, stars across the sky.

> (Lightwork, 2006, p. 54)

In David's final moment of consciousness, it is as if signification is unchained from desirous interpretation, beauty from the eye of the beholder.

10
Supplement: Naming Critical Acts

Reading, and its complex, changing relationship to ideology, has figured as a theme in all of these chapters. In this final, supplementary chapter, I will consider in more detail the naming that critical readings perform. In previous chapters, I have used the terms 'theatre-maker' and 'theatre-making' to encompass the production, writing, performance, and also criticism of theatre. I want, in this one, to comment more explicitly on how naming within theatrical works provokes and invokes naming in critical discourse. In naming theatrical paradigms and genres, what kind of self-naming has recent criticism performed, and what kind should it perform?

While the chapters book-ended by this one and the Introduction have focused on works of theatre, those works have often echoed, mirrored, projected, interpellated, and parodied critical naming. Characters like Lutzky the Naturalist PhD in *Imperceptible Mutabilities in the Third Kingdom* (*IMTK*) and Kevin, *Say Nothing*'s doctoral student of Peace and Conflict Studies, mock academics. Somewhat bumbling, street-unwise David Rée broadly resembles Ibsen's Jörgen Tesman (*Hedda Gabler*), but is more sympathetic (which is a relief, since he was 'authored' by Rebellato and Lavender, artists doubling, like so many do, as academics). Compared to Tesman's immersion in domestic crafts in Brabant in the Middle Ages, Rée's work on genetic codes is relevant to the point of heroism.

Even from these few examples, we can begin to see that it is not academics (or institutions of learning) *per se* who are regarded as the cause of the taxonomy that has been variously derided, attacked, pathologically and ironically embraced in the preceding chapters. While universities may be a training-ground, it is in theological, scientific, industrial, governmental, and artistic institutions that real taxonomic damage is done. Whether emanating from doctors and pseudo-doctors (*The Baltimore*

Waltz, Venus, How to be Funny, and, though author Soans might disagree, the psychiatrist in *Talking to Terrorists*), religious devotees (Miss Faith in *IMTK*), businessmen (*The Receipt*) and soldiers (*Pugilist Specialist*) whose every action is programmed, museum guides (*Two Undiscovered Amerindians Visit...*, *The Colored Museum*) and appointed Narrators (*Kind Ness, World in Pictures*) who act as anthropologists, it is taxonomy itself that seems to be the target. (Taxonomy in *Under the Knife* emanates from all of these areas: Church authorities who refuse to let bodily needs and realities dictate the treatment of social diseases, snake oil salesmen, museum guides, military doctors, and various brands of narrator).

Taxonomy, as its etymology attests, is arrangement (*taxos*) and distribution (*-nomia*). The taxonomizers depicted here abstract the commodities of labour from embodied endeavour, overwriting the stories behind that labour. In a world that seems increasingly complex, the logic ordering it seismically shaken, taxonomy (these texts and performances suggest) puts on new disguises to assert old divisions, and invents new divisions to reassert traditional hierarchies. Criticism, as portrayed in these works, and as stated by some of those artists, particularly the US-based ones who, as we have seen, provide their own commentaries (Wolfe, Fusco, Parks, Chong, Vogel, Skipitares), is as fervently taxonomic as ever.

Reflecting on critical naming of the genealogy of 'new American drama', Marc Robinson makes salient points about genre, and about efforts to map perceived departure from 'convention':

> Even the smallest of these families eventually acquires a name, occasionally self-declared but more often the invention of a sympathetic critic or editor. [...] Theaters of the Ridiculous and of the Absurd; the New Realists and the Neo-Formalists; Black theater and Gay theater; the Language writers and the Theater of Images. When the categories fail, geography is a fallback: Here are histories of off-off-Broadway, of the California school, and, more precisely, of such important incubators for new work as the Judson Poets' Theater, La Mama, and the Padua Hills Playwrights Festival. Some categories flash brightly, linger awhile and then die, replaced by new names for similar groups of writers: At one time or another, readers of this anthology have probably surveyed the Theaters of Crisis, of Commitment, and of Protest; or Theaters of Visions, of Wonders and of the Marvelous. [...] Granted, few of these names are specific enough, few expressive of the imaginative range within each group; and none do justice to the idiosyncrasies of the individual writers. Indeed, in the effort to stake out territory,

critics and editors often ignore what's least familiar about a particular writer in favour of the lowest common denominator. [...] As admirers of Adrienne Kennedy wonder if she really has anything other than race in common with Amiri Baraka, and as Richard Foreman's partisans point out all the ways his self-referential work differs from that of Lee Breuer, the critical energy in the theatrical community undergoes a subtle but important change. The hated monolith 'conventional theater' no longer seems relevant – it's a fair question whether it was ever possible to define such a thing. Anyone hoping to understand this art must now move beyond identifying only what their creators reject, and start examining what they offer in its place. All the usual prefixes – 'anti,' 'post,' 'non,' 'off-off' – only point us in the right direction. Once we arrive at this rich theatrical territory, we have to devise a new language and draw our own maps. That effort makes formalists of us all – if only so we draft our maps correctly, by first revisiting the basics of theatre craft. [...] The design of space, the passage of time, the rhythms of speech and movement: these 'invisibles' of theater, once meant to disappear when stories or characters are compelling enough, instead emerge from the background to tell their own stories [...]. These writers incorporate into their plays their questions about the form [...]: What kind of a charge is released when one character encounters another? What do we mean when we speak of stage presence? What defines the stage itself?

(Introduction to Messerli and Wellman, 1998, pp. 12–13)

Robinson raises two sets of questions here. Firstly, there are questions about the changing nature and value of genre categories and 'denominators'. I will discuss Robinson's claim that 'critics and editors often ignore what's least familiar about a particular writer in favour of the lowest common denominator' and his entreaty to 'move beyond identifying only what [artists] reject' and, going beyond 'post-' words, to 'examine what they offer in its place'. Secondly, there is the fusion of, or confusion between, the critic and the artist. Should we even think of critical effort as separate from artistic effort, given that the 'effort to stake out territory', to 'devise a new language and draw our own maps' aligns critics with artists and writing with performance/performativity, and given the extent to which contemporary theatre portrays criticism, and 'incorporate[s ...] questions about the form'? How is the critic's 'effort' affected by the reflexivity of the artist?

As Robinson notes, 'post-s' and 'beyond's, paradigm terms that designate limbo and the lack of a mapped future, have been prevalent during the last two decades. Concurring with Herbert Blau's view that 'future theories are unlikely to be bold', Michael Vanden Heuvel suggests that we live amidst 'an environmental totality of forces and tendencies only predictable within the shadowy limits of the indeterminacy principle', and that the study of performance must respond to the fact that ours is a culture which cannot be mapped according to 'logic' or 'law' (2000, p. 135). One can only get to grips with the future by examining how it has been constructed, prepared for, delimited, and squandered, in the recent past. Rejecting what he sees as a postmodernism that is 'totalizing' in its 'deconstructive' logic, Vanden Heuvel's strategy, brilliantly executed, is to frame performance in the vocabulary and methods used to conceive thermodynamic systems. He aligns himself with philosopher of science Robert Crease and theatre phenomenologist Bert States in asserting that theatre is not 'a metaphor for what goes on in science: theatre and science stand in mutual relationship, in which the same features appear, mutatis mutandis' (ibid., p. 146).

Metaphors of indeterminacy from one field or tradition can certainly vitalize another, and acknowledging the translation by tracing the metaphors enhances the exchange. However, as McKenzie argues throughout *Perform or Else*, there are dangers in assimilating metaphors too easily: not least, the danger of sublimating differences between discursive traditions. Performing his own struggle against the temptation to construct a paradigm, McKenzie sets himself the 'challenge to fold generalization back on itself in order to avoid reducing performance to any one model' (2001, p. 52). His audacious 'mission' for comprehension beyond paradigmatic construction is a multi-faceted metaphorical journey beyond paradigm in which he cites and situates previous journeys toward paradigm. His 'journey-situating' journey is fuelled by a wilfully destabilizing suspicion of the 'paradigm' as an analytical tool.

A number of critics and editors at the start of the twenty-first century attempt to describe theatre and/or performance via paradigms while at the same time complicating the notion of the paradigm. Contributions to, and formulations of, a theoretical basis for performance studies have embraced the instability of epistemological foundations so often that these efforts might be seen as a paradoxically inchoate foundation of performance studies. 'More than any other mode of work', claims Nick Kaye in 1994, 'performance may be read, in itself, as tending to foster or look towards postmodern contingencies and instabilities' elucidated by Derrida and Lyotard (Kaye, 1994, p. 23). Several years later, McKenzie, like several other performance theorists of the early twenty-first century, draws on Deleuze as he launches his rocket to go beyond Kaye's efforts to ground performance's flights from grounding. The theoretical bedrock that McKenzie plumbs, and performs his own failure to plumb, consists in significant part, as it did for Kaye, of those destabilizing ideas about language that rocked academic disciplines.[1] Several theorists, including Kaye and Michel Benamou (see Benamou and Caramello, 1977, pp. 3–5), constructed models of 'postmodern performance' in which the emergence of a kind of performance/performativity is conceived as a paradigmatic actualization of postmodernism. I would argue, along the same lines as Robinson, that 'post-' terms are not identifiers to any meaningful extent. While postmodernism was initially seen as a designator of a specific set of properties, a discursive metastasis has taken place since the mid-1990s (or earlier), via which postmodernism has been increasingly attributed with agency, with the capability to nurture feelings/designations of uncertainty and limbo, and to breed other 'post-s'.

The call for contributions to the first *Beyond Postmodernism* symposium (2005) describes postmodernism as 'a compliant theory of the contemporary'.[2] 'Compliant theory' is a slippery phrase. It implies that postmodernism has capability, but that capability is presented as ambiguous: is postmodernism itself compliant, or does it render those who advocate it compliant? The slipperiness of the phrase 'compliant theory' works to intensify rather than counteract the slipperiness of postmodernism itself. Because of its paradoxically nebulous force as a marker of displacement, a paradigm of the implausibility of all paradigms, postmodernism is not something that one can comply with or dissent from. The term 'compliant theory' is used in the call for contributions in opposition to the desire to 'dissent from postmodernism': that postmodernism coerces compliance, or *is* compliance, serves to render 'dissent' emancipatory. The image of a battle between compliance and dissent presumes the possibility of an agency vis-à-vis postmodernism that is problematically romantic. By 'agency', I mean both the ability to intervene in a situation through action and the ethical implications of intervention: who is doing what to whom?

As Rebecca Herzig observes, 'most recent efforts' in science 'disavow the focus on individuated men that characterized earlier accounts of scientific change, and instead emphasize the formative role of conflict, dissent, and negotiation. In lieu of narratives of individual genius, we now find decentralized subjects, whose actions appear as effects of shifting networks of relations' (Herzig, 2004, p. 134). As addressed in Chapters 5 (on Skipitares) and 9 (on Lightwork), I agree that such progressive complications of agency are necessary to challenge long-standing myths of 'individual genius'. However, in debate about postmodernism, agency continues to be contorted in ways that problematically exploit such complications. The perpetual currency of postmodernism as an idea, or cluster of ideas, is largely attributable to the manoeuvres through which writers have exploited the performative elasticity of agency afforded within *discourse about* postmodernism. A look at some of these manoeuvres will show that strange things have been done *to* compliance and dissent that have been blamed on postmodernism. The endowing of postmodernism with capability is enabled (in the examples below) by a rhetorical relinquishing or denial of agency by the commentator and a corresponding projection of that agency onto postmodernism and its alleged proponents.

In their Introduction to *Postmodernism: The Key Figures*, a book comprising 50 short, insightful essays on figures from across the arts and philosophy, Hans Bertens and Joseph Natoli admit: 'Although we clearly cannot do without them', they begin, 'few of us are straightforwardly happy with the terms postmodern, postmodernism, postmodernity' (2002, p. xi). In the same vein, the subsequent essays point out their, and their subjects', misgivings about the label, before applying it with gusto. Ronald Bogue's contribution begins by stating that 'there is good reason not to label Deleuze and Guattari "postmodern".' After spelling out that 'good reason', he concludes: 'theirs is a postmodernism of resistance' (ibid., pp. 98–9). Jim Collins states that Robert Venturi is an architect who resists being labelled a 'postmodernist'. Collins goes on to claim, however, that, as Venturi's is 'a gentle manifesto', it is more properly seen as a 'post-manifesto', and therefore an example of 'postmodern discourse' (ibid., p. 311). The contributions on theatre artists are sceptical both in their application of 'p-terms' and their attitude to postmodernism. Greg Giesekam observes that, 'paradoxically', Wooster Group 'productions have become canonized as postmodern classics, despite insistence by company members that they have no great interest in theory' (ibid., p. 327). In contrast, Philip Auslander begins by telling us that 'the word "postmodernism" and its cognates seldom appear in discussions of Ping Chong's performance work.' By the fifth paragraph, Chong's assimilation to the label seems to be complete. It begins: 'Like any good postmodernist, Chong [...] ' (ibid., pp. 82–3).

Ambivalences and contradictions within constructions of postmodernism are acknowledged in the Natoli and Bertens collection, but are overridden by the need to characterize postmodernism as a coherent entity. The prefacing of application of p-terms by disclaimers and qualifications occurs so frequently throughout this volume that it seems *de rigeur.* Scepticism about the validity of applying 'postmodern' as a label appears to be an unnamed rule allowing the assimilation of each 'figure'.

A project such as *Postmodernism: The Key Figures* enhances the power of postmodernism by showing how encompassing a label it can be. The versatility of postmodernism as a label adds to the sense that postmodernism is somehow doing the labelling itself, almost without the agency of the critic. The endorsing blurb on the back cover of the book, by Steven Shaviro, is emblematic:

> The word 'postmodern' resists precise definition, and a definitive survey of postmodernism would be a contradiction in terms. But this book does the next best thing, giving lucid and comprehensive summaries of a broad range of postmodern artists and thinkers.

Shaviro's acknowledgement of the 'contradiction' between these two sentences is presented as a badge of authenticity. The implication seems to be that a particular brand of inconsistency, a kind of wilful failure to shake off the inadequacy of one's own (or perhaps any?) statement-making, is needed to describe postmodernism because of its peculiar 'resistance' to 'definition'. While the 'figures' referred to in the book's title are the people discussed, the word 'figures' refers equally well to the discursive motifs employed. Time and again, we are told that people and *oeuvres* discussed are not textbook cases of postmodernism, but the contradictory gesturing toward both assimilation and the refusal of assimilation makes the book itself a textbook example of postmodern discourse.

A significant proportion of debate about the nature of postmodernism has taken place in the many academic anthologies and surveys that the subject has occasioned. Justifying the utility of an annotated collection, survey, handbook, or reader was not a hard task for editors or publishers in the 1990s, given the institutional demands to map evolving complexities of argument.[3] The proliferation of 'secondary' literature about postmodernism reflects its continuity with the 'primary' literature. Elucidations of postmodernism from as early as the mid-1980s on seem, despite being expository, to be already stemming tides of conceptual uncertainty. By 1985, Lyotard writes of the need not 'to close the debate but to situate it, in order to avoid confusion and ambiguity'.[4] By 1987, Ihab Hassan in *The Postmodern Turn* finds himself sweeping up conceptual debris with one hand while desperately struggling to stop leaks in logic with the other. Counterposing a string of names of figures exemplifying postmodernism with names of precursors they replace or oppose, Hassan resorts to the list, glued together with dollops of sceptical disclaimer, as a repair kit.[5]

I can think of no other conceptual term (not even 'performance') that has been so sustained by attempts to define it. Fittingly, the editors of the Routledge *Encyclopedia of Postmodernism* state that their 'volume does not adhere to a single definition of postmodernism as much as it documents the use of the term across a variety of academic and cultural pursuits'. The *Encyclopedia* navigates that brand of discourse, across a 'variety of academic and cultural' domains, that consists of defining postmodernism.[6] It is a brand that acknowledges the partiality, provisionality, and conditionality of definition itself before (with obligatory use of the word 'paradoxically') going on to tentatively list characteristics – or, more precisely, forms of negation – that 'we' can just about agree are postmodern. The items on the *Encyclopedia's* list – processual terms such as fragmentation, dehierarchization, deconstruction, and totalizing appropriation – are the items on so many previous lists.

Encompassing and hard to encompass as postmodernism is, and always has been, we can go some way toward contextualizing a perceived failure to think beyond 'the postmodern turn' by remembering, and reconsidering, its relationship to 'the linguistic turn'. What emerges during the nineteenth and twentieth centuries from distinct, but increasingly intersecting, developments in philosophy, linguistics, and psychology is a dichotomous sense that everything is language, but that language is slippery – complex, empowering, treacherous, or inadequate, depending on the point of view. In 'Structure, Sign, and Play in the Discourse of the Human Sciences' (an influential essay in his 1967 book *Writing and Difference*), Derrida identifies that 'moment when language invaded the universal problematic, the moment when, in the absence of a centre or origin, everything became discourse' (1978, p. 280). On the second page of his Preface to *The Anti-Aesthetic*, a reader at the cusp (if there is one) of primary/secondary literature on postmodernism, Hal Foster states that, 'as the importance of a Foucault, a Jacques Derrida, or a Roland Barthes attests, postmodernism is hard to conceive without continental theory, structuralism and poststructuralism in particular' (1983, p. x). From a perspective radically less sympathetic than Foster's to 'continental theory', Peter Dews's interrogation of Derrida, Lacan, and Lyotard, *Logics of Disintegration*, reaches a similar conclusion: that postmodernism can only be understood in terms of the provocative effect of Saussure's structuralist linguistics as a point of departure for a variety of theoretical projects (1987, pp. 33–4).

If the phenomena that we package as postmodernism have taught academics anything, they have hopefully taught us about the power that lies in our institutionalized packaging of debate. Only by resisting the packaging of difference into the coherence of inherited models of dissent can we begin to intervene in those uncertainties for which the reifying word 'postmodern' has been forced to stand.

Synthesizing as it does varied constructions of performance, but attempting to slough off their tendency toward paradigm, is McKenzie's *Perform or Else* a turning-point at which writing about theatre/ performance failed to turn, resigning itself to being paradigm-led in a post-paradigmatic world? There are few signs as yet of cessation of quests for the perfect paradigm. Hans-Thies Lehmann tries, in line with my concerns about the collapsing of theatre and science, to distance himself from 'the illusion that art, like science, could conform to the developmental logic of paradigms and paradigm shifts' (2006, p. 24). He quickly proceeds to erect 'a new paradigm of postdramatic theatre'.[7] Lehmann's delineation of aesthetic properties is useful and highly accomplished, but pursuing the goal of a secure paradigm means that he is constantly shepherding specific examples into his general formulation. His paradigm of 'postdramatic theatre' labours to exclude any questions of agency that might inform or result from aesthetic choices. Citing Julia Kristeva to argue that 'the political' is 'always' about setting rules, whereas art is 'always' about 'transgression' of rules, Lehmann insists that the only 'law' the aesthetic can be made to obey is the law of his paradigm of postdramatic theatre, which categorically insists on ignoring 'thematization' to get to the purity of 'aesthetic behaviour' (ibid., p. 178).

As I have argued throughout this book, 'the 'invisibles' of theatre – what Robinson (1997) describes as 'the design of space, the passage of time, the rhythms of speech and movement' – have increasingly come to the fore as themes because they are recognized by artists and others *as political*. Mr Smith's complaint (in *IMTK*) that 'there used to be uh flap' of time to slip through, and Wiley's failure (in *The Receipt*) to sell space because he refuses to provide the right entry/exit dockets, are striking reminders of the extent to which space, time, and language provide the conditions for the enunciability of character and environment, and must 'appear' before agency can be effective.

Having frequently argued against 'lowest common denominator' genre, style, and identity descriptors, I applaud Robinson's assertion that criticism of theatre has too often relied on such denominators. There are, though, more problematic examples than the ones (Kennedy and

Baraka; Foreman and Breuer) that he offers. The term 'AIDS play', which I avoided using in my chapter on *The Baltimore Waltz* (*BW*), is one such example.

In the first paragraph of her introduction to *The Way We Live Now: American Plays and the AIDS Crisis* (1990), M. Elizabeth Osborn positioned *The Baltimore Waltz* as an important 'AIDS play' before it had even been professionally produced. When the play premiered in New York in 1992,[8] it won the Obie Award for Best New American play despite a slew of vitriolic reviews from respected critics. Entertainingly, John Simon begins: 'There are plays that are merely bad, and others that are downright repellent.[9] Paula Vogel's *The Baltimore Waltz* establishes itself firmly in the latter category.' Melanie Kirkpatrick, in the *Wall Street Journal*, bemoans the fact that Vogel's 'mostly witless vignettes' were to be 'inflicted on theatregoers' in several cities.[10] Clive Barnes, in the *New York Post*, describes the play as 'a farrago of annoying nonsense'.[11] Puzzled by what they perceive to be an oblique agenda on Vogel's part, all three reviewers accuse her of making light of a serious issue: AIDS. Simon insists that 'some subjects, such as AIDS and the Holocaust, are not laughing matters, and should be protected from the likes of Paula Vogel'. Kirkpatrick and Barnes both point to publicity for the production that describes *The Baltimore Waltz* as 'a second-generation AIDS play'. Barnes mocks: 'A what? Second-generation? This is "[...] a play about AIDS and how to live and laugh with it," a play to put a little gaiety into gayness.' In a more measured tone, Kirkpatrick arrives at a similar conclusion: 'I've puzzled over this [second-generation] designation and concluded that perhaps it's a comment on the play's attempts to be humorous, something few "first-generation" AIDS plays dared to try.' The humour, she argues, is 'an insult to our intelligence'. Decidedly less hostile, a review of the production in *Theatre Journal* by David Román also focuses on the treatment of AIDS in the play, referring to AIDS 18 times.[12] Román – whose *Acts of Intervention* (1998) is a passionate, multi-faceted account of performance vis-à-vis AIDS activism and gay culture, and who (as I will discuss) has written on the political complexities of identifying 'generations' of AIDS and 'post-AIDS' discourse (see note 14, below) – asserts that Vogel memorializes her brother 'without ever trivializing the devastation of AIDS'.

Whether one sides with Osborn and Román, or with the reviewers of the Circle Rep production and its (New York) revival by Signature Theatre, *The Baltimore Waltz* exposes some of the problems that attend the attaching by critics and publicists of the term 'AIDS play'.[13] Quoting what is on the poster, or assuming that, since it has been anthologized as such, it must be seen as an AIDS play, stops short of genuine criticism, and ignores the fact that, however its merits are assessed, *BW* is about the politics of discourse to which any mention (let alone discussion) of AIDS is subject. Long before it could be isolated as a disease, AIDS, as Vogel dramatizes, became a social phenomenon that generated its own discourse.[14] While 'AIDS' is a name that critics often cannot see beyond, a set of perceptions and projections underlie critical discourse that are usually unnamed. Camps – a word I use here to convey associations less often named in critical discourse than schools (the Frankfurt School), or methodologies (semiotics) – are in the eye of the beholder. Not only may we not know we are in one, we may not know that we might be perceived to be in one, or even of its existence. They are, like the demographic segments identified by marketing experts, a combination of factual evidence, socially situated attitude, and invention. Camps raise the question: when are the rules of naming named, and who names them?

Theatre production proceeds by a series of translations: one person's thoughts and movements (a writer, a character) are put onto the body and into the mouth of another (a performer) by directors who interpret authors in an environment that works with an actual space to render a design plan. Theatre is expression via a chain of citations and sub-stitutions. Something similar to (and I will argue, continuous with) theatre's citational, substitutional logic operates in theatre criticism (a term I use here to embrace theorists, historians, and kinds of analyst and commentator that might resist being defined either as theorist or historian). Critical discourse is constituted in significant part by naming conventions, or rituals. One of the rituals of academia is reader-review of proposals and articles in which the person submitting and/or the person evaluating the submission does not know the name or identity of the other. Most who have been through this process know how curious a process it can be – often incredibly informative, but sometimes perplexing. (I had the strange experience of being told, with no hint of irony, and in an otherwise helpful reader's report, who I was: my gender, nationality, vocational background, and with whom I identified. Every designation was so wonderfully wide of the mark that I was left to ponder how I had created such an impression.)

The portrayal of criticism within critical discourse itself consistently plays down the role of such naming rituals in circulating authority. While criticism usually portrays itself as containing and harnessing cita-tion, the authority of the critic (their right to speak, and their status as speaker) is achieved through various forms of citation performed within and/or auxiliary to, critical discourse. These forms include: the citation of sources and of examples to endow analysis with cogency; those catalogues of previous works that often accompany academic articles about theatre companies; and the biographical notes on contributors or curriculum vitae that record the work of the critic. All these naming rituals are like a passport that the critic or artist must brandish. The assumption of place within critical discourse is predicated on the appropriate submission of these passports, while *movement* within critical discourse entails participation in dialogue that consists largely of contestation of place. That contestation, in turn, consists of sequential citation and counter-citation that names both oneself and the critical other(s).

I am interested in the way these forms of citation underpinning academic discourse name and decline to name themselves *alongside* concepts of citation that academic discourse theorizes and critiques. Each decade has its own obsession with citation. For much of the 1990s, Judith Butler's feminist analysis of gender as citation was the most cited thing in the humanities. For Butler, as for Derrida, citation is a 'recitation, the citing of a prior chain of acts, which are implied in the present act and which perpetually drain any "present" act of its present-ness' (1993, p. 244). It is interesting to consider this definition of performative citation in relation to what is perhaps the citation crisis of the 2000s: the crisis around intellectual property. Issues of copyright, plagiarism, and intellectual property are certainly not new to academia, but new ways of disseminating co-operative, often anonymous or dubiously authored, internet-friendly sources has impacted hugely on how academics seek to manage citation. And lest this be seen as a matter confined to student essays, Richard Schechner, in a piece posted on the internet regarding 'Philip Auslander's' *Theory for Performance Studies*, asserts: 'At one very important level, scholarship is about citation, referencing, and giving credit to predecessors and parallels.'[15]

Camps, citation rituals, and questions of the territory and property that critics shield and usurp, are subjects of Jill Dolan's essay 'Geographies of Learning', in which Schechner is a 'key figure'. Published in 1993 and much discussed since, it is an essay I want to read in relation to some subsequent reflections on the role of art, criticism, and theatre. In the second paragraph of her article, Dolan poses a question that sets the tone for what is to follow: 'How can theatre studies avoid being dispersed into metaphor while developing new ones to use, to enable us to include more identities, practices, and theories under our increasingly broad purview?' (Dolan, 1993, p. 417). Combating the threat of 'being dispersed into metaphor' is pragmatically and strategically vital for Dolan, who goes on to describe the 'midnight raiding' of theatre studies by other disciplines. These disciplines, while appropriating the-atrical concepts, regard theatre itself, particularly its practice and study in universities, as 'elitist' and 'undertheorized', which, Dolan admits, it has been. Observing the reception of Schechner's speech at the 1992 ATHE Conference – on the problems of theatre studies, and how perfor-mance studies must be embraced as a more 'progressive' model – Dolan interrogates Schechner's claims, and those of others advocating perfor-mance studies models. Agreeing that inclusion and breadth are needed, she remains worried by Schechner's 'imperialist' manner, and, in a 'gen-tle amendment', argues for 'a dialectical movement' that 'reconfigures both fields'. In the remainder of the article, Dolan considers how theatre might profitably reappropriate metaphors from other fields that have themselves used theatrical metaphors, and how theatre and performance studies might work through their own practices of identity development and exchange with the help of feminist and post-colonial thinking about location and identification.

Dolan points out that much feminist theory of the late 1980s and early 1990s – the period that she, and I, situate as 'post-identitarian' – can be traced back to 'The Technology of Gender', a 1987 essay by Teresa de Lauretis. Deploying a cinematic metaphor of framed space, de Lauretis (as already cited in relation to Chong and Skipitares) describes in this essay 'the movement in and out of gender' as 'a movement between the (represented) discursive space of the positions made available by hege-monic discourses and the space-off, the elsewhere of those discourses' (1987, p. 26). How crucial the binary is to this much-cited idea in post-identitarian gender discourse. In the repeated movement between one position to another, between space and space-off, the fixity of the binary facilitates the dialectical negotiation of gender. Not only does de Lau-retis not abandon binary logic in her re-conception of gender beyond simple positionality, she adds to the structuring role of the binary by grounding one binary (between space and space-off) in another, namely the binary between the stasis of spaces and the movement of individ-uals. Dolan also cites Biddy Martin and Chandra Mohanty's resonant re-conceptualization of community as a space of negotiation between 'being home [...] the place where one lives within familiar, safe, protected boundaries' and 'not being at home [...] a matter of realizing that home was an illusion of coherence and safety' (ibid., p. 420). Dolan appropri-ates this new binary logic (as I call it in my Introduction) to ground her own arguments about the reconfiguration of theatre and performance studies. Though she uses the term 'poststructuralist', she deftly identifies the promises and pitfalls of what she calls 'poststructuralist theory'.

Like other ground-breaking feminist theorists, Dolan finds that, for all their deconstructions, 'poststructuralist' theories are replete with formulations and blueprints that can help to (re-)ground not only feminism and theatre, but theory and disciplinarity.

As Dolan points out, the contemporary, academy-based critic must negotiate changing interfaces between civic and vocational contexts. I want to consider two other, similarly wide-ranging reflections on producing theatre in institutions, and in the shifting sands of civic space. Very different in tenor and style from Dolan's, and from each other, each is a combination of testimony and entreaty offered by experienced theatre practitioners. Anne Bogart is Artistic Director of SITI Company and a Professor at Columbia University; Gwenda Hughes is the former Artistic Director of the New Vic in Stoke, and has led other regional theatres since working with TIE and socialist-feminist theatre companies in the 1970s.

In their reflections on making art in institutional contexts, Hughes and Bogart call for a reclaiming of embodied language, invested articulation. Bogart refers to 'a culture of the inexact', Hughes to a world in which 'words', including 'culture', have 'become untethered from their value'. Both wonder if an 'American corporate management-speak virus' is to blame, along with the increasingly 'slippery' speech of politicians (Hughes cites New Labour).[16] As its subtitle suggests, Anne Bogart's second collection of essays, *and then, you act: making art in an unpredictable world*, contains a call for articulation that signals through what she perceives to be 'a culture of the inexact' (2007, p. 17). An essay, titled 'Articulation', focuses on the specific contingencies, and larger, 'inherited' agendas, within which all expression operates. An articulation, as Bogart conceives it, is an act of communication illuminating, and opening a space within, those contingencies and agendas. She asserts that 'articulation poses a threat to corporate interests' controlling the 'commercial arena' in which 'language is dumbed down, commodified and cheapened'; and insists that if 'we assume that the words we inherit are good enough rather than embarking upon a close examination of the vocabulary, we are cheating ourselves'. Nonetheless, if the 'performance of articulation' is to be 'positive action in the world', each cultural 'performer' must 'stand up and articulate what they are, rather than what they are not'. Therein, I would say, lies the challenge of the postmodern condition: interrogating 'vocabulary' without becoming mired in scrutiny. 'When you can point articulately in a specific direction', Bogart argues, 'others will know where you are headed. [...] The pointing is the point' (ibid., p. 21).

In September, 2006, I participated in an event at the intersection of theatre, government policy, and social activism, where ideas about language, art, and the body forced their way in. A number of retired, current, and future regional theatre directors, producers, actors, designers, literary managers, administrators, and academics were gathered for two days in one room to discuss the impact on regional theatre in Britain of the landmark Arts Council report of 1984, the 'Glory of the Garden'.[17] It is often the case at conferences that a spread of energy amongst delegates forces a subject only fleetingly mentioned by presenters to the centre of the debate. Here, it was the sardonic, quotational utterance of a particular word, 'culture', that provided the first clue as to where things were going. After a few hours, the bleak, running gag was that, thanks to policy-making and funding bodies, the word 'art', which anyway had come to refer less and less strongly to work made by artists, had been superseded by the word 'culture'. The word 'culture', in the opinion of many at the conference, has itself been bureaucratized and disembodied, operating as a euphemism for an arts policy driven by the economics of tourism and consumption.

Certainly, conferences like this that bring workers from different sectors together are spaces in which contentious articulation can occur that does something *to* the civic. Often, a particular contribution will harness the energy in the room, and on this occasion it was a paper by Gwenda Hughes. I should put quotation marks around 'paper' and 'by', as most of the words she spoke were letters to and from funding bodies, spectators, front-of-house staff, other theatre practitioners, and policy-makers. Hughes presented the paper in a dry, reportage tone, but it was structured with the rhythms of competing comic turns within a variety show. It was a dry but riotously funny performance of how to cope with, and even enjoy, politics, pettiness, penury, and triviality, attempting to tick government boxes and to please over-enthusiastic, over-familiar, and aggrieved patrons while pursuing artistic and civic enrichment. Hughes's reading of the collaged letters and moments of reflection illustrated the communicative gymnastics that the Artistic Director of a regional theatre is required to perform:

Extract from letter To Gerry Robinson, Arts Council England, Re: Restructuring and Prospectus For Change Document. 1999:

These days it is easy to take a cheap shot at any public document by accusing it of 'spin'. However, the proposition that the new arrangements will 'properly address democratic needs', makes me feel

distinctly spinned at. I'm sure a system which makes the arts regions coterminous with government planning regions makes neat, logical sense but does not necessarily address democratic needs any more than standing next to a musician on the bus will make one musical. Yours sincerely,
Gwenda Hughes

Dear Sir,
Could you please let me know the dates and times of the performances of the Alan Ayckbourn play JOKING APART, due at your theatre this coming October. Yours faithfully, A. W.

P.S. Have you noticed that your postcode ST5 could be interpreted thus: 5 is the fifth letter of the alphabet, ie. E, so ST5 becomes STE short for Stephen. OJG has the letters OJ. Turn to JO the start of Joseph. So ST5 OJG = Stephen Joseph (Alan Ayckbourn's theatre in Scarborough).

....

About a month after I wrote the following letter in Spring 2005, I told our Board of my intention to leave at the end of 2006. Not because I had another job, not because I don't respect, admire and care about the people I work with. I do beyond measure. I adore larking about a rehearsal room with actors. Unlike a lot of directors, I really, really like management. But I am indeed battle weary and need to lie down somewhere quiet for a little while.

Dear Mr S,
Your letter is without doubt, one of the most pleasant and polite letters of complaint I've ever had. I am saddened that you think we are just concerned with putting 'bums on seats' through our programming. I also share your sadness at the death of Arthur Miller.

I take the job of making the organization financially stable very seriously, because it is public money we are spending and because I am responsible for the employment of over seventy employees. These are not louche, arty types like me who expect to have periods of unemployment because we work in the theatre and also expect to move to where the work is, but the cleaners, the caterers, the box office staff, the administrative staff, the carpenters, the costume makers. [...] I don't mean to be rude, but there is a kind of intellectual snobbery around the use of the dismissive phrase 'bums on seats'. What is wrong with wanting and trying to sell as many tickets as possible for work we have spent a long time creating? What is wrong with wanting as many people as possible to engage with a company that, after all, they are paying for through their taxes? Why is it an ignoble ambition to want a full theatre?

[...]

I don't think any theatre that has produced, among others, KISS OF THE SPIDERWOMAN, TOP GIRLS, BROKEN GLASS, WHO'S AFRAID OF VIRGINIA WOOLF, BLUE REMEMBERED HILLS, TRANSLATIONS, DEALER'S CHOICE, PRIVATES ON PARADE, THE DUCHESS OF MALFI, SIZWE BANZI IS DEAD and three operas can be said to be going for easy, comfortable entertainment. [...] This theatre is for everyone and that is a passionately held belief at the heart of our artistic policy. It is for committed playgoers like you and also for those who just fancy an occasional, diverting night out at something like STEPPING OUT. It is for the young offenders, the people with learning disabilities, the asylum seekers and others at the margins of our community that we work with through our Borderlines Programme. [...] Mr S your letter clearly came from the heart and so does this reply. I care deeply about theatre. After all I have worked in it for over thirty years now and believe me, no one goes into a career in subsidised theatre for the big bucks.

Like Bogart's essay, Hughes's presentation allowed messy issues of agency to resonate in ways that illuminate, and intervene in, formations of 'culture'.

While Dolan names institutional frameworks, Bogart and Hughes each name what is involved in prising articulation *from* institutional frameworks that supplant agency and implant vocabulary: corporate lingo that commodifies; medical discourse that depersonalizes; culture management that abstracts. In their particular ways, each of these three essays speaks through theatre, but opens lines of communication that extend into civic space. Theatre-oriented interventions into the degradation of language, agency, meaning, and value, they are also civic trajections, transmissions across civic space that illuminate that space. As examples of critical, and meta-critical naming, they speak across domains and discourses. In doing so, they point up, and invite consideration of, the translations they make and those that must be undertaken by readers who choose to cross with them. If theatre is to function as civic trajection, if its acts of articulation are to impact on institutions and formations of community, it must do something *to* the civic in ways that discourse about postmodernism has tended not to do.

In continuing to articulate the rules of naming and how they are applied, critics inevitably construct the territory on which they think they stand. Entailment relationships between theatre and the study of theatre are extraordinarily intense, and remain a recurrent item for discussion at theatre conferences across the world. Such debate has often featured calls to bridge the gap between theory and practice, between the world of the artist and of the scholar.[18] Expressions of desire to come together have contended with sardonic, or angry, reassertion of gaps.[19] We should remember Doreen Massey's assertion that spaces in the era of so-called 'globalization' less frequently nurture or accommodate in ways that Dolan, Mohanty, and Martin would like them to; rather, they are meeting/contact/collision zones, in which new forms of naming mark and erase the translations we make as we travel and collide. While less romantic than an idea of space as 'home', Massey's idea of zones allows for the grounding in a lack of groundedness desired, and modelled, by the art and criticism of Hughes, Bogart, and many of the other theatre-makers I have discussed.

Notes

Chapter 1   Introduction: Improper Naming

1. The allusion of Ru, Vi, and Flo to the flowers adorning Ophelia (described in *Hamlet* Act IV Scenes v and vii) is probably more than a coincidence, as an early version of the play held in the Beckett Collection at Reading University Library suggests that Beckett originally called the characters Viola, Rose, and Poppy.

2. In Kane's slightly earlier plays – *Blasted* (showcased in 1993), *Phaedra's Love* (produced in 1996), and *Cleansed* (produced in April 1998) – they are given names. The characters in *Crave* (produced in August 1998) are referred to only by letters (C, M, B, A); and in the posthumously produced *4.48 Psychosis* (2000), there are no character names. The 'I' that speaks throughout *4.48 Psychosis* is singular but split: three performers speak the 'I', arguably reflecting a triad voiced by the 'I' itself: 'Victim/ Perpetrator/ Bystander' (Kane, 2001, p. 231).

3. These insights derive in part from a response from Vogel by email to my question about the name 'Anna'.

4. Prefiguring Lehmann, Bonnie Marranca states, in her introduction to the three-text collection *The Theatre of Images* (a work each by Robert Wilson, Lee Breuer, and Richard Foreman), that 'value came to be increasingly placed on performance with the result that the new theatre never became a literary theatre, but one dominated by images – visual and aural. This is the single most important feature of contemporary American theatre' (Marranca, p. ix).

5. Mac Wellman, 'Writers' Bloc', *Village Voice* 18 May 2004, retrieved: www.villagevoice.com (para 6 of 9).

6. In an essay written in Paris in 1968, while students (some of them his) were protesting against unaccountable, centralized, faceless authority, Barthes announced that 'the birth of the reader must be at the cost of the death of the author'. He makes an oft-cited distinction between the classic 'writerly' text, which makes the reader a passive consumer, and the 'readerly' text that invites the reader to (as David Lodge puts it) participate 'in the production of meanings that are infinite and inexhaustible' (Barthes, 1988, p. 167). It is an opposition, in my view, that supercedes Barthes's very useful concept of the 'scriptor'. For Barthes, the limited agency available to the scriptor is the ability to combine existing texts in new ways. One of Barthes's intriguing claims is that the scriptor has no past prior to, but rather is *born with* the text.

7. Increasingly, Forced Entertainment have played on the recycling of items from earlier works to generate, and sometimes to obstruct, the production of new drama. These items include the cut-out stars in 2004's *Bloody Mess*, first used in 1987 in *200% & Bloody Thirsty*; and a skeleton suit used in *Who Can Sing a Song to Unfrighten Me?* (1999) that returns in 2008's *Spectacular*.

8. On the day in 2006 when I took some students to see *The World in Pictures*, I found a press pack from Forced Entertainment in my pigeonhole thanking me for doing so and helping us interpret its portrayal of failure. In 2008, almost immediately after we had booked to see *Spectacular*, we received a DVD documentary that reflected in a similar vein.

9. McKenzie's 'catachristening' emerges from his dazzling reading of the famous argument between Butler and Žižek regarding catachresis (the use of words in the wrong context, and in forced, provocatively paradoxical, figures of speech) (see McKenzie, 2001, pp. 209–13).

10. 'Trans-apparent' is arguably a more fitting, though neologistic, translation of the French title *La Transparence du Mal* (1996).

11. The phrases '*font date*' and '*fait date*' are taken from a 1977 essay by Pierre Bordieu, 'The Production of Belief: Contribution to an Economy of Symbolic Goods', in which conjugations of the expression '*faire date*' are key:

> The ageing of authors, works or schools is something quite different from the product of a mechanical slippage into the past. It is the continuous creation of the battle between those who have made their names [*fait date*] and are struggling to stay in view and those who cannot make their own names without relegating to the past the established figures [...] To 'make one's name' [*faire date*] means making one's *mark*, achieving recognition.
>
> (Bordieu, p. 106).

12. Full text of Charles Mee's plays and other works are available at www.charlesmee.org.

13. Massey gave this lecture as part of the Liverpool BBC Free Thinking Festival, at Liverpool's Foundation for Art and Creative Technology (FACT), 5 November 2006.

14. This quotation is from the description of *The Desire Paths* on Graeme Miller's section of the site: www.artsadmin.co.uk.

15. Commenting on the relationship of political identification to aesthetic properties, Slavoj Žižek describes how names such as 'Fascist', imported and exported to and by different organizations for political purposes, function as shells that masquerade as, and stand in for, substance via separation of the sign from its historical operation (afterword to Rancière, 2004, p. 78). What Barthes loved about Brecht is what Wolfe loves: Brecht's penchant, via techniques such as *verfremdungseffekt*, for 'detaching the sign from its effect'. Through such detachment, names like 'Fascist' endure, but are made to work hard.

Chapter 2   Authorship: A Trick of the I

1. See Derrida (1982), p. 15. For a fuller commentary on this discussion by Derrida, see Philip Auslander's important essay '"Just be your self": *Logocentrism* and *differance* in performance theory' (Auslander, 1997, pp. 28–9). Challenging '[t]heorists as diverse as Stanislavski, Brecht and Grotowski, all [of whom] implicitly designate the actor's self as the *logos* of performance',

Auslander argues that performance cannot be based on the self because it has, like any textual mode, to construct the self (ibid., p. 30).
2. This quotation from Vogel appears in the earlier, single-play edition of the playtext: Paula Vogel, *The Baltimore Waltz* (New York: Dramatists Play Service Inc., 1992), p. 7.
3. As Vogel described in a speech to the 2000 annual conference of the Association for Theatre in Higher Education (Washington DC: 3 August 2000), the texts patched within her rendition of Anna's daydream include *The Danube*, a play by Maria Irene Fornes, the Stanley Kubrick 1964 film *Dr Strangelove*, and Ambrose Bierce's story, 'An Occurrence at Owl Creek Bridge'. As David Savran points out, 'all of the action' in Bierce's story 'takes place in the mind of a soldier during the moment in which he is being hanged.' '[A]ction' in Vogel's play takes place in Anna's mind while Carl is in the process of dying (Vogel, 1996, p.x). In *The Danube*, characters repeat phrases and statements from a language instruction tape: as in Vogel's play, the machinic recitation of the tape, and of the characters' efforts, are a key atmospheric element and structuring device. *Dr Strangelove* is a manic scientist like Vogel's Todesrocheln. Strangelove's mechanical hand, which causes him to make involuntary movements that include Nazi salutes, informs the thoughts of Anna as she sits in Todesrocheln's waiting-room:

> ANNA: When I was a child, I could wait blissfully unaware for hours. I used to read signs and transpose letters, or count tiles in the floor. And in the days before I could read, I would make up stories about my hands – Mr. Left and Mr. Right. (*Beat.*) Mr. Left would provoke Mr. Right. Mr. Right would ignore it. The trouble would escalate, until my hands were battling each other to the death. (*Beat. Anna demonstrates.*) Then one of them would weep. Finally, they became friends again, and they'd dance....
>
> (Vogel, 1996, p. 47)

4. Email interview, 5 May 2001.
5. In *Under the Knife*, those moments include the die-in monologue of the AIDS corpse (Skipitares, 1996, p. 114), and the 'speaking back' on speechlessness in which Fanny Burney confides '[...but I could not utter a syllable' (ibid., p. 103).
6. Vogel refers to the contingencies of theatrical presence at several points in her interview with Savran in *The Playwright's Voice*.
7. Image- and narrative-construction are kept dialectically in view, and in tension, in Anna Deavere Smith's work. In the closing monologue of *Fires in the Mirror*, Carmel Cato (father of Gavin, whose death sparked the riots in Crown Heights) is looking for narratives, not images. He wants narratives to give him a direction. Smith's work is indirect – it fractures directionality, making images out of narratives. Her subjects want to assert their orientation on events, but Smith dis-, re-, and reversibly orients them.
8. Vogel states that 'Barthes's *Mythologies* was a huge book for [her]' (Savran, 1999, p. 269).

9. Vogel tussled with, and yielded to, 1992 director Anne Bogart and set designer Loy Arcenas, who wanted to change the bed to a sofa:

> Our greatest battle came in the tale of the sofa. I had written *Baltimore Waltz* with the image of a bed in my mind [...] a bed that changed its function, like a good Russian formalist device should, in the same magically estranging way that as children my brother and I transformed our beds into tents, houses and forests. [...] Anne won the battle – but the sofa floated, became the Eiffel Tower, became the bed – in our articulation of difference, she won the argument, but I felt that somehow a bed floated on stage.
>
> (Dixon and Smith, 1995, p. 94)

Vogel's description of the 'battle' as 'our articulation of difference' is symptomatic of the entire process of staging *The Baltimore Waltz*, at the heart of which is a dialectic of interiority and dialogue, between realizing trauma and maintaining equilibrium.

Chapter 3   Assimilation: Sounding Through the Surface

1. 'Laughter through tears' is a translation of an idiomatic Russian phrase – 'смех через слезы' – often used by Meyerhold to describe his work.
2. In *Nuit Blanche: A Select View of Earthlings*, projections of 'cave drawings' and of 'the sounds and images sent, as a record of life on earth, into outer space on the Voyager II spacecraft headed for Jupiter' are juxtaposed with naturalistic scenes that each take place in a particular room on a particular day in history (Berson, 1990, pp. 8, 13). Fragile links between the diverse characters/locales seem like trivial coincidences one minute, paradigmatically vital the next. Links are made by emblematic visual and textual details, recurring images, objects, and names. One unresolved scene (Scene Seven), 'fade[s ...] to black' as a character named Franklin brandishes a knife; a few minutes later, in a new locale, a Man in Dark Glasses is seen with 'a hunting-knife' (ibid., pp. 17, 24). Such links thread radical discontinuities of time, place, and action.
3. This quote is from a review of *Kind Ness* by Ping Chong and Company at Group Theatre, Seattle: Misha Berson, 'For a bit of the unusual, try some *Kind Ness*', *The Seattle Times*, 23 April 1993, p. 10.
4. *Archie* comics feature the escapades of fictional teenager Archie Andrews, who first appeared in *Pep Comics* in 1941, before spawning a whole series of other comics and related outlets. There are broad parallels between some of the characters in *Kind Ness* and some of those in *Archie*. Daphne, for example, has echoes of the posh, flighty, two-faced Veronica ('Ronnie'), and Rudy of 'Jughead' (Forsythe Pendleton Jones III), who is very clever but coarse and lazy.
5. The 'Americanness' of *KN* extends to its production venues. In the six years following its first production in 1986 and 1992, *KN* played in a variety of American cities – Boston, New York, Syracuse, Hartford, Milwaukee, Minneapolis, Seattle, Philadelphia, Easton, Lincoln – and (unusually for Chong's work) made only one excursion abroad (to France).

6. Sally Banes, 'The world according to Chong', *The Village Voice* 28 February 1984, p. 83.
7. The phrase 'the artifice of human culture' is used by Ping Chong in his Foreword to *East/West Trilogy*, a performance manuscript provided by Ping Chong and Company in 1997, p.ii.
8. I am grateful to Liz Diamond for her reflections on Parks's work, and her directing of it, with me (during conversations by telephone and in person).
9. For a few spectators of the 1993 Yale Repertory production to which I refer in this paragraph, this particular echo might have been strengthened by the fact that Reggie Montgomery, who played the Foundling, also played the Masterpiece Theatre Host in the seminal Crossroads Theatre production of *The Colored Museum* in 1989.
10. In the week of Thanksgiving, 2006, I participated in Parks's *365 Days/365 Plays*, the year-long performance event in which theatres around the United States (taking a week at a time) produced all of the short plays that Parks wrote, one a day, a couple of years previously. The play in which I performed (thanks to the Foundry Theatre, Manhattan) turned up wry echoes of Parks's own theatrical history-making which, previously having been a spectator of Parks's work, made me feel only a little like the Lesser Known impersonating the Greater. 'November 26' features Mrs Lincoln being dressed by her 'Negro dressmaker and housemaid, Mrs. Keckley' to get ready for that fateful theatre visit to see *Our American Cousin*. I played a dress.

Chapter 4   Demonstration: Illustrative Irony

1. In Chong's *Nosferatu: A Symphony of Darkness* (1985), a plague-like atrophy insinuates the apartment of suburbanites Nina and Jonathan. The stage darkens and a series of hieroglyphs are projected on a screen in the form of equations: [shoes] + [axe] = [paper] ... [airplane] + [fish] = [lantern]. Along with the yuppies, we are left to decode as Chong depicts the attempts of a spiritually plagued society to scrabble for meaning via the machinic manipulation of signs.
2. See C. Carr's description of this event (Carr, 1993, pp. 177–8).
3. Piper's 'calling cards' consist of neatly printed text on $2 \times 3\ 1/2$-inch cards, which she would present to people in social gatherings, whenever she felt prompted by a remark made in her presence. The text I quote is from *My Calling Card #1* (1986–90). The card ends a few lines later: 'I regret any discomfort my presence is causing you, just as I am sure you regret the discomfort your racism is causing me.'
4. Pirandello's *Six Characters* (1921) appear to confront the theatre company attempting, in lacklustre fashion, to bring them to life. The Stage Manager's demonstrative framing of the actions of the residents of Grover's Corners in *Our Town* (1938) conspicuously breaks the fourth wall, reflecting Wilder's view that the theatre of the time was 'inadequate' and 'evasive'. In *Tango Palace* (1963), Fornes's darkly witty, role-playing allegory, 'androgynous clown' Isidore teaches culture to 'earnest youth' Leopold, Isidore flipping cards on the floor after delivering each item of text written on the cards. I am grateful to Steve Bottoms for his insights on ironic demonstration in

American drama; and to various people for their take on the old stereotype that Americans don't get irony. Some insist that the situation is now reversed, and that Americans show Brits 'the way'; some suggest that there are only regional ironies (Liverpool irony or New York irony), or that Americans *only* get irony when it is in theatre, or in the paratheatre of groups like Billionaires for Bush.

5. Produced in partial fulfilment of a PhD at the University of Kent, David Woods's report on *How to be Funny* begins:

> For centuries the greatest philosophers, scientists and psychologists have attempted to define humour. Plato began rather negatively with the Superiority Theory, Kant and others claimed all comedy was incongruity whilst Freud declared relief to be the unifying factor in humour. True to academic bent the different camps and their followers take it in turns to knock each other's theories down finding examples that don't fit (a snake in a fridge is incongruous but not funny for example). I attempted the opposite and sought to find a unifying and universal solution. The result of the research – a thirty five second practical performative demonstration, involves the deflation of a balloon, a duck caller and a rubber wind bag in the act of sitting down three times.
>
> (2005, p. 2)

6. A dazzlingly inventive absurd comedy about love, intellectual property, physics, and the Wombles (cute, and only vaguely wombat-like, legends of British television who live on Wimbledon Common and recycle things they find), Unlimited's *Tangle* features four characters demonstrated by four actors who switch between their own voice and that of the characters. The fictional characters include Jocelyn, 'a quantum teleportation physicist', who jostles with Professor Hamish Beresford, her 'colleague and mentor'. Hamish steals ideas that will win him adoration and recognition. In one of his speeches, actor Chris Thorpe/character Hamish confides:

> It occurs to him then. He thinks about teleporting himself. He considers the possibility that he could arrive with all this scrubbed away. He wonders about the atoms that make up his emotions, if they do. He wonders what it would mean if the process somehow wiped him. Emotionally clean. He hopes it will.

I saw the play at the Unity Theatre, Liverpool, in 2006. This quotation is from an unpublished script provided by Unlimited Theatre.

7. A comparative review by James Moy of Brenda Wong Aoki's *Obake! Tales Of Spirits Past And Present* (at the Smithsonian's National Museum of Natural History) and *New World [B]Order/El Nuevo [B]Order Mundial* by Guillermo Gómez-Peña and Coco Fusco (at Dance Place), both performed on 24 October 1992, in Washington, DC, argues that Aoki complies with the museum context. 'Whereas Aoki's audience strolls past dioramas displaying stuffed horses and plaster Indians before entering the theatre for her performance, Guillermo Gómez-Peña and Coco Fusco purposefully keep their audience waiting in the lobby. At the appointed hour, with bullhorn in hand, they announce that admission will be according to race. "Full blooded people of

color born in America" are called to the door and given privileged seating.'
The review concludes that 'whereas Wong Aoki offered her predominantly
white audiences a few comfortable glimpses of Asian life, Gómez-Peña and
Fusco sought to remind the spectator that the position of the oppressed is
not an amusing matter' (Moy, 1993b).

8. The film, *The Couple in the Cage: A Guatanaui Odyssey*, was made in 1993 and
is directed by Coco Fusco and Paula Heredia.

9. Elaine Aston's important essay 'Feminist Performance as Archive: Bobby
Baker's "Daily Life" and *Box Story*' (see Aston, 2002; and the extract reprinted
in Barrett and Baker, 2007, pp. 129–33) reads Baker through gender-conscious
theorizing by Phelan and Schneider of the permanence of performances and
of art objects. Aston asserts that Baker performatively archives in ways that
Charcot, studying 'his' female hysterics, could not see; but also that Baker's
performances of 'ruptured fictions' pose voluminous questions about how to
place her work.

10. See, for example, the 'Mr. Hirsch' section of Finley's *I'm an Ass Man*, in which
a woman relates being forced to perform oral sex on her neighbour. Finley
describes how she 'used melted ice cream sandwiches that smash and pop
through their wrappers onto the girl's dark dress, to symbolize the neighbour's
climax' (2000, pp. 20–3). Finley's humour is as savage as Wolfe's in *The Colored
Museum*, and both stimulated rethinking amongst theatre scholars in the mid-
and late-1980s about the ethics of irony in performance, and about political
(in)correctness.

11. Itabari Njeri, 'Black Not Like Me', *Los Angeles Times*, 12 June 1998, pp. 47–8.

12. For a discussion of the 'Snap!' as deployed by snap queens, by Miss Roj, and
within *In Living Colour*, see Johnson (1995).

13. Frank Rich, 'The Colored Museum' (performance review), *New York Times*, 3
November 1986. Reprinted *New York Theatre Reviews 1986*: pp. 131–2.

14. A steady stream of characters flows, for example, from Mimi Goese's pieces. As
in *CM*, most of them appear to have seized bits of cultural coding and grafted
them on to themselves as a mask. *Bombardment* features four personae: a
circus Big Man; a diva; a rapper; and Pinocchio. As well as markers of style
and convention that associate each of these four personae with a particular
artistic genre, they are also, like Wolfe's characters in *CM*, socially emblematic.
A diva, for instance, might be seen as quintessentially female and classical,
rap as distinctly young and urban. Goese assaults the boundaries of tradition
and of identity through performative manoeuvres that merge (opera with rap)
or deflate (the spectacular frivolity of the circus). Interaction with the debris
left by earlier personae helps to shape later ones, who emerge amidst tin foil
and other remnants of previous incarnations. They consume themselves in
packaging.

15. Wolfe's use of the word 'silhouette' resonates with the re-contextualized and
sometimes palimpsestic silhouettes of visual artist Kara Walker. Like Wolfe,
Walker focuses on her own, and the contemporary's, contradictory relationship to historical forms of caricature. I am grateful to Michael Peterson for
helping me see the connections between Wolfe and Walker.

16. While there is not room here to encapsulate feminist debate in the years
since de Lauretis's 'space-off' emerged, I want to note that the question of
how attempts to recentre hegemonic discourse should situate themselves

entirely within that discourse, or whether there can be a strategic 'elsewhere' conceived as being outside it, remain vitally contested amongst feminists. Mediating this debate, Rebecca Herzig (2004) argues that the idea of being outside epistemology is a paradoxical key to performance studies constructions of resistance: paradoxical because they try to account for it within discourse.

17. Brecht titled his essay on the subject 'Street Scene: A Basic Model for an Epic Theatre' (Willett, 1964, pp. 121–9).

18. As well as analyses of irony in scholarly publications such as Clare Colebrook's *Irony*, an article by Zoë Williams lucidly reviews types of irony – including the confusion and ire, both in academic and popular contexts, that the concept of irony continues to provoke (Zoë Williams, 'The final irony', *The Guardian*, 28 June 2003, retrieved at www.guardian.co.uk).

19. Ideas of hybridity are intricately applied and interrogated in José Esteban Muñoz's *Disidentifications: Queers of Color and the Performance of Politics* (1999).

20. Harris's reading puts generations of female/feminist/feminine perspectives in dialogue, applying Joan Rivière's alignment of 'genuine womanliness' with 'masquerade' and Linda Kintz's reading of Rivière three-quarters of a century later to read a review of *How to Shop* by Kintz's contemporary, Susan Melrose (Harris, 1999, pp. 121–4).

21. In relation to cases of alleged obscenity within rap music, Judith Butler cites Henry Louis Gates, Jr.'s legitimating view of rap as a form of 'signifying'. She agrees with Gates that 'the African-American genre of "signifying" is misunderstood by the court, and such genres ought to be properly recognized as works of literary and cultural value'. While I agree with the thrust of Gates's argument, he, and particularly Butler, elide 'genre' with individual 'works' in ways that occlude the work they profess to defend (Butler, 1997, p. 174).

22. In his practice-based research thesis on Ridiculusmus (see Chapter 8), Jonathan Haynes (company member Jon Hough's stage name) insightfully describes the additional layer of narrative recuperation of creativity that academic analysis places over the already recuperative effects of theatrical narrative. Haynes/Hough writes: 'The MA performance, I believe, was a mere gloss, behind which personal histories (what David Williams calls "the real personality" which can "flare or appear in performance") and variegated selves are playing out some intricate dance or, less prosaically, their own relationship. At the same time, Jonathan Haynes sits like a voyeur on the edge or in the "off" area of the devising room. His role now is the academic filter, sifting the guilty and nervous observations of Jon Hough and moulding them into an accepted academic form' (Jon Haynes, unpublished MA thesis, p. 11).

Chapter 5   Diagnosis: Putting Medical History Under the Knife

1. See, for instance, the stage directions at the start of *Pugilist Specialist* that I discuss toward the end of Chapter 7, which include the note: '*No naturalistic movement accompanies the entrances, exits, or travel*' (Shaplin, 2003, p. 13).

2. Thanks to Jeanne Harrison, with whom I saw *Under the Knife*, for introducing me to the work of Theodora Skipitares.

3. See Note 11 to Chapter 1.

Chapter 6 Programming: The Designated Blueprint

1. These quotations are from Miller's Artsadmin site: www.artsadmin.co.uk.

2. These debates about genre are touched on in the *TDR*-derived sourcebook *Happenings and Other Acts*, edited by Mariellen Sandford. Sandford's book contains a substantial essay on European Happenings-makers (such as Wolf Vostell) by Günter Berghaus: 'Happenings in Europe: Trends, Events, and Leading Figures' (Sandford, 1995, pp. 310–80).

3. Kaprow's *18 Happenings in Six Parts* is often cited, as in remit statements and calls for participation to PSi #13 Happening/Performance/Event (November 2007, New York University), as a landmark early Happening. It features 'simultaneous and sequential compartmentalization' of activities into spatial and temporal units (see Kirby in Sandford, 1995, pp. 3–4). It emerged, in 1959, from Kaprow's years of study with Cage at Black Mountain College.

4. *Graphis* is described by participant-performer Letty Eisenhauer and creator Dick Higgins in Sandford, 1995, pp. 123–9.

5. The peculiar, nostalgic, love and derision of minor celebrity is particularly evident in post-punk popular music, in the work of bands such as The Fall and Half Man Half Biscuit. Half Man Half Biscuit songs such as 'D'ye ken Ted Moult?', 'I Hate Nerys Hughes', and 'Bob Wilson, Anchorman' incorporate swingeing but joyous citation of ordinary British culture.

Chapter 7 Disclosure: Transcript and Testimony

1. These company statements are taken from the Recorded Delivery website: www.recordeddelivery.net.

2. *Come Out Eli* is a piece of documentary theatre featuring the actors' in-time re-performance of the recorded testimony to which they are listening on headsets. The interviewees to whom they listen reflect on one of a 15-day siege at the turn of 2002/3, and on the area of Hackney, in London, where the siege took place. Four days after the escape of his hostage Paul Okere, and an exchange of gunshots with police, Eli Hall was found dead in the burnt-out building.

3. *Fires in the Mirror* (1992) and *Twilight: Los Angeles, 1992* (1993) are parts of a project Smith titled *On the Road: A Search for American Character*, as outlined in her introduction to *Fires in the Mirror* (Smith, 1993a, pp. xxiii–xli).

4. See the foreword to the script of *Unprotected* (Wilson et al., 2006).

5. As she explains on the Recorded Delivery website, and alludes to in Soans (2005, p. 101), Blythe encountered the 'recorded delivery' technique in a workshop with Mark Wing-Davey, and wanted to use it in performance. It is a technique that, like Smith's performances, plays up the hesitations and non-fluencies that dramatic speech conventionally cleans up.

6. Katie Laris, performance review of *Fires in the Mirror: Crown Heights, Brooklyn and Other Identities* by Anna Deavere Smith, *Theatre Journal* vol. 45, no. 1 (March 1993), pp. 117–19.
7. Michael Billington, performance review of *Bloody Sunday* by Tricycle Theatre, *The Guardian*, 12 April 2005; accessed www.guardian.co.uk.
8. Solomon raises her concerns about 'self-aggrandizing actors impersonating real folks' in *The Laramie Project* in a performance review of *Undesirable Elements* by Ping Chong and Company: Alisa Solomon, 'The Making of Americans', *Village Voice*, 5 December 2000, retrieved at www.villagevoice.com.
9. The framing and self-framing of Smith in the early 1990s is fraught with contradictions. She emerges as a natural scientist and a spirit channel; a non-author who is supremely interpretative; a Black woman in touch with the material reality of the streets, but who is quasi-transcendentally objective and culturally liminal; and as deeply vulnerable yet above human foibles. Richard Stayton claims in 'Anna Deavere Smith' (*American Theatre*, July/August 1993, pp. 21–2) that she 'seems to tap into your mind'; a television critic, reviewing the television version of *Fires* broadcast as part of the PBS series *American Playhouse*, describes her as 'a chameleon and an exorcist' (John Leonard, 'The Search for Signs of Intelligent Life in Brooklyn', *New York*, 3 May 1993, p. 68). Attilio Favorini claims: 'Perhaps more than any other human being on the planet, [Smith] carries Crown Heights within her' (Favorini, 1996, p. 105). An article by Karen de Witt, 'The Rainbow Finds A Voice That Rarely Speaks of Itself', strikes a similar note (*The New York Times*, 14 May 1997, p. C1+).
10. Wilson et al. (2006), unnumbered page preceding playtext.

Chapter 8   Monstrosity: Branding the Phatic

1. Michael Pollick, 'What is Phatic Communication?' (2007), posted on the online knowledge compendium *wiseGEEK*: www.wisegeek.com/what-is-phatic-communication.
2. Joyce McMillan, '*The Receipt*', *The Scotsman*, 9 August 2006, accessed at: www.edinburgh-festivals.com/reviews.
3. The *Fringe Firsts* are awarded each week during the Edinburgh Festival Fringe by a team of critics for *The Scotsman* newspaper. *The Receipt* received won in the first 'batch' of 2006 awards; it subsequently won the 2006 *Total Theatre* Award for Innovation.
4. David Woods, 'An analysis of the current practice of Ridiculusmus theatre company', MA thesis, University of Kent, 2003, p. 108.
5. Quotations are from a video of *Say Nothing* in performance at the Traverse Theatre, Edinburgh in August 2000, generously provided by Ridiculusmus and by Gloria Lindh at the agency Your Imagination.
6. *A Night in November* was originally produced in 1994 and *Stones in his Pockets* in 1996. Both productions were directed by Pam Brighton for the Belfast-based DubbelJoint Theatre Company. Texts of the two plays are published together: see Jones (2000).
7. Woods, MA thesis (2000), p. 108.

8. Ibid., p. 109.

9. All quotations in this paragraph are from Charlotte Cripps, 'The Commodification of Ideas', *The Independent*, 29 September 2003, an interview article about *Ideas Men*, accessed at: www.independent.co.uk/arts-entertainment/theatre-dance/features.

10. *Receipt* quotations are from a DVD of a performance at the Assembly Rooms in Edinburgh in August, 2006. The DVD was kindly provided by Will Adamsdale and the agency Fuel.

11. *The Office*, created by Ricky Gervais and Stephen Merchant, features Gervais as the now-legendary character David Brent. Two series, and a two-part special, were made for the BBC (2001–03). Other versions (both official and unofficial adaptations) have run in various countries, including the US *Office* that began in 2005.

12. Nathan Barley is a 26-year-old webmaster, guerrilla film-maker, screenwriter, DJ and (in his own words) 'self-facilitating media node'. The show is largely about his desire to be the epitome of urban cool and his terror that he might not be.

13. In Kubrick's satire of Cold War politics, Sellers plays US President Merkin Muffley, British Group Captain Lionel Mandrake, and Strangelove himself (a German scientist who advises the President).

14. *The Corporation* was written and directed by Mark Achbar, Jennifer Abbot, and Joel Bakan. It had a fairly wide cinema release; was released on DVD in 2004; and was broadcast on Channel 4 television in the United Kingdom.

15. Before *No Logo* (London: Flamingo, 2000), Klein wrote for many years about corporations and global markets for *Village Voice* and many other newspapers and magazines.

16. This section of the show – about the phatic function of paper bags, newspaper supplements, and other consumer items – was not in the original production at the Edinburgh Fringe from which I quote elsewhere. It was incorporated as an opening monologue in the version I saw at the Unity Theatre in Liverpool in February 2007 as part of a tour (New York, Melbourne, and various UK venues). I am grateful to Josephine Large, with whom I saw the show in Liverpool, for her insights.

Chapter 9 Graphting: Plotting the Body as Puzzle

1. *Here's what I did* was conceived and directed by Andy Lavender, created by the company, and written by Dan Rebellato.

2. The Human Genome Project was, according to its leaders, 'completed' in 2003, once the 20,000 or so genes in human DNA had been identified.

Chapter 10 Supplement: Naming Critical Acts

1. The move 'from Piaget to Lacan', states McKenzie, 'displaces the presence of the subject into the insistent deferral of signifying chains' (2001, p. 41); 'while Austin sought to ground the performative and the illocutionary in subjective presence, Deleuze and Guattari move instead toward collective

assemblages of enunciation, utterance machines irreducible to subjective or intersubjective relations' (ibid., p. 209).

2. The first *Beyond Postmodernism* symposium took place at Birkbeck College, London, in September 2005, and the second at Central School of Speech and Drama in April 2006.

3. Introducing the reader he edits, for example, Thomas Docherty points to the 'the enormous and eclectic body of interests upon which the postmodern debate has made a significant mark' and to the 'prevalence' of 'populist, rather superficial and essentially misleading characterizations of the postmodern' to show 'how necessary is the production of the present *Reader*' (1993, p. xiii).

4. Jean-François Lyotard, 'Letter to Jessamyn Blau', *The Postmodern Explained to Children: Correspondence, 1982–1985* (Sydney: Power Publications, 1992), pp. 64–8 (p. 64). Reprinted in Docherty, 1993, pp. 47–50 (p. 47).

5. Another example of postmodern discourse that acknowledges the difficulty of defining the p-word outright, Hassan's *Postmodern Turn* suggests, as a makeweight, or perhaps stopgap, that 'names, piled here pell-mell, may serve to adumbrate postmodernism, or at least suggest its range of assumptions: Jacques Derrida, Jean-Francois Lyotard, [...] Donald Barthelme, Walter Abish, John Ashbery, David Antin, Sam Shephard, and Robert Wilson' (1987, pp. 84–5).

6. *Encyclopedia of Postmodernism*, ed. Victor E. Taylor and Charles E. Winquist (London: Routledge, 2001), pp. xiii–xvi.

7. Lehmann disclaims his own use of the term 'paradigm' somewhat torturously by insisting that it is 'an auxiliary term used here to indicate the shared negative boundary demarcating the internally highly diverse variants of the post-dramatic theatre from the dramatic' (2006, p. 24).

8. The 1992 Circle Repertory Company production was directed by Anne Bogart, and performed by Cherry Jones (Anna), Richard Thompson (Carl), and Joe Mantello (Third Man).

9. John Simon's review suggests that the Circle Rep production did not make clear to him the estranging function of the rabbit. His interpretation is so tenaciously literal that it seems unwittingly comic:

> Why are homosexual encounters treated in this oblique fashion? The bunny trope, moreover, does not work. Whenever the siblings go through Customs, Anna must hold Carl's rabbit, lest the Customs officers, suspecting it of harboring contraband, tear it apart. First, women carrying bunnies can be just as suspected of smuggling as men. Second, there are X-ray machines specifically designed to protect bunnies from needless disembowelment.
>
> (John Simon, 'Old Wine in New Bottles,' *New York*, 2 March, 1992, p. 57)

Simon seems to miss the key point that there are no 'homosexual encounters'. Rather than 'encounters' treated in 'oblique fashion', the play depicts the reverse: the construction of obliqueness that produces the impression of homosexual activities. Simon's real gripe seems to be that Vogel is fashionable, and has 'garnered more grants and awards than a sofa gathers lint'.

His jibe belies (a) the fact that, while she was a renowned playwright, playwriting teacher and mentor, productions of her work, and indeed critical discussions of it, were surprisingly few and far between; and (b) Vogel's resistance to belonging to any camp – feminist or otherwise, despite her espousal of many tenets of feminism. Written several years before *How I Learned to Drive* (which premiered in 1997, and which many see as resisting orthodoxies on child abuse), *Hot 'N' Throbbing* (first produced in 1994) depicts a mother separated from a violent husband writes pornographic stories that are disturbingly infiltrated by the burgeoning sexuality of the couple's son and daughter. The play was attacked from a variety of angles both as 'anti-pornography' and as 'pro-pornography' (Vogel, 1996, p. 231).

10. Melanie Kirkpatrick, 'The Baltimore Waltz', *The Wall Street Journal*, 14 February 1992, reprinted *New York Theatre Critics' Reviews 1992*, p. 39.
11. Clive Barnes, 'Waltz Trips on Intentions', *New York Post*, 13 February 1992, reprinted *New York Theatre Critics' Reviews 1992*, p. 37.
12. David Román, 'The Baltimore Waltz', performance review, *Theatre Journal* vol. 44, no. 4 (1992), pp. 520–2.
13. Reviews of *BW*'s second New York incarnation in 2005, as the centrepiece of Signature Theatre's Vogel season, followed the pattern of reviews of the 1992 production. Charles Isherwood, in the *New York Times*, was not alone in regarding the play's 'whimsy-spiked satire' as a bemusingly 'idiosyncratic' depiction of AIDS (Charles Isherwood, 'Death-Defying Fantasy Fueled by Love When AIDS Was a Nameless Intruder', *New York Times*, 6 December 2004; retrieved at www.theater2.nytimes.com).
14. In an essay titled 'Not-about-AIDS' (Román, 2007), first published in *GLQ* in 2000, Román cites Eric Rofes's book *Dry Bones Breathe*, which theorizes the distinction between post-AIDS and the end of AIDS, pointing the way toward a discourse beyond the AIDS-as-crisis model that does not collapse that distinction. In an earlier essay (Román, 1992), Román suggests that 1987 'marks a turning point in AIDS activism', and 'in the history of the drama of AIDS'. That was the year of *Pouf Positive*, Robert Patrick's short and powerful attempt to write 'a funny AIDS play', and the year in which Larry Kramer, author of celebrated AIDS play *The Normal Heart*, 'shifted gears and inaugurated the spectacularly effective, and often seriously funny, AIDS theatrics, the direct action AIDS activist organization ACT UP (AIDS Coalition to Unleash Power)'. Román argues that 'Patrick's aim, not unlike ACT UP's own, is to focus on the anger and to anger the focus against the limited discursive fields by which we live with, and struggle against, AIDS' (Román, 1992, pp. 305–9).
15. Richard Schechner, 'Plagiarism, Greed, and the Dumbing Down of Performance Studies' (Draft), posted at www.interregnum.dk, a site for discussion relating to PSI #14 (Performance Studies International's 14th Conference, which took place in Copenhagen, 20–24 August 2008). Auslander's alleged passing-off of *Theory for Religious Studies*, by William E. Deal and Timothy K. Beal' as his own work is the subject of extensive discussion by a range of scholars in the Spring 2009 issue of *TDR: The Drama Review*.
16. The text of Hughes's speech runs: 'And there are other words that seem to me to have become untethered from their value: quality, innovation, access, diversity. Important, precious things certainly, but seemingly now more significant in their repetition than their meaning like a chant or mantra: nam

yoho renge quyo, nam yoho renge quyo, Lord Jesus Christ have mercy upon me a miserable sinner, quality, innovation, access, diversity, quality, innovation, access, diversity. What's to blame for this? An American corporate management-speak virus? New Labour, whose relationship with the language of truth and the truth of language has always, it appears, been flexible, a little slippery? They are culpable in so many other ways, why not in this? All I know is that it leaves me profoundly unsettled, but not clever enough to articulate why'.

17. *The Glory of the Garden: Regional Theatre in Britain since 1980* took place at Liverpool John Moores University, September 2006, and was co-ordinated by Ros Merkin.

18. Prompted in part by the fact that these discussions are often a sideshow rather than the main event, a 1997 conference in which I participated at Columbia, *Thinking and Doing*, brought together an impressive array of artists, scholars, artist-scholars, and scholar-artists to reflect on the conference title.

19. At the 2006 Conference of the Theatre and Performance Research Association (TaPRA), at Central School of Speech and Drama (London), invited respondent Lloyd Newson derided academics in both his closing and opening remarks for their wilfully obscure and often irrelevant preoccupations. Alarmingly, many academics in the audience seemed predisposed to defer to an artist, even to enjoy the attack, leading me to wonder at the masochistic tendency of academics and at the strange dance of cynicism and idealism that we so often do.

Bibliography

Aston, Elaine (2002) 'Feminist Performance as Archive: Bobby Baker's "Daily Life" and *Box Story*', *Performance Research* (vol. 7, no. 4), pp. 78–85.

Auslander, Philip (1997) *From Acting to Performance* (London: Routledge).

—— (2006) 'The Performativity of Performance Documentation', *PAJ* 84 (vol. 28, no. 3), pp. 1–10.

—— (2008) *Theory for Performance Studies* (Abingdon: Routledge).

Banes, Sally (1993) *Greenwich Village 1963: Avant-Garde Performance and the Effervescent Body* (Durham, NC: Duke University Press).

—— (2000) 'Institutionalizing Avant-Garde Performance: A Hidden History of University Patronage', in James Harding (ed.), *Contours of the Theatrical Avant-Garde: Performance and Textuality* (Ann Arbor: University of Michigan Press), pp. 217–38.

Barrett, Michèle and Bobby Baker (eds) (2007) *Bobby Baker: Redeeming Features of Daily Life* (Abingdon: Routledge).

Barthes, Roland (1973) *Mythologies* (London: Paladin).

—— (1988) 'Death of the Author', reprinted in David Lodge (ed.), *Modern Criticism and Theory: A Reader* (London: Longman), pp. 166–72.

—— (1989) *The Rustle of Language*, trans. Richard Howard (Los Angeles: University of California Press).

Baudrillard, Jean (1996) *The Transparency of Evil: Essays on Extreme Phenomena* (Bath: Verso).

Beckett, Samuel (1986) *The Complete Dramatic Works* (London: Faber)

Benamou, Michel and Charles Caramello (eds) (1977) *Performance in Postmodern Culture* (Madison, WI: Coda Press).

Bennett, Susan (1990) *Theatre Audiences: A Theory of Production and Reception* (London: Routledge).

Benston, Kimberly W. (1987) 'The Aesthetics of Modern Black Drama: From Mimesis to Methexis', in Errol Hill (ed.), *The Theatre of Black Americans* (New York: Applause), pp. 61–78.

Berson, Misha (ed.) (1990) *Between Worlds: Contemporary Asian-American Plays* (New York: Theatre Communications Group).

Bertens, Hans and Joseph Natoli (eds) (2002) *Postmodernism: The Key Figures* (Oxford: Blackwell).

Bhabha, Homi (1994) *The Location of Culture* (New York: Routledge).

Bigsby, Christopher (1999) *Contemporary American Playwrights* (Cambridge: Cambridge University Press).

Bogart, Anne (2007) *and then, you act: making art in an unpredictable world* (New York: Routledge).

Bolton, Gavin (1984) *Drama as Education* (London: Longman).

Bordieu, Pierre (1993) *The Field of Cultural Production* (Cambridge: Polity).

Bottoms, Steve (2006) 'Putting the Document into Documentary', *TDR: The Drama Review* (vol. 50, no. 3), pp. 56–68.

Brook, Peter (1977) *The Empty Space* (Harmondsworth: Penguin).

Burke, Gregory (2007) *The National Theatre of Scotland's* Black Watch (London: Faber).

Butler, Judith (1993) *Bodies that Matter: On the Discursive Limits of 'Sex'* (New York: Routledge).

—— (1997) *Excitable Speech: A Politics of the Performative* (New York: Routledge).

Cage, John (1961) *Silence* (Middletown, CT: Wesleyan University Press).

Calle, Sophie (2004) *Exquisite Pain* (London: Thames & Hudson).

Carlson, Marvin (2004) *Performance: A Critical Introduction* (2nd edn) (New York: Routledge).

Carr, C. (1993) *On Edge: Performance at the End of the Twentieth Century* (Hanover, NH: Wesleyan University Press).

Carroll, Noël (1983) 'A Select View of Earthlings: Ping Chong', *The Drama Review* (vol. 27, no. 1), pp. 72–81.

—— (1990) *The Philosophy of Horror, or Paradoxes of the Heart* (New York: Routledge).

Champagne, Lenora (ed.) (1990) *Out from Under: Texts by Women Performance Artists* (New York: Theatre Communications Group).

Charon, Rita and Maura Spiegel (2003) 'Editors' Preface: Discursive Bodies, Embodied Text', *Literature and Medicine* (vol. 22, no. 2), pp. 133–9.

Chaudhuri, Una (1995) *Staging Place: The Geography of Modern Drama* (Ann Arbor: University of Michigan Press).

Chong, Ping (1986) *Nosferatu: A Symphony of Darkness*, Videotape by Ping Chong and Penny Ward, ed. Johannes Holub. Provided by Ping Chong and Company.

—— (1988) *Kind Ness*, in James Leverett and Gillian Richards (eds), *New Plays USA* 4 (New York: Theatre Communications Group).

—— (1990a) 'Notes for "Mumblings and Digressions: Some Thoughts on Being an Artist, Being an American, Being a Witness..."', *MELUS: The Journal of the Society for the Study of Multi-Ethnic Literature in the United States* (vol. 16, no. 3), pp. 62–7.

—— (1990b) *Nuit Blanche: A Select View of Earthlings*, in Misha Berson (ed.), *Between Worlds* (New York: Theatre Communications Group).

—— (1997) *East/West Trilogy*. Unpublished bound volume comprising scripts of *Deshima*, *Chinoiserie*, and *After Sorrow: Viet Nam* and foreword by Ping Chong. Provided by Ping Chong and Company.

—— (2004) *The East/West Quartet* (New York: Theatre Communications Group).

Cixous, Helene (1984) 'Aller à la Mer', *Modern Drama* (vol. 27, no. 4), pp. 546–8.

Cole, David (1976) 'The Visual Script: Theory and Techniques', *TDR: The Drama Review* (vol. 20, no. 4), pp. 27–50.

Corrie, Rachel, Alan Rickman and Katharine Viner (eds) (2006) *My Name is Rachel Corrie* (New York: Theatre Communications Group).

Crimp, Martin (1997) *Attempts on her Life* (London: Faber).

Dayal, Samir (1996) 'Diaspora and Double Consciousness', *The Journal of the Midwest Modern Language Association* (vol. 29, no. 1), pp. 46–62.

De Certeau, Michel (1984) *The Practice of Everyday Life* (Berkeley: California University Press).

De Lauretis, Teresa (1987) *Technologies of Gender: Essays on Theory, Film, and Fiction* (Bloomington: Indiana University Press).

Derrida, Jacques (1978) 'Structure, Sign and Play', in *Writing and Difference*, trans. Alan Bass (London: Routledge & Kegan Paul, 1978), pp. 278–93.

———— (1982) *Margins of Philosophy*, ed. and trans. Alan Bass (Chicago: University of Chicago Press).

———— (1985) *The Ear of the Other: Otobiography, Transference, Translation*, ed. Christie V. McDonald, trans. Peggy Kamuf (New York: Schocken).

Dews, Peter (2007) *Logics of Disintegration: Post-Structuralist Thought and the Claims of Critical Theory* (London: Verso).

Diamond, Elin (1997) *Unmaking Mimesis: Essays on Feminism and Theater* (London: Routledge).

Dixon, Michael and Joel A. Smith (eds) (1995) *Anne Bogart* (New Hampshire: Smith & Kraus).

Docherty, Thomas (ed.) (1993) *Postmodernism: A Reader* (Hertfordshire: Harvester Wheatsheaf).

Dolan, Jill (1993) 'Geographies of Learning: Theatre Studies, Performance and the "Performative"', *Theatre Journal* (vol. 45, no. 4), pp. 417–41.

Douglas, Mary (1984) *Purity and Danger: An Analysis of the Concepts of Pollution and Taboo* (London: Routledge).

Drukman, Steven (1995) 'Doo-a-diddly-dit-dit:' An interview with Liz Diamond and Suzan-Lori Parks', *The Drama Review* (vol. 39, no. 3), pp. 56–75.

Elam, Harry J., Jr. (1992) 'Signifyin(g) On African-American Theatre: *The Colored Museum* by George Wolfe', *Theatre Journal* (vol. 44, no. 3), pp. 291–303.

Elam, Harry J., Jr. and Robert Alexander (eds) (1996) *Colored Contradictions: An Anthology of Contemporary African-American Plays* (New York: Plume).

Etchells, Tim (1999) *Certain Fragments: Contemporary Performance and Forced Entertainment* (London: Routledge).

———— (2006) *Instructions for Forgetting*, Performance script, *TDR: The Drama Review* (vol. 50, no. 3), pp. 108–29.

Fabre, Geneviève (1983) *Drumbeats, Masks and Metaphors* (Cambridge, MA: Harvard University Press).

Favorini, Attilio (1996) '*Fires in the Mirror*' (performance review), *Theatre Journal* (vol. 48, no. 1), pp. 105–7.

Finley, Karen (2000) *A Different Kind of Intimacy* (New York:Thunder's Mouth Press).

Forced Entertainment (1998) *Interactions: Making Performance*, Video (Sheffield: Forced Entertainment).

———— (2001) *First Night*, Performance DVD (The Place, London: FE).

———— (2002) *The Travels*, Performance script (Sheffield: FE).

———— (2006) *The World in Pictures*, Performance DVD (Nuffield Theatre, Lancaster: FE).

———— (2008) *Spectacular*, Performance DVD (Nuffield Theatre, Lancaster: FE).

Foster, Hal (ed.) (1983) *The Anti-Aesthetic: Essays on Postmodern Culture* (Seattle: Bay Press).

Foucault, Michel (1972) *The Archaeology of Knowledge* (New York: Tavistock; first published 1969).

———— (1991) 'What is an Author?' (an interview with Paul Rabinow), in Paul Rabinow (ed.), *The Foucault Reader* (Penguin: London), pp. 101–20.

———— (1992) *The History of Sexuality, vol. 1: The Will to Knowledge* (London: Penguin; first published 1976).

Frieze, James (1998) 'Making Space/Losing Face: Mimi Goese and the Penultimate Dis-', *PAJ* 60 (vol. 20, no.3), pp. 1–9.

Fuchs, Elinor (1996) *The Death of Character: Perspectives on Theater after Modernism* (Bloomington: Indiana University Press).

Fusco, Coco (1994) 'The Other History of Intercultural Performance', *TDR:The Drama Review* (vol. 38, no. 1), pp. 143–67.

——— (1995) *English is Broken Here: Notes on Cultural Fusion in the Americas* (New York: New Press).

Gates, Henry Louis, Jr. (1988) *The Signifying Monkey* (New York: Oxford University Press).

Hall, Stuart (1986) 'On Postmodernism and Articulation: An interview with Lawrence Grossberg', *Journal of Communication Inquiry* (vol. 10, no. 2), pp. 45–60.

Hansberry, Lorraine (1986) *A Raisin in the Sun*, in Mary Remnant (ed., *Plays by Women: Volume 5* (London: Methuen), pp. 51–107.

Harris, Geraldine (1999) *Staging Femininities* (Manchester: Manchester University Press).

Hassan, Ihab (1987) *The Postmodern Turn* (Columbus: Ohio State University Press).

Heaney, Seamus (1975) *North* (London: Faber & Faber), p. 59.

Herzig, Rebecca (2004) 'On performance, productivity, and vocabularies of motive in recent studies of science', *Feminist Theory* (vol. 5, no. 2), pp. 127–47.

Jameson, Fredric (1990) *Late Marxism: Adorno or the Persistence of the Dialectic* (London: Verso).

Jiggets, Shelby (1996) 'Interview with Suzan-Lori Parks', *Callaloo: A Journal of African-American Arts and Letters* (vol. 19, no. 2), pp. 309–17.

Johnson, E. Patrick (1995) 'SNAP! Culture: A Different Kind of Reading', *Text and Performance Quarterly* (vol.15, no. 2), pp. 122–42.

Jones, Marie (2000) *Stones in his Pockets/A Night in November: Two Plays* (London: Nick Hern Books).

Kane, Sarah (2001) *Sarah Kane: Complete Plays* (London: Methuen).

Kaufman, Moisés and Members of the Tectonic Theater Project (2001) *The Laramie Project* (New York: Vintage).

Kaye, Nick (1994) *Postmodernism and Performance* (New York: St. Martin's Press).

Kennedy, Adrienne (1988) *Adrienne Kennedy in One Act* (Minneapolis: University of Minnesota Press).

Kelly, Mary Kate (1999) 'Performing the Other: A Consideration of Two Cages', *College Literature* (vol. 26, no. 1), pp. 113–36.

Kirby, Michael (1995) 'On Acting and Not-Acting', (first published 1972) reprinted in Phillip Zarrilli (ed.), *Acting Re(Considered)* (London: Routledge), pp. 43–58.

Kirshenblatt-Gimblett, Barbara (1998) 'The Ethnographic Burlesque Author', *TDR:The Drama Review* (vol. 42, no. 2), pp. 175–80.

Klein, Naomi (2000) *No Logo* (London: Flamingo)

Kripke, Saul (1980) *Naming and Necessity* (Cambridge, MA: Harvard University Press).

Kristeva, Julia (1996) 'Artaud: Between Psychosis and Revolt', Public Lecture: The Drawing Center, New York City.

——— (2003) *Intimate Revolt:The Powers and Limits of Psychoanalysis* (New York: Columbia University Press).

Leach, Robert (1989) *Vsevolod Meyerhold* (Cambridge: Cambridge University Press).

Lehmann, Hans-Thies (2006) *Postdramatic Theatre* (Abingdon: Routledge).

Lévi-Strauss, Claude (1966) *The Savage Mind* (Paris: Plon).

Lightwork (2006) *Voici ce que j'ai fait un jour de mon corps (Here's what I did with my body one day: A genetic detective story)*, Unpublished production script with accompanying performance DVD.

Linden, Ann (2002) 'Seducing the Audience: Politics in the Plays of Paula Vogel', in Joan Herrington (ed.), *The Playwright's Muse* (London: Routledge), pp. 231–52.

Lyotard, Jean-François (1979) *The Postmodern Condition: A Report on Knowledge* (Minneapolis: University of Minnesota Press).

Malkin, Jeanette (1999) *Memory-Theater and Postmodern Drama* (Ann Arbor: University of Michigan Press).

Mann, Emily (1983) *Execution of Justice* (New York: Samuel French).

Marranca, Bonnie (1977) *The Theatre of Images* (Baltimore, MD: Johns Hopkins University Press).

Martin, Carol (2006) 'Bodies of Evidence', *TDR: The Drama Review* (vol. 50, no. 3), pp. 8–15.

Marx, Karl (1976) *Capital: A Critique of Political Economy vol.1* (Harmondsworth: Penguin; first published 1867).

Massey, Doreen (2005) *For Space* (London: Sage).

McCormack, Brian (2002) 'Postcolonialism in an Age of Globalization: Opening International Relations Theory to Identities in Movement', *Alternatives: Global, Local, Political* (vol. 27), pp. 99–115.

McGregor, Douglas (1966) *Leadership and Motivation: Essays of Douglas McGregor* (Cambridge, MA: MIT Press).

McKenzie, Jon (2001) *Perform or Else: From Discipline to Performance* (London: Routledge).

Mehta, Xerxes (1984) 'Some Versions of Performance Art', *Theatre Journal* (vol. 36, no. 2), pp. 164–98.

Mercer, Kobena (1990) 'Welcome to the Jungle: Identity and Diversity in Postmodern Politics', in Jonathan Rutherford (ed.), *Identity: Community, Culture, Difference* (London: Lawrence & Wishart), pp. 43–71.

Messerli, Douglas and Mac Wellman (eds) (1998) *From the Other Side of the Century II: A New American Drama 1960–1995* (Los Angeles: Sun and Moon Press).

Mohanty, Chandra, Ann Russo and Lourdes Torres (eds) (1991) *Third World Women and Feminism* (Bloomington: Indiana University Press).

Morgan, Peter (2006) *Frost/Nixon* (London: Faber).

Morley, David and Kuan-Hsing Chen (eds) (1996) *Stuart Hall: Critical Dialogues in Cultural Studies* (London: Routledge), pp. 262–75.

Moy, James (1993a) *Marginal Sights: Staging the Chinese in America* (Bloomington: University of Indiana Press).

—— (1993b) 'Comparative performance review: *Obake! Tales Of Spirits Past And Present* by Brenda Wong Aoki'; '*New World {B}Order/El Nuevo {B}Order Mundial*' by Guillermo Gómez-Peña and Coco Fusco, *Theatre Journal* (vol. 45, no. 3), pp. 378–9.

Muñoz, José Esteban (1999) *Disidentifications: Queers of Color and the Performance of Politics* (Minneapolis: University of Minnesota Press).

Nancy, Jean-Luc (1991) *The Inoperative Community* (Minneapolis: University of Minnesota Press).

Norton-Taylor, Richard (1999) *The Colour of Justice* (London: Oberon).

—— (2005) *Bloody Sunday: Scenes from the Saville Enquiry* (London: Oberon).

Omi, Michael and Howard Winant (1994) *Racial Formation in the United States: from the 1960s to the 1990s* (New York: Routledge).

Orloff, Kossia (1984) 'Women in Performance Art: The Alternate Persona', *Heresies: A Feminist Publication on Art and Politics* (vol. 5, no. 1; issue 17), pp. 37–9.

Osborn, M. Elizabeth (ed.) (1987) *On New Ground: Contemporary Hispanic-American Plays* (New York: Theatre Communications Group).

―――― (ed.) (1990) *The Way We Live Now: American Plays and the AIDS Crisis* (New York: Theatre Communications Group).

Parks, Suzan-Lori (1995) *The America Play and Other Works* (New York: Theatre Communications Group).

―――― (1998) *Venus* (New York: Dramatists Play Service).

―――― (2006) *365 Days/365 Plays* (New York: Theatre Communications Group).

Pearce, Michele (1994) 'Alien Nation: An interview with Suzan-Lori Parks', *American Theatre* (vol. 11, no. 3), p. 26.

Pellegrini, Ann (1997) *Performance Anxieties: Staging Psychoanalysis, Staging Race* (New York: Routledge).

Phelan, Peggy (1993) *Unmarked: The Politics of Performance* (London: Routledge).

Rancière, Jacques (2004) *The Politics of Aesthetics* (London: Continuum).

Rayner, Alice (1995) 'Improper Conjunctions: Metaphor, Performance, and Text', *Essays in Theatre* (vol. 14, no. 1), pp. 3–14.

Reinelt, Janelle (2006) 'Towards a Poetics of Theatre and Public Events', *TDR: The Drama Review* (vol. 50, no. 3), pp. 69–87.

Ridiculusmus (2008) *Tough time, nice time* (London: Oberon).

Robinson, Marc (1997) *The Other American Drama* (Baltimore, MD: Johns Hopkins University Press).

Román, David (1992) '"It's My Party and I'll Die If I Want to!": Gay Men, AIDS, and the Circulation of Camp in U.S. Theatre', *Theatre Journal* (vol. 44, no. 3), pp. 305–27.

―――― (1998) *Acts of Intervention: Performance, Gay Culture, and AIDS* (Bloomington: Indiana University Press).

―――― (2007) 'Not-about-AIDS', in Janelle G. Reinelt and Joseph R. Roach (eds), *Critical Theory and Performance* (revised edn) (Ann Arbor: University of Michigan Press), pp. 372–94.

Ruhl, Sarah (2006) *The Clean House and Other Plays* (New York: Theatre Communications Group).

Sandahl, Carrie (2003) 'Queering the Crip or Cripping the Queer? Intersections of Queer and Crip Identities in Solo Autobiographical Performance', *GLQ: A Journal of Lesbian and Gay Studies* (vol. 9, nos. 1–2), pp. 25–56.

Sandford, Mariellen R. (ed.) (1995) *Happenings and Other Acts* (London: Routledge).

Savran, David (1999) *The Playwright's Voice: American Dramatists on Memory, Writing and the Politics of Culture* (New York: Theatre Communications Group).

Sell, Mike (2005) *Avant-Garde Performance and the Limits of Criticism* (Ann Arbor: University of Michigan Press).

Shank, Theodore (1982) *American Alternative Theatre* (New York: Macmillan).

Shaplin, Adriano (2003) *Pugilist Specialist* (London: Oberon).

Shaviro, Steven (1995) 'Two Lessons from Burroughs', in Judith Halberstam and Ira Livingston (eds), *Posthuman Bodies* (Bloomington: Indiana University Press), pp. 38–54.

Simon, Herbert A. (1977) *The New Science of Management Decision* (Englewood Cliffs, NJ: Prentice-Hall; first published 1960).

Skipitares, Theodora (1996) *Under the Knife, PAJ* 53 (vol. 18, no. 2), pp. 93–117.

Smith, Anna Deavere (1993a) *Fires in the Mirror: Crown Heights, Brooklyn and Other Identities* (New York: Bantam Doubleday).

—— (1993b) *Fires in the Mirror: Crown Heights, Brooklyn and Other Identities.* Directed by George C. Wolfe for *American Playhouse* PBS Television/WGBH Boston.

—— (1994) *Twilight: Los Angeles, 1992* (New York: Bantam Doubleday).

—— (1997) 'Not so Special Vehicles', Keynote address to Association for Theatre in Higher Education Conference, 1993. Reprinted W. B. Worthen (ed.), *Modern Drama* (New York: Harcourt, Brace & Jovanovich), pp. 1074–81.

Soans, Robin (2005) *Talking to Terrorists* (London: Oberon).

Solomon, Alisa (1990) 'Signifying on the Signifyin': The Plays of Suzan-Lori Parks', *Theater* (vol. 21, no. 3), pp. 73–80.

Stein, Gertrude (1970) *Selected Operas and Plays of Gertrude Stein*, ed. John Malcolm Brinnin (Pittsburgh: University of Pittsburgh Press).

Taylor, Diana (2003) *The Archive and the Repertoire: Performing Cultural Memory in the Americas* (Durham, NC: Duke University Press).

Torgovnick, Marianna (1990) *Gone Primitive: Savage Intellects, Modern Lives* (Chicago: University of Chicago Press).

Treadwell, Sophie (1993) *Machinal* (London: Nick Hern).

Vanden Heuvel, Michael (2000) '"Mais je dis le chaos positif": Leaky Texts, Parasited Performances, and Maxwellian Academons', in James Harding (ed.), *Contours of the Theatrical Avant-Garde: Performance and Textuality* (Ann Arbor: University of Michigan Press), pp. 130–53.

Vogel, Paula (1996) *The Baltimore Waltz and Other Plays* (New York: Theatre Communications Group).

Voloshinov, V. N. (1973) *Marxism and the Philosophy of Language* (Cambridge, MA: Harvard University Press).

Watkins, Beth (1998) 'Women, AIDS, and Theatre: Representations and Resistances', *Journal of Medical Humanities* 19 (vol. 2, no. 3), pp. 167–80.

Westfall, Suzanne R. (1992) 'Ping Chong's Terra In/Cognita: Monsters of the Stage', in Shirley Geok-lin Lim and Amy Ling (eds), *Reading the Literatures of Asian America* (Philadelphia: Temple University Press), pp. 359–71.

Willett, John (ed. and trans.) (1964) *Brecht on Theatre* (London: Methuen).

Wilson, Esther, John Fay, Tony Green and Lizzie Nunnery (2006) *Unprotected* (London: Josef Weinberger).

Wolfe, George C. (1987) *The Colored Museum* (New York: Broadway Play Publishing).

—— (1991) *Spunk* (New York: Theatre Communications Group).

—— (1993a) '"I Just Want to Keep Telling Stories", Interview by George H. Rowell', *Callaloo: A Journal of African-American Arts and Letters* (vol. 16, no. 3), pp. 602–23.

—— (1993b) *Jelly's Last Jam* (New York: Theatre Communications Group).

Woods, David (2005) *How to be Funny*, PhD thesis, University of Kent at Canterbury.

Žižek, Slavoj (2008) *Violence* (London: Profile).

Index

Titles of plays are listed alphabetically under the name of the playwright or producing company. Titles of films are listed under the name of the director.